ADULT EDUCATION AND THE WORKING CLASS: EDUCATION FOR THE MISSING MILLIONS

This book has two purposes: first to argue that there is a greater need now than ever before for liberal adult education for the working class. Such provision would both help to ameliorate the gross inequalities of our society and provide some counter-balance to the increasingly utilitarian and vocational orientation of post-school education. Secondly, the book aims to describe and analyse in some detail the community-based programme for various 'disadvantaged' working class groups that has recently been developed by a British Pioneer Work team concerned with adult and continuing education. The methods, objectives and overall practice described in this case study are of relevance to those working in all sectors of adult and community education. This book is edited by two members of staff concerned with Pioneer Work development from the outset, and the contributors include other members of the Pioneer Work team of lecturers and researchers.

Richard Taylor is Director of Extramural Courses and Kevin Ward Co-ordinator of Pioneer Work, both at the Department of Adult and Continuing Education, University of Leeds.

RADICAL FORUM ON ADULT EDUCATION SERIES
Edited by Jo Campling, Series Consultant: Colin Griffin

ADULT EDUCATION AND THE WORKING CLASS

EDUCATION FOR THE MISSING MILLIONS

Edited by Kevin Ward and Richard Taylor

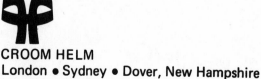

CROOM HELM
London • Sydney • Dover, New Hampshire

© 1986 Richard Taylor and Kevin Ward
Croom Helm Ltd, Provident House, Burrell Row,
Beckenham, Kent, BR3 1AT
Croom Helm Australia Pty Ltd, Suite 4, 6th Floor,
64-76 Kippax Street, Surry Hills, NSW 2010, Australia

British Library Cataloguing in Publication Data
Adult education and the working class:
   education for the missing millions.
   1. Adult education — Great Britain
   2. Labor and Laboring classes — Education —
   Great Britain
   I. Taylor, R.K.S.   II. Ward, Kevin
   374'.941'0880623   LC5256.G7
   ISBN 0-7099-2461-5

Croom Helm, 27 South Main Street,
Wolfeboro, New Hampshire 03894-2069, USA

Library of Congress Cataloging-in-Publication Data
Adult education and the working class.

   Includes index.
   1. Labor and laboring classes – Education (Higher) –
Great Britain. 2. Adult education – Great Britain.
3. Adult education – Great Britain – Citizen participation.
I. Taylor, R.K.S. (Richard K.S.) II. Ward, Kevin.
LC5056.G7A38   1986   374'.941   86-11537
ISBN 0-7099-2461-5

Printed and bound in Great Britain by
Biddles Ltd, Guildford and King's Lynn

CONTENTS

Notes on Contributors

All contributors are members of staff in the Pioneer Work section of the Department of Adult and Continuing Education, University of Leeds. Keith Forrester is lecturer in industrial relations and involved in both trade union and Pioneer Work courses; Lindsey Fraser is research assistant on the DES funded research project assessing students' and tutors' experiences on the Pioneer Work programme from 1984 to 1986; Jean Gardiner is lecturer with responsibility for developing women's Pioneer Work courses; Jill Liddington is lecturer with responsibility for developing Pioneer Work courses with retired people; Richard Taylor is senior lecturer and co-ordinator of Pioneer Work; and Kevin Ward is lecturer with responsibility for developing courses for unemployed people.

Individually, they have published widely in the fields of: adult education; labour history; women's issues; social policy; politics; peace studies; industrial relations; and social and community work.

Editor's Introduction

The development of working-class adult education has long been a central objective of radical adult educators. From the early days of University Extension and the WEA, adult education has attempted to devise structures and programmes which would involve those who had not had the opportunity of higher education and who would benefit from educational provision for personal, social and political - as well as educational - reasons.

Generally, however, the provision of such adult education has been both small scale and restricted. Insufficient resources have been made available for the provision of anything approaching mass working-class adult education. Indeed, as is well known, AE as a whole has always been seen as an ancillary and minor part of the education service. Equally important, however, working-class AE has been restricted largely to either leisure/recreational areas in the LEA sector, or to day release courses for, predominantly, white, male trade unionists.

There is thus a longstanding need for the development of AE provision for the whole working class. Of course, this entails far more resources being made available. But it also requires a fresh, more dynamic and more realistic perception of the diversity of the working class and its educational needs. Whilst the relationship to the ownership and control of the means of production remains the fundamental determinant of social class inequality in contemporary society, other dimensions of inequality have come to be seen in recent years as of considerable significance. Thus, employment status, gender, age and ethnic origin, amongst other things, have been recognised, belatedly, as crucial aspects of inequality and oppression.

In the educational context such perceptions are of critical importance: if the educational service in general is to contribute towards the creation of a more egalitarian, informed, democratic - and hence more civilised - society, then acknowledgement of the importance of educational provision for such sectors is a very high priority.

This book confronts these issues squarely, in the context of AE provision. Having analysed briefly the chronic inequality which characterises British society at all levels and in all sectors, a more detailed overview of AE practice in thse fields is undertaken. A central concern of contemporary AE, and indeed of society at large, is to make appropriate provision for the unprecedentedly large numbers of unemployed people, and Chapter 2 analyses critically, in the national context, the responses made by such agencies as the MSC and the range of educational providers, as well as examining definitions of unemployment and the need for fundamental re-thinking about work and non-work.

The focus of the book, however, is upon the experience of the 'Pioneer Work' section of the Department of Adult and Continuing Education at the University of Leeds. There have been many experimental programmes in community adult education in recent years but few have been documented, and valuable lessons have thus been lost. Such work is, by its very nature, innovative and experimental, and analysis of both 'success' and 'failure' is therefore crucial if future 'good practice' is to be achieved.

The 'Pioneer Work' experience is of particular significance in that it has succeeded in providing, within an action-research framework, large numbers of community-based courses, within a coherent methodological framework. The course programmes have been designed, on an inter-agency basis, to test various approaches to innovative provision. All provision has been community-based and has recruited overwhelmingly working-class participants. The aim has been to focus on four particular, though obviously overlapping, working-class groups: the unemployed; women; ethnic minorities; and the retired. Work with the unemployed has made up the majority of the provision.

In Chapter 3 the overall structure and objectives of Pioneer Work are examined, and this is followed, in Chapter 4, by a detailed examination, with useful and thought-provoking case studies, of the development of the work with the unemployed. Chapter 5 recounts briefly the work developed with trade unions, and particularly with the TUC Centres for the Unemployed. Chapter 6 analyses both the practice and the concepts underlying the provision of Pioneer Work courses designed specifically for women. And Chapter 7 explores one very successful aspect of Pioneer Work development, courses for working-class retired people.

Chapter 8 explains the approach underlying the research project into work with the unemployed, funded by the DES, and Chapter 9, after reviewing the Pioneer Work experience and its significance, concludes with some challenging recommendations for a national initiative to develop working-class adult education.

The great strength of this book lies in its detailed and coherent analysis of a wide range of successful community adult education in practice. Here, other radical adult educators will learn not only of the principles and perspectives underlying the Pioneer Work development, but also the practical details of how such work can actually be established, even within the extreme difficulties of resource constraints, institutional 'blockages', working-class 'alienation' et al.

The authors have achieved that most difficult of feats - the integration of theory and practice within the parameters of a clearly defined case-study approach. The lessons here for others interested in these crucially important areas are both numerous and significant. If progress is to be made in the development of working-class adult education, broadly defined as it is here, then the experience of Pioneer Work will be of central importance to both policy makers and other adult educators.

Jo Campling
Series Editor

PREFACE

The central concerns of this book are with the community-based programme of adult education organised by the Pioneer Work section of the Department of Adult and Continuing Education of the University of Leeds. As the following chapters make clear this has been very much a collective, team approach, and has involved too inter-agency working at both the formal and informal levels.

This book has thus arisen out of the collective experience and commitment of a large number of people involved with the development of Pioneer Work and should be seen as a 'collective work' in that sense. Whilst it is thus not possible to acknowledge individually the help and support of all those concerned, we would like to thank all those involved as teachers, organisers, researchers and - not least - course participants.

Particular thanks should go to: our Pioneer Work full-time staff colleagues, Gina Bridgeland and Ron Wiener; all the 'Group 2' organising tutors, especially Roger Higginbottom, Rob Imeson, Mohindra Nimba and Bernie Stinson; to LEA and other local authority officers and fieldworkers in both Bradford and Leeds; to the staff of the Educational Advice Service for Adults in Bradford; to colleagues in Bradford and Ilkley Community College; to the TUC officer, Services for the Unemployed; to Tim Dant, for assistance with research methods; and to the numerous voluntary organisations in both Bradford and Leeds without whose hard work and commitment the Pioneer Work programme could not have been successful.

Within the Department of Adult and Continuing Education we have had unstinting support from Diane Jacks, from Olive Mowat, and from all the clerical staff concerned. A vote of thanks is due to all those who helped prepare this manuscript, at short notice and in long hours of overtime - and in particular to Jaswant Bhavra.

For any inaccuracies or misinterpretations we are, of course, solely responsible.

Richard Taylor
Kevin Ward
(editors)

Chapter 1

PROBLEMS OF INEQUALITY: THE NATURE OF ADULT EDUCATION
IN BRITAIN

There can be no doubt that Britain has long been, and remains,
characterised by deep and structural inequalities.(1)
Moreover, Britain is a peculiarly class-ridden society. The
importance attached to social rank and the means by which it
is identifiable are unmatched in any other modern
industrialised society. In no comparable society do the
outward signs of social status play such a universally and
overtly significant role in the determination of social
relations. Accent, manners, dress, overall life style and,
not least, educational background - of which more later - all
serve to distinguish between the subtly defined range of
hierarchies within the social system. Complicating these
structures of inequality is a plethora of other significant
divisions: including those of gender, of race, of age, and of
geographical location.

     In order to situate education in general, and adult
education in particular, in its overall socio-economic
context, it is necessary therefore, to explore and delineate
briefly these dimensions of inequality. At the foundation of
the whole complex pattern of inequality lies the single,
simple fact of the capitalist structure of British society.
Whilst the nature of this capitalist structure has changed
enormously, of course, over the last two hundred and more
years, it remains the case that in both economic and political
terms class relations are based upon the division between the
ownership and control of the means of production (and
increasingly of financial institutions) by the capitalist
class, and the structural exploitation of those who live by
selling their labour power, the working class. There is, of
course, a multiplicity of mitigating, qualifying and ancillary
aspects of class division in contemporary society: but this
division is the base from which all other inequalities
stem.(2)

     The British ruling class 'is rooted in the ownership
and/or control of property which can be used as capital and
which, thereby, generates a substantial income ... The crucial

element in their class situation ... is their relationship to capital, considered as a productive resource ... Power has not passed to neutral technocrats; it remains in the hands of a capitalist upper class'.(3)

What are the economic dimensions of this structural inequality? Precision is impossible because of the large number of variables (and, indeed, 'unknowns', such as tax avoidance). Most analysts would concur with Westergaard's calculation that, in the late 1970s, 'the share of the richest 1% in all real post-tax income .. (is) .. about 8% - rather more than the aggregate share of the poorest fifth of the population.' Thus, as Westergaard goes on to say,

> The concentration of current resources for livelihood in the hands of a tiny minority is enormous; the gap between them and the poor yawns wide; and there is wealth enough piled up at the extreme top to eliminate mass poverty in the low reaches of the scale, if will and radical measures were directed to that.(4)

It is, however, important to note that the share of the 'top 1%' has declined substantially in terms of both income and personal wealth during the twentieth century: according to one authority, from 60% of personal wealth in 1923 to 30% in 1972. But the crucial corollary of this is that the redistribution of wealth has been confined to those in the immediately adjacent groups in the socio-economic hierarchy.(5)

At the other end of the scale, according to Townsend, the leading authority on the incidence of poverty in contemporary Britain, '25% of households and 23% of persons were in poverty. Or, to put it another way, more than half the population in Britain will experience poverty at some point in their lives'.(6)

It should be noted that government activity, via the institutions of the Welfare State, does mitigate this picture, but only to a very limited extent, and only significantly in respect of the very poorest people in society.(7) Contrary to the popular view, the effects of taxation are 'broadly neutral' and the bulk of Welfare State provision for a large majority of the population is funded 'by "horizontal" rather than "vertical" redistribution - from ordinary wage-earners at work'.(8)

The overall conclusion must therefore be that gross inequalities of wealth persist. And, indeed, under the Conservative governments in the 1980s, in part because of the recession but also as a deliberate result of ideological principle relentlessly applied, such disparities have <u>widened</u> significantly.

With this economic inequality has gone political

2

inequality. The power of decision-making resides overwhelmingly with those who are integrated either materially or ideologically - or both - into the economic ruling class. The historical origins and subsequent nature of this ruling class have been a matter of fierce debate. To what extent the nineteenth century industrial bourgeoisie was an autonomous and separate (and even hegemonic) class, or alternatively, was always entrapped within a continuingly dominant aristocratic class structure, has been at the kernel of this argument.(9) However, in this context, the precise nature of the ruling class is not of paramount importance. Similarly, although there have been significant changes in the composition of the contemporary ruling class (not least in the rise within the Conservative Party of the lower middle class ideologues of the new right at the expense of both the Conservative radicals of the McLeod era and the old Tory patrician paternalists), the salient point here is the continuing dominance of the political representatives of the capitalist system. Successive analyses have demonstrated the homogeneous elite nature of the major decision-making bodies in the modern state: the higher civil service, the judiciary, the executive itself, etc.(10) Not only do decision-makers have a predominantly elite background, they also operate within the relatively narrow ideological parameters of the existing socio-economic system.(11)

Clear and major inequalities exist, therefore, in both the economic and political contexts, stemming from the class structure which is inherent in the capitalist system. But, as noted earlier, there are other important areas of inequality which must be analysed. There are two major aspects of the contemporary 'class socialisation' process which are in direct tension with each other. There is no doubt that, over the last thirty years or so, the immense, unquestioned and self-confident social dominance of the British upper class has diminished considerably. This is manifest in a thousand and one ways: for example, the decline of 'domestic service'; the virtual disappearance of the 'Oxford/BBC' accent; the abolition of the amateur/ professional division in most major sports. Above all, perhaps, the change has been seen in the growth of a genuinely mass culture, in which fashion, music, and leisure have to a large, though by no means total, extent spanned class divisions and been subject at least equally to generational tensions. Moreover, the transmission of mass culture through the rapidly developing technology of the mass media has ensured that in one sense there has been a democratisation of culture.

All this would point to the breaking down of important cultural barriers within the hierarchy of class inequalities. (And similar arguments might be held to apply to the expansion of secondary, and especially tertiary, education, as is discussed below in the overall context of educational developments.) Even here, though, substantial qualifications must be made. Quite opposite tendencies are, in fact, evident.(12) The importance of cultural (as opposed to physical) control by the ruling class has increased greatly during the twentieth century. The mass culture is, in reality, thoroughly imbued with capitalist values and assumptions. From their obsession with royalty and high society to their concentration upon competitive and individualistic values, the mass media, at least in their popular forms, act as a highly effective means of socialising the populace into acceptance of the existing socio-economic system. Moreover, the organisational structure and practice of media industries, in common with the general pattern of monopolistic development, have become concentrated in fewer and larger units as they have expanded. Paradoxically, therefore, with the massive increase in size and influence of the media, control has fallen increasingly to those already powerful within the overall capitalist structure.(13) One important effect of this process has been the 'homogenisation' of culture. No longer is the mass of the working class exposed to any significant 'counter culture'. There is no socialist mass circulation daily or Sunday newspaper; the socialist local press has disappeared; the cultural organs of the cooperative and labour movements have also been swept away. As cultural socialisation has increased in range and importance so it has become more uniform. The counter culture does of course exist - and indeed has flourished amongst the tertiary educated radical strata of the 1960s and beyond - but it has minimal contact with the working class.(14)

There are four aspects of social structure, in addition of course to education, which are of particular importance in the context of the analysis of inequality: geography, gender, age and race. Geographical inequalities within Britain have been evident throughout the twentieth century, but have become particularly acute since the 1930s.(15) In broad terms, the South East of England has become ever more dominant economically as the newer industries of the 1930s, and the increasingly important financial, commercial and administrative centres of power, became located in and around London. Parallel with this went the decline of the traditional heavy industries upon which the manufacturing base of the industrial revolution had been created in the nineteenth century. From around 1870, as Britain was first challenged and then rapidly overtaken by her industrial competitors, the industrial basis of British capitalism has been in relative decline.(16) When the recession came in the 1930s it was the older industrial areas which suffered: the Midlands and the South East remained relatively unaffected. The present recession has seen a partial change in this pattern. 'To the old industrial areas ... have been added new regions. And within each region of the country there are the unemployment blackspots of the inner cities'. This is a problem resulting not only from the decline of old industries and the (inadequate) creation of new employment: it reflects 'above all the collapse of the UK's international manufacturing role'.(17)

To regions of longstanding industrial decline - the North East and the North West of England, South Wales, Clydeside, Northern Ireland - must be added in the 1980s not only new areas (in particular the West Midlands, in the 1960s a centre of industrial affluence), but also pockets of severe inner city deprivation throughout virtually the whole of Britain. The indices of inequality here are numerous, and uniformly depressing. Not only are living standards generally considerably lower, and unemployment rates higher, social problems also abound. Infant mortality rates are higher, vandalism and petty crime greater, and general social alienation, especially among young people, is rife. In the 1960s and 1970s some attempts, however inadequate, were made at regional development in an attempt to counteract such trends. With the onset of the recession and Thatcherism even the pretence of such objectives has been abandoned, save in ad hoc response to specific eruptions of discontent (eg. Toxteth). In the 1980s the 'Two Nations' problem has reappeared, as the result of a complex of economic, political and social factors.

In relation to gender issues, there are two broad areas of inequality, both of which reinforce the existing patterns of structural inequality already discussed. There is, first, the generally patriarchal nature of society which results in discrimination, to some degree, against all women simply by virtue of their gender. This can be seen as a pervasive, though widely differentiated (as between classes, etc), form of social and political inequality. Secondly, there is overwhelming and voluminous evidence of economic, material disadvantages for women within the existing system, at all levels. These two areas are not of course separate and distinct, and the second may indeed be held to derive, at least to some extent, from the first.

Without entering here into the ideological complexities of the varying positions within the Women's Movement (liberal feminism, radical feminism, socialist feminism, etc),(18) it is undoubtedly the case that on both the general and the specific level women are discriminated against, and that that discrimination constitutes an important part of the overall inequalities within the social system. Whether the focus is on social institutions such as the nuclear family, or upon women's roles as workers, the pattern of disadvantage is the same. In the family, the woman is still for the most part

5

expected to fulfil a subsidiary, domestic, 'supportive', and
child-rearing role.   In occupational terms,   hard evidence is
even more dramatic.   'The few women in "higher   professional"
jobs   in 1978,   for example,   earned on average 20% less   than
their   male counterparts,   but women in manual work 40% to 50%
less   than   men   in   corresponding   wage-earner   grades'.(19)
Moreover,   both   in the professions and in manual   occupations
women   are   likely   to be found in the more lowly   paid   jobs:
school teaching (especially primary),   nursing, service sector
(cooks,   cleaners,   caterers,   etc).   'Because of assumptions
about gender appropriateness much of the work women perform is
seen   as   "women's work" in that it so closely   resembles   the
domestic work they perform in the family'.(20)
        It should also be borne in mind that the 'working   woman'
is no longer the exception.   By the 1980s 42% of the workforce
was female;   62% of working women were married and half of all
married   women   went out to work.(21)   The large majority   of
these workers - approximately 75% - were employed in low   paid
service sector occupations.   Even though women constitute more
than   40% of the workforce they earn only 25% of   the   total
wage   and salary bill.   Overall,   then,   women labour under a
double disadvantage: most women are socially and economically
disadvantaged and therefore suffer the inequalities common   to
the working class as a whole;   but most women workers are also
employed   in   low paid occupations relative to other   workers
(and   are   often   discriminated   against   overtly   by   Trade
Unions);(22)   and,   finally,   all   women are victims of   the
endemic   discrimination   of an   overwhelmingly   male-dominated
society.
        Generation   and   age provide another set   of   factors   by
which   inequalities experienced by working-class people become
more   severe.   The   great   majority   of   the   nine   million
pensioners   in Britain finished their full-time education aged
14   or younger;   and,   in the decades since they   left   school
fifty,   sixty or even seventy years ago,   they have had little
or no involvement in educational activity.   Growing up before
the   educational   expansions   following the 1944 Act   and   the
educational investment of the 1960s,   working-class people   of
their   generation have paid through their rates and taxes   for
other,   younger,   people's   education - but seldom reaped   the
benefit themselves.
        The ageing process itself also brings further inequalities
and   dependencies   on   the state.   The basic   weekly   pension
remains well below the one-third of average earnings which Age
Concern   suggests it should rise to;   and with fewer than   one
pensioner   in six being entitled to an   occupational   pension,
many   retired   people   are   forced   to   live   around   the
Supplementary   Benefit   level - yet feel too   proud   to   claim
their   entitlements.   Particularly vulnerable in   retirement,
and as they grow increasingly elderly,   are single pensioners,

women - and in particular elderly single women living on their
own. It is on these groupings, along with those of the ethnic
minority   elderly,   that   Pioneer   Work   has   focussed   its
attention.
     The   problem of racism in Britain is of major proportions
and of some considerable complexity.   (It should   always   be
stressed, however, that, as Salman Rushdie has said, 'Racism
.... is not our problem. It is yours. We simply suffer the
effects of your problem'.)(23) Obviously, the problem is by
no means confined to Britain, but there is a unique context
and depth to the British experience because of the legacy, as
much cultural as economic, of British imperialism. The deep-
rooted racialist attitudes (and hence racist legislation) stem
in large part from the imperialist mentality, and they affect
all social classes (vide 'Alf Garnett' and Enoch Powell, for
example).   In this context it is inappropriate to enter into
the complex and problematic area of racial inequality in
Britain.   But note should be taken again of the 'double
disadvantage' experienced   by black people in   Britain.*
Most of the black people in Britain - 40% of whom were born in
this country - are concentrated in run-down inner-city areas:
49% of black immigrant workers live in Greater London, and
another 22% in West Yorkshire, the West Midlands and South
East Lancashire.(24)   And they tend to experience all the
worst   aspects   of   contemporary   urban   poverty: high
unemployment, poor schooling, poor health, inadequate housing,
and so on.   The unemployment rate among black people, for
example, was 17.2%, compared with the national figure of 9.9%,
in 1981. If this whole complex of disadvantage is added on to
the 'cultural racism' referred to earlier, it becomes clear
that, for the two million or so black people in Britain, and
especially for the non-professional majority, there is a very
considerable structural inequality.(25)
     There are of course many other areas of disadvantage and
inequality within contemporary British society.   Nothing has
been said here, for example, of religious discrimination or of
the web of disadvantage experienced by the physically and
mentally disabled; and the whole dimension of Welsh, Scottish
and, especially, Northern Irish, problems has been omitted.
Nevertheless, enough has been said to indicate the stark
reality of a grossly unequal society.   And, it must be
emphasised, ours is a society which is becoming, under the
impact of the recession and the policies of the Conservative
governments of the 1980s, considerably more unequal in all

---

*   Throughout the text, 'ethnic minorities' refers to the
whole range of ethnic minority groups, including white as well
as Asian and West Indian.   'Black' refers to both Asians and
West Indians, although, when particular case studies etc are
being discussed, reference is made to the specific ethnic
minority group concerned.

of the areas discussed briefly above. It is within this context of inequality that education must be analysed.

Before doing so, however, it is important to note here the way in which the microcosmic Pioneer Work development - which is the central concern of this book - relates to this macrocosmic societal inequality. As will be argued in Chapter 3, adult education has long had an orientation towards broadly working-class, social purpose provision.(26) And in the 1980s and beyond there is as strong a series of reasons as ever before to concentrate resources and attention upon the development of such work.

The concerns of Pioneer Work, however, have been somewhat more specific. All the groups of people with which Pioneer Work is involved are indeed working class: but they are also subject to double disadvantage. They are working class and unemployed, or female, or black, or retired, (and often a combination of two or more of these). What they have in common of course is that they are 'unwaged', dependent in one way or another upon the state (through child allowance, pensions etc), and are, generally, in the most disadvantaged sections of the working class. But what is beyond doubt is that such disadvantaged groups have major educational, as well as social, economic and psychological, needs. The more that the educational system as a whole can devote attention to developing relevant, effective and successful modes of provision, the more it will help eventually to undermine the structures of overall inequality in society.

Like all other institutions and processes within capitalist society, the educational system has been subject to contradictory pressures. Essentially, education has expanded rapidly since the later part of the nineteenth century because changing economic, technological and commercial requirements have necessitated a higher degree of numeracy, literacy, cultural and general educational and technological skills on the part of the workforce. In this sense, the educational system exists in order to provide an appropriately equipped workforce for the changing society. This functional, utilitarian role has necessarily had the effect of socialising the large majority of the adolescent population into semi-skilled or unskilled employment (or indeed on occasion into unemployment). As Miliband has pointed out, the net effect of this is to produce the belief amongst the working class that 'they are the prisoners, not of a social system, but of an ineluctable fate'.(27)

Over and above this class-confirming role in relation to the working class, the educational system, via the leading public schools, plays an equally important part in determining the elite socialisation of the upper class. Not only do such schools train their pupils for future leadership roles, they also instil intrinsically bourgeois values of competition,

8

hierarchy, and individualism. Moreover, the very narrowness of the social recruitment (and the predominance of single sex boarding schools) is a powerful factor in producing class solidification. The importance of the public schools, socially and politically, can be seen from the very high proportion of leading decision-takers whose educational backgrounds include public schools (followed very often by Oxford or Cambridge). Thus, for example, from the 2.5% (approximately) of the population attending public schools have come, in the 1970s: 64% of Conservative MPs; 77% of Conservative Cabinet Ministers (1970 Cabinet); 89% of senior Royal Navy officers (and 86% and 62% of equivalent Army and RAF officers); 82% of Ambassadors; 80% of High Court and Appeal Court judges; 67% of Church of England bishops; 68% of directors of forty major industrial firms; 80% of directors of clearing banks; 77% of directors of merchant banks; 83% of directors of major insurance companies; and 55% of governors and directors of the Bank of England.(28) (Over two-thirds of senior civil servants - Under-Secretary and above - also have a public school background, although this proportion has been declining consistently since 1945.)

Against this whole pattern of class-confirming socialisation via education, there exists a series of quite other tendencies within education. At the ideological level there has been a predominantly liberal approach to the educational process from within the profession as a whole, and, to an extent, from politicians and civil servants. Thus, there has been a commitment to a conception of education as a critical, open-ended, enriching experience, in which, at all levels, both curriculum and teaching methods are characterised by liberal pedagogic criteria: a belief in objectivity and the impartial explication of all viewpoints; a focus on developing to the full the individual's abilities; the encouragement of a critical and enquiring approach; an emphasis upon knowledge for its own sake rather than for vocational or utilitarian purposes, etc. In practice these commitments have been restricted largely though not exclusively to the higher levels of the educational system. As Westergaard and Resler have noted,

> Public provision of education has been expanded to meet in the main utilitarian demands ... Elite education, by contrast, has always seen objectives which were beyond this ... (ie. of the 'liberal' type referred to above). The price paid for the expansion of the latter has been further entrenchment of the notion that, except for a minority, education must be seen to pay off.(29)

Such precepts are being challenged by the Conservative governments of the 1980s, of course, as is discussed below in relation both to universities and to adult education. But historically such a division has certainly applied. And there has been a marked discrepancy, therefore, between the practical, vocational education for the mass, and the cultural, liberal education for the elite.

Nevertheless, the liberal orientation in tension with the utilitarian reality remains one of the central contradictions of the overall educational system.

Closely related to this has been the educators', and indeed the politicians', insistence that the educational process in Britain (and in the western democracies generally) was essentially 'democratic and free', in the sense that its intellectual autonomy and control over curriculum content were sacrosanct, and were not subject to state interference. This was, it has been argued, in sharp contrast to the practice of totalitarian regimes, especially those of the USSR and similar societies. Thus, far from being a bulwark of an inegalitarian and exploitative society, whose function was to socialise the respective classes into their appropriate economic and social roles, education, on this argument, is seen as a key means of ensuring the individual's free access to the whole range of knowledge, and therefore of critical importance in the overall democratic structure. Within this context, it is argued, there has been an increasing equality of opportunity in the twentieth century, resulting, with the huge expansion of educational opportunities, in increased social mobility. The talented working-class person, it is argued, has the opportunity to rise via the educational system to a far higher social and economic position. In this sense education is thus the key attribute of the 'open society'.

There is some validity in these claims. There is a high degree of educational independence and commitment to liberal educational values in Britain, compared with the restrictive and totalitarian educational systems of many other societies. Similarly, not only has the British secondary education system expanded, especially since the 1944 Education Act, but the introduction of a comprehensive educational structure in the 1970s, incomplete though it was, marked a major advance towards a more egalitarian approach.

In the tertiary sector the expansion of student numbers at universities, and the creation of the polytechnic structure in the 1960s, have resulted in a major increase in the numbers of people who have undertaken degree level work. Students attending universities, for example, have increased in number from 50,246 in 1938/9, to 138,711 in 1964/5, and to 297,200 by 1980/81.(30)

Strong qualifications have to be made to these arguments, however. On the general level, it is true of education as a whole that institutions and the policies they pursue are predominantly conservative, and fall within the prevailing

10

consensual framework, in terms of ideological parameters, priorities and objectives. (A more detailed discussion of these points, and the related and key issue of 'objectivity and commitment' in teaching, is to be found below in the context of adult education.) On the more specific point of educational expansion, it must be noted, first, that the introduction of a comprehensive system, however radical its intensions might have been, could not alone have ended unequal social and economic structures. Whilst the outside context remains, the educational system must fulfil the economically functional and socialising roles discussed earlier. To the extent that the comprehensive reorganisation reduces inequalities and raises the educational, cultural (and by implication the <u>political</u>) horizons of the working class, so the educational <u>system</u> will come into conflict with the established order.

Not that there is much sign of this problem arising at present. Contrary to popular belief, social mobility has not increased markedly in Britain since 1945. There was 'no change of substance in the amount of movement up and down the social scale till about the time of World War II. And there seems now to have been little increase in social circulation after that either, leaving class disparities in individual opportunity sharply marked'.(31) Similarly, whilst university student numbers have risen sharply, especially since the 1950s, the age participation rate (APR) of working-class students has hardly changed. Professor Edwards has stated that 'the sharp escalation in numbers of students in the period from 1955-1970 ... was not accompanied by any closing of the gap between manual and non-manual workers. This means, of course, that the great majority of the increased flow of students came from the same social classes as before'.(32) In fact, between 1957 and 1975, the APR of sons of professional parents rose from 25.7% to 57.5%, and for daughters of professional parents, from 10% to 38%; whereas the APR for the sons of unskilled workers rose from 0.6% to 1.4%, and for the daughters of unskilled workers from nil to 0.8%.(33) A wealth of evidence suggests that these differences in the APR have little or nothing to do with differences in inherent abilities between the children of different social classes, but are the result of differing social environment.

By and large, therefore, the educational system, with all its contradictory orientations, is essentially integrated into the deeply inegalitarian socio-economic structure, and plays its part in maintaining that structure in the variety of ways already discussed. Post-school education is no exception to this general pattern. There is a clearly defined hierarchy of institutions with gradations of status, salary structure and so on. Further Education Colleges, with a relatively low status and funding, concentrate upon GCE and related courses for adolescents and, on a smaller scale, for adults, and upon low level vocational courses, and are at the bottom of the status ladder in the post-school educational structure. Colleges of education, colleges of higher education, polytechnics and universities constitute the other major rungs on that ladder.

Where though does adult education (AE) come in this spectrum? AE is notoriously difficult to define. It is not a single concept; nor is it, of course, organised and provided through a single agency, or even a group of similar agencies. The Russell Report situates AE as follows: '... there is a spectrum called further education which at one end is clearly vocational ... and at the other is personal, social, cultural and non-vocational'.(34) AE lies towards the latter end of this spectrum, though no fine dividing lines can be drawn.

Just as its definition is uncertain, so is its position in the hierarchy touched on briefly above. Since 1944 the Local Education Authority (LEA) sector has been the largest provider of statutory AE. But the LEAs involvement has been heterogeneous in the extreme, varying greatly in both quality and quantity, as well as in orientation. There are essentially five major styles of operation(35): local, free-standing 'area' adult education centres, colleges or institutes; community colleges, community schools or village colleges; departments of adult studies (or similar title) in FE colleges; polytechnic or colleges of higher education 'extension'; and residential AE institutions. The range of provision is very wide: but, at the risk of over-generalisation, it is probably the case that most AE work undertaken through these LEA organisations is institution-based, recreational/leisure activity (eg. the traditional evening class programme), or GCE or other relatively low level AE courses for adults on a part-time basis, or community-based innovative AE for disadvantaged sections of the community (eg. the unemployed; the literacy programme; English as a Second Language (ESL) and numeracy provision for ethnic minority groups, etc).

A point of central importance here and throughout this discussion of AE is that, whilst LEA provision may form the major share of AE, the total AE provision is of minuscule size. Around 1% of local authority total expenditure is on AE and, in the light of the persistent pressure on local authority finance in recent years, it is likely that this figure has been further reduced recently.(36) The proportion of finance expended by other institutions - the universities in particular - on AE is even less. AE is thus a marginal, as well as a diffused, activity, and is well-named 'The Poor Cousin'.(37)

Nevertheless, approximately two million people each year attend LEA adult education provision of some sort. How does this reflect upon the earlier discussion of education and socio-economic inequality? The first point is to reiterate the small scale of AE work. Even if the whole of such provision was made for the disadvantaged (which of course it is not), this would make relatively little impact of itself in the wider context. Secondly, whilst precise statistical information is not available, it is quite clear that the large majority of provision is institution-based, traditional in format, and does not on the whole attract the educationally disadvantaged. Thirdly, whilst most LEAs offer concessionary rates for disadvantaged adult students (eg. the unemployed, the disabled, etc), fees for LEA classes are high, and are a major disincentive to attendance for working-class adults. Finally, the small proportion of resources expended on community-based AE work, valuable though such provision can be, is inadequate, not only for the substantial needs of the adult disadvantaged, but also for there to be any real pressure on the institutions (and the LEAs) to move away from the traditional, institution-based approach.

On a slightly different dimension it is also relevant to note that the large bulk of LEA adult education provision is designed neither to provide access to higher education and/or qualifications (thus contributing to increasing social mobility and the breaking down of the structures of inequality in the wider society), nor to develop subject matter and curricula likely to induce any questioning of the existing social order. There are three important qualifications to this latter point: all educational provision, irrespective of content, provides educational benefit in the sense of developing social skills, an inquiring attitude of mind, etc (the notion of process being at least as important as content); and, secondly, community-based provision, whatever its ostensible characteristics, is often designed, very carefully and successfully, to achieve the beginnings of that critical and questioning attitude referred to above; finally, there are numerous examples of LEA financed provision on projects achieving significant advances within this dimension (eg. the literacy scheme; the funding of residential adult colleges with a strong community and working-class orientation such as the Northern College, near Barnsley). Nevertheless, the general point remains.

Before moving on to discuss the 'Responsible Bodies' (RBs), the universities and the WEA, it is important to note the large and important contribution made to AE by the voluntary sector in all its many forms. There has been a long tradition within the labour movement of educational endeavour, motivated in part precisely by the desire to mitigate at least some of the effects of a grossly unequal social and educational structure. From the Chartists onwards, education has been seen as of key importance by working-class socialists. The organisational forms developed to articulate this belief have included the plethora of organisations in and around the Cooperative Movement, the various workers' colleges (Ruskin, Coleg Harlech, etc), the Socialist Sunday Schools, and many more. AE activity within the voluntary sector has not been confined to the labour movement. Women's organisations, ethnic minority groups, church organisations and many others have all played an active role in AE, as well as community development. Whilst it is impossible to quantify such work, it has certainly made a contribution to the life of the community. However, the lack of resources available has been a considerable barrier to anything beyond small scale activity.

It is in the area of RB work (ie. WEA districts and university departments of adult education, designated RBs by the DES and in receipt of grants for teaching) that the concerns of AE with educational inequalities and the consequent need for concentration upon social purpose education for disadvantaged groups, and generally for the working class, have been strongest. The WEA was founded in 1903 as a result primarily of the success of Albert Mansbridge in convincing leading politicians, churchmen and other notables, of the need for a movement specifically geared to the education of the adult working class.(38) Throughout its history the WEA has had close connections with both the universities and the trade unions, and has always espoused liberal educational objectives. This has involved a complex, and at times contradictory, commitment to objectivity in teaching, to the pursuance of 'knowledge for knowledge's sake', and to the facilitation through education of the emancipation of the working class and the overall democratising of society.(39)

The essentially liberal and politically integrated perspective of the WEA resulted in the breakaway just before the First World War of the National Council of Labour Colleges (NCLC), which had an explicitly Marxist orientation and concentrated exclusively on the provision of economics, politics and industrial relations classes for trade unionists.(40) The large bulk of the work, however, and the funding from the state necessary to maintain it, was through the WEA. From the early years of the twentieth century until 1945 the overwhelming majority of working-class adult education took place within the framework of the WEA, and, specifically, within the structure of the three year tutorial class (ie. a group of not more than 24 students meeting once a week for two hours over three years of 24 meetings per year, taught by a university lecturer). The reasoning behind this policy was that only a sustained course could enable the previously poorly educated working-class adult to reach a standard appropriate to a serious university course. Moreover, to achieve the 'social purpose' objectives, educational provision had to be of a high standard.

Whilst the WEA expanded rapidly during the inter-war years, its central concern with working-class education, over a sustained period, and with a 'social purpose' orientation, was diluted. Shorter courses began to predominate, and non working-class students, interested in a whole range of subjects, enrolled in large numbers for WEA classes.

The post-war period saw a great expansion of all AE (from a low base of course). Within this experience two organisational changes were of profound importance for the WEA: the very rapid growth of LEA provision following the 1944 Education Act; and the establishment of University Extramural Departments (or Departments of Adult Education as most later became known), with the consequence of a distancing of the hitherto close relationship between the WEA and the universities.

The WEA grew in the post-war period (from 99,000 students in 1945/6 to 167,000 in 1973/4). But the programme was composed increasingly of shorter courses, and the tutorial class has now all but disappeared from the WEA, with the exception of the London and Yorkshire North districts. The numbers of manual workers attending WEA classes declined further, and, although it is difficult to calculate figures for the 1970s and 1980s, partly because of the large numbers of TUC 'Health and Safety' courses organised by the WEA in part of that period, there is no doubt that the proportion of manual workers has declined still further in more recent years.

The Russell Report in 1973 advocated that the WEA should concentrate, in accord with its own submission to the Committee, upon four main areas of provision for the disadvantaged and relinquish much of its general provision to other providers. The four areas specified were: education for the socially and culturally deprived living in urban areas; industrial studies work with the TUC and individual trade unions; political and social education; and 'courses of liberal and academic study below the level of university work'. It was also envisaged that there would be closer liaison between the WEA and the LEA, and a further weakening of the links between the WEA and the universities. Whilst the WEA has made some notable efforts to achieve provision in these areas, and by no means without success,(41) its task has been made impossible by a combination of adverse circumstances. Among the main elements have been: the failure of government to implement the Russell Report and the consequent absence of increased funding; the subsequent constrictions on finance from both central and local government, which have been continuous and increasing, reaching the point in the 1980s where the very existence of liberal AE is under threat (this is discussed below in the context of university adult education - UAE); the decline of the voluntary basis of the WEA and its increasing domination by older, generally more conservative and middle-class lay members; and the continuance of the trends in provision already noted towards short courses outside the social purpose tradition.

Overall, then, the ability of the WEA to play a major AE role in the erosion of educational inequality is limited and has been so for many years. This is not to say that the WEA has declined as an AE provider: quite clearly that is not the case. But it is to claim that the WEA's central, de facto, function is no longer the provision of social purpose AE for the working class.

Although UAE had its origins in the Extension Movement of the 1870s,(42) the modern structure and provision of UAE did not take shape until the post-1945 period.(43) UAE has developed within the context of its parent institutions, and has been characterised by the same complex blend of elitism, pure research orientations, technocratic and managerial subject developments, and a still powerful commitment to the 'liberal tradition' of education, primarily though not exclusively within the context of the arts and social sciences. (In the 1980s the average proportion of science and technology courses within UAE provision was approximately 15%). Nevertheless, one of the central characteristics of UAE has also been its position on the border territory between the generally introverted world of the university and the more pragmatic and prosaic wider society.

A number of trends relevant to the concern here with UAE and its relationship with inequality can be discerned. There have been declines in the longer courses, including tutorial classes, as noted earlier; and corresponding increases in shorter course provision.(44) The reasons for this decline need not concern us here.(45) There is no doubt that the universities, from the time of the creation of most of the major UAE departments in the earlier part of the post-war period, took explicit policy decisions to broaden their AE scope and to provide both shorter, less demanding courses in subject areas popular with the middle class, and to enter into the professional, vocational, high level areas of educational provision.(46)

Changes in subject balance within UAE provision show a related pattern. Concentration in the broad social studies area has been replaced by subjects which have a strong participative element and/or offer some partial escape from social and political realities.(47) Some of this change has resulted from the creation of the Open University but it must be remembered that the numbers involved in the OU Social Science and Arts degree schemes are not very great, and, more importantly in our context, the large majority are not working class. This decline in UAE social studies provision, coupled with the erosion of the sustained course and the marked decrease in emphasis by providers upon working-class AE, has reflected a widespread disillusionment with and withdrawal from political and social concern by significant sections of the working class. Of course, 'activists' and 'politically aware' adults have always been a small minority amongst the working class. And it would be a mistake to hark back, by implication, to some mythical golden age. Nevertheless, the contemporary picture is one of particular working-class cynicism and apathy, which has, if anything, increased during the prolonged recession and the austerity of Thatcher's Britain. (See, for example, the Labour Party's 1983 election result.)(48)

With the exception of three minority areas of UAE work - industrial studies, the development of 'Return to Learn' courses for women, and community adult education, which are discussed at the end of this section - trends within UAE in the post-war period have not countered such tendencies. Indeed, UAE has been a part of the educational dimension of this move away from working-class, social purpose AE. Two developments in particular have characterised UAE in the post-war period: post-experience vocational education (PEVE); and professional adult education work. It is in the former field, with the provision of short, intensive high level courses, predominantly in the science and technology fields, that UAE has seen the most significant expansion, especially from the mid 1970s onwards. The motivations underlying this development are partly financial, of course. In times of economic cutback, 'profitable' PEVE provision is very appealing to hard-pressed university authorities. But there is also a more fundamental ideological reason for this shift of emphasis: the universities have responded to the demands of both government and industrial and financial capital for a more utilitarian and 'practical' approach. UAE has thus altered its provision in order to integrate more fully into the developing managerial, technological elitism of the contemporary university structure.

Whatever the nature of this provision there can be no doubt that it represents a move away from social purpose, working-class, liberal adult education. And the same can be said, whatever its other merits may be, of the development of professional continuing education: the provision of full-time postgraduate courses carrying a Diploma or Master's qualification, in addition to a CQSW, for those involved in social work and related fields; and short courses for specific professional groups - magistrates, prison officer personnel, etc.

A further area of UAE specialism, of some importance, has been in professional adult education itself: the provision of courses at post-graduate level for those engaged professionally in AE, and the development of research programmes and related activities in the field of AE. Whilst departments vary widely in the degree of emphasis given to such work, it is generally the case that there has been a move away from subject specialisms and towards the discipline of AE itself amongst full-time UAE staff in recent years, and, significantly, especially amongst senior UAE staff. Such developments reflect the increasing tendencies of universities to disciplinary specialisms, defined relatively narrowly, in contrast to the broader liberal tradition. The salient point in this context, again, however, is that such developments necessarily reduce further the degree to which UAE gives priority to working-class, social purpose AE.

This whole pattern of UAE provision and structure has been considerably affected by the financial and organisational changes of the early 1980s. This is not the place for a detailed discussion of these complex, and largely negative, developments, either in the context of the whole university system or the specific area of UAE. Whatever the complexity of the detail, however, the overall outline is clear enough. The UGC cuts of 1981, of 14%, have resulted in the loss of one-sixth of university academic staff, increased workloads and worsening staff:student ratios, and serious demoralisation within the university sector as a whole (parallel to the situation in the whole of the educational world as a result of the Thatcher governments' policies). Following the 'cuts' of 1981 there have been continuous further reductions in funding, culminating, in 1985, in the publication of the government's Green Paper on Higher Education outlining its policy for the remainder of the century. Among other things this postulates the closure of some departments, and possibly whole universities; a drastic reduction in student numbers; a division between elite universities with a high research profile and the remainder, which are planned to become almost exclusively teaching institutions; and a modification of the 'Robbins principle' to the effect that not only should students be able enough to benefit from a university education, but that that benefit must justify the cost.(49)

UAE departments have been affected by these UGC cuts by slightly more than the average university department. However, over and above this, the DES announced in 1984 its plans for the introduction of a 'new formula' for the allocation of RB grant (to both the universities and the WEA), and a reduction of 14.3% overall in the total allocation of grant, again applicable to both the universities and the WEA, over a three year period. The 'new formula', in keeping with

18

general government policy, assigns RB grant to UAE departments on the basis of 'output' (measured in terms of Effective Student Hours - ESHs). There are 'weightings' for such considerations as rural locations, long courses, and fee subsidies for certain categories of students. But these are very much ancillary to the main scheme. In addition, 'bonus points' are awarded for the use of internal university academic staff; and 5% of the total budget (c. £250,000 at 1984/5 figures) is to be held in reserve partly for contingencies but mainly for allocation for specific, one-year, innovative projects.

The net effects of the 'new formula' are likely to be largely deleterious, though this must remain conjecture until 1988-90. The principal results are likely to be twofold. There will be a fairly rapid reduction in the numbers of full-time UAE staff and a change in full-time staff roles so that less teaching and more organising and 'catalyst' work is undertaken. This is because the use of part-time teaching staff is far cheaper, especially if internal university staff can be used at no charge or a nominal fee; alternatively, part-time tutors can be recruited from the large numbers of unemployed and intellectually able graduates. Secondly, and in our context even more important, there is likely to be strong pressure to provide short, undemanding, popular classes for which large numbers can be recruited easily. This will maximise ESHs at minimal organisational cost.

This latter point, in particular, will undermine seriously UAE involvement in working-class AE. Such work is labour-intensive, high-risk, and recruits only low numbers, largely because of the built-in alienation of the mass of the working class from education. Such alienation is a result of previously negative experiences, both of education itself and of the institutional structures of the state at a whole number of levels.

This then is the context of UAE in the 1980s; and, on the whole, a pretty gloomy context it is. In common with the rest of the educational system UAE is under extreme pressure, and the social purpose, working-class AE (which is the focus of attention here because of its relationship with structural inequality) is under the greatest threat of all.

Nevertheless, there are areas of such work which have survived, and indeed to an extent prospered, despite this negative context. These are all relatively minor areas of provision; and they take place within an overall AE system which is itself, it must again be emphasised, the 'poor cousin' of the educational structure. And that structure itself has been the subject of severe financial reductions in the 1980s. So the significance of these areas of work must not be exaggerated. In one sense they are 'drops in the ocean'. But, as later chapters go on to argue, they do have some significance as catalysts, and examples of at least some 'good practice'.

There are three such areas to which particular attention should be drawn: industrial studies; 'Return to Learn' or 'New Opportunities' courses for women; and community adult education. The remainder of this book is an exploration, analysis and critique of one Department's work in the last of these areas. But it may be useful, finally in this introductory overview, to situate the other and closely related aspects of provision.(50)

Mention has already been made of the TUC's move away from the 'liberal approach' to industrial studies for trade unionists. This has resulted in a diminution of the proportion of AE work with trade unionists that is undertaken by the UAE sector, and a large increase in the role training courses undertaken by other agencies (FE colleges, etc). Whilst it is possible to adopt a liberal approach within the TUC course framework, and many WEA and UAE lecturers have managed successfully so to do,(51) there is no doubt that the TUC approach is necessarily constricting, given its training orientation, and tends to be inimical to social purpose working-class AE.

Despite this generally restrictive context, UAE departments (and the WEA, and some other agencies) do provide genuine, sustained liberal adult education courses for trade unionists. At the Leeds, Sheffield and Nottingham departments, for example, there are sizeable programmes of three-year day release courses for the National Union of Mineworkers, organised on the basis not of role training, but of analysing trade unions, industrial relations, and the labour movement within the wider society, from historical, political, economic, sociological and legal perspectives.

The numbers passing through such courses are of course relatively small. But it is arguable that, in the traditions of 'education for citizenship' for the active sections of the working class, such people have the potential to influence far greater numbers within working-class communities. In that sense such educational experiences can be seen as of some significance within the wider society.

The marked increase within UAE (and the WEA) over the 1970s and 1980s of provision for, and usually by, women has been a part of the overall growth of women's consciousness and the women's movement.(52) 'Return to Learn' or 'New Opportunities' courses have had several purposes: to help in the process of liberating women from subservient, domestic roles, and gaining confidence and understanding by coming together as women to study and to discuss common problems and issues. At its best, such provision has combined social and political concerns within an educational and genuinely liberal context, and has produced some of the most educationally valuable and exciting AE courses of recent years. Some emphasis within this provision has been placed upon access to higher education, and to professional or voluntary training in various fields.

Returning to the central theme of this chapter - the relationship between general, structural inequalities and the role of UAE provision - it should be noted, however, that the large bulk of such provision has attracted largely <u>middle class</u> women. This is, of course, a problem for the <u>women's</u> movement as a whole, as it is indeed for the whole of the left in Britain in the 1980s.(53) And it applies with particular force to single issue movements, such as the peace movement.(54)

However, there have been some significant attempts in recent years to broaden this provision and to devise structures which will appeal to working-class women. Progress has been made, for example, in the Southampton and Leeds UAE departments in this area. (The experience of this type of work in West Yorkshire is discussed in some detail in Chapter 6).

All these areas of work relate to the broader concept of community adult education(55) construed within the context of social purpose AE for working-class adults. The remainder of this book is devoted to a critical analysis of one UAE Department's relatively small scale attempts, in the 1980s, to utilise these concepts to construct programmes of community-based AE for working-class adults.

Pioneer Work, which has organised a wide range of innovative, community-based courses with disadvantaged working-class groups in two major northern cities, provides, in the opinion of the contributors to this book, a case study which will be of value to other adult educators wishing to develop analogous work elsewhere.

REFERENCES

1. See J Westergaard and H Resler, Class in a Capitalist Society: a Study of Contemporary Britain, Penguin, 1976; A B Atkinson, Unequal Shares: Wealth in Britain, Penguin, 1972; P Townsend, Poverty in the United Kingdom, Penguin, 1979; (eds) N Bosanquet and P Townsend, Labour and Inequality: a Fabian Study of Labour in Power 1974-1979, Heinemann, 1980.

2. It should be noted, however, that some feminists have argued that gender inequality is as fundamental, or even more so, than social class inequality.

3. J Scott, The British Upper Class, in (eds) D Coates,

G Johnston and R Bush, A Socialist Anatomy of Britain, Polity Press (Basil Blackwell), 1985, pp 29-30.

4.   J Westergaard, Income, Wealth and the Welfare State, in (eds) D Coates and G Johnston, Socialist Arguments, Martin Robertson, 1983, pp 153-4.

5.   J Urry, The Class Structure, in (eds) Coates, Johnston, and Bush, A Socialist Anatomy of Britain, p 60. Urry goes on to state that 'the next 4% increased their share from about one-fifth to one-quarter, while the next 5% doubled their share from about 7% to 14/15% and the next 10% tripled theirs from 5% to 15%'.

6.   Ibid, p 64.

7.   See Westergaard, in (eds) Coates and Johnston, Socialist Arguments.

8.   Ibid, pp 160-1.

9.   See P Anderson, Origins of the Present Crisis, in (eds) Anderson and Blackburn, Towards Socialism, Fontana and New Left Books, 1965; and E P Thompson, The Peculiarities of the English, reprinted in Thompson, The Poverty of Theory, Merlin Press, 1977.

10. See, for example, R Miliband, The State in Capitalist Society, Weidenfeld and Nicolson, 1969; J Urry and J Wakeford, Power in Britain, Heinemann, 1973.

11. This is well exemplified in Miliband, The State in Capitalist Society.

12. The argument which follows draws heavily upon Miliband's work.

13. See G Murdock and P Golding, For a Political Economy of Mass Communications, in (eds), R Miliband and J Saville, Socialist Register 1973, Merlin Press, 1973.

14. For arguments about the importance of this new radical middle-class stratum see D Coates, The Context of British Politics, Hutchinson, 1984, Chapter 7.

15. See D Massey, Geography and Class, in (eds) Coates, Johnston and Bush, A Socialist Anatomy of Britain.

16. There are numerous analyses of this decline and the reasons for it. See, for example, A Glyn and J Harrison,

The British Economic Disaster, Pluto Press, 1980;
Laurence Harris, British Capital: Manufacturing,
Finance and Multinational Corporations, in (eds) Coates,
Johnston, and Bush, A Socialist Anatomy of Britain;
A Glyn and B Sutcliffe, British Capitalism, Workers and
the Profit Squeeze, Penguin, 1972; R Bacon and W Eltis,
Britain's Economic Problem: too few producers,
MacMillan, 1978.

17. Massey, Geography and Class, p 82.

18. See S Perrigo, The Women's Movement: Patterns of
Oppression and Resistance, in (eds) Coates, Johnston
and Bush, A Socialist Anatomy of Britain.

19. Westergaard, in (eds) Coates and Johnston, Socialist
Arguments, p 157.

20. Perrigo, The Women's Movement, p 127.

21. Ibid, p 126.

22. See R Hyman, Class Struggle and the Trade Union Movement,
in (eds) Coates, Johnston and Bush, A Socialist Anatomy
of Britain; J Beale, Getting it Together, Pluto Press,
1983; A Phillips, Hidden Hands, Pluto Press, 1983.

23. S Rushdie, cited in Kum Kum and Reena Bhavnani, Racism
and Resistance in Britain, in (eds) Coates, Johnston
and Bush, A Socialist Anatomy of Britain, p 146.

24. Coates, The Context of British Politics, p 175.

25. For further detailed information on both gender and
racial disadvantage see ibid, Chapter 8.

26. See, for example, R Fieldhouse, The Workers' Educational
Association: Aims and Achievements, 1903-1977, Syracuse
University Publications in Continuing Education, USA,
1978; and G F Brown, Working class Adult Education, in
(eds) A H Thornton and M Stephens, The University in
its Region: the Extramural Contribution, Department of
Adult Education, University of Nottingham, 1977; and
The Joint Committee of University and Working Class
Representatives, Oxford and Working Class Education,
Oxford, 1908.

27. Miliband, The State in Capitalist Society, p 242.

28.   Source: T Noble, Modern Britain: Structure and Change,
      Batsford, 1975, p 314.

29.   Westergaard and Resler, Class in a Capitalist Society,
      p 333.

30.   P Gosden, The Education System since 1944, Martin
      Robertson, 1983, Chapter 5, The Universities, p 136.

31.   Westergaard and Resler, Class in a Capitalist Society,
      p 314.

32.   Professor E G Edwards Higher Education for Everyone,
      Nottingham, 1982, p 82.

33.   Source: ibid.

34.   Adult Education: A Plan for Development, HMSO, 1973,
      para 4 (popularly known as the Russell Report, after its
      Chairman, Sir Lionel Russell).

35.   This categorisation is taken from A Stock, The
      Organisation of Education for Adults in England and
      Wales, in (ed) M Tight, Opportunities for Adult Education,
      Croom Helm, 1982, pp 58 - 61.

36.   The Russell Report estimated the figure as 1.1% of total
      local authority expenditure on all services. Michael
      Newman cites this figure (The Poor Cousin, Allen and
      Unwin, 1979), and states that he was unable to ascertain
      any more recent figure from the DES.

37.   The title of Newman's book, ibid.

38.   On the WEA see: R Fieldhouse, The Workers' Educational
      Association; B Jennings, Knowledge is Power: a Short
      History of the WEA, Department of Adult Education,
      University of Hull, 1979; M Stocks, The Workers'
      Educational Association: the First Fifty Years,
      Allen and Unwin, 1953.

39.   For a full discussion of the liberal tradition in this
      context see Chapters 2, 3 and 9 of R Taylor,
      K Rockhill and R Fieldhouse, University Adult
      Education in England and the USA: a reappraisal of the
      liberal tradition, Croom Helm, 1985.

40.   See J P M Millar, The Labour College Movement, NCLC, nd;
      W W Craik, Central Labour College, Lawrence and Wishart,
      1964.

41.   For example: the large programme of trade union work
       initiated in conjunction with the TUC in the 1970s;
       provision for mentally and physically disabled adults;
       programmes of work in Peace Studies in the 1980s; the
       WEA project on work with unemployed adults in the North
       East, specially financed by the DES in the 1980s, etc.

42.   See N A Jepson, The Beginnings of English University
       Adult Education, Michael Joseph, 1973.

43.   For a full discussion of UAE, concentrating upon the
       post-1945 developments, see Taylor, et al, University
       Adult Education in England and the USA, Chapter 4.

44.   Thus, by 1983/4, courses of two or three years' duration
       had fallen to 718, those of 20+ meetings totalled 2,998,
       and those of 19 meetings or fewer had risen to 5,812.
       Source: UCACE Annual Report, 1983-4.

45.   See Taylor, et al, University Adult Education in England
       and the USA, Chapter 4, for a discussion of these.

46.   As early as 1945, a conference of Vice-Chancellors of
       the Universities of Oxford, Cambridge and London
       expressed the view that UAE should become more diverse,
       specifically to meet the 'special needs of those engaged
       in the professions or in industry'. (cited in J A Blyth,
       English University Adult Education 1908-1958: a unique
       tradition, Manchester University Press, 1983).

47.   For details of these changes, see Professor R Dyson,
       Determining Priorities for University Extramural
       Education (inaugural lecture), University of Keele, 1978.

48.   For a discussion of this and related issues see, for
       example, E J Hobsbawm, et al, The Forward March of
       Labour Halted?, Lawrence and Wishart, 1981; (ed)
       J Curran, The Future of the Left, Polity Press, 1984;
       the essays by D Coates and R Miliband in Socialist
       Register 1983, Merlin Press, 1983; and Coates, Johnston
       and Bush, A Socialist Anatomy of Britain.

49.   The Green Paper produced a storm of criticism from
       diverse quarters, including Enoch Powell, who denounced
       its utilitarian and instrumentalist ideology as
       'barbarism' in the House of Commons.

50.   For a somewhat more detailed discussion, see Taylor
       et al, University Adult Education in England and the
       USA, Chapter 5.

51.   For arguments to this effect, see R Fieldhouse and
       K Forrester, The WEA and Trade Union Education, The
       Industrial Tutor, Vol 3, No 9, Spring, 1984.

52.   See J Thompson, Learning Liberation, Croom Helm, 1984.

53.   See D Coates, The Context of British Politics,
       pp 132-136 for discussion of this.

54.   See R Taylor, The British Peace Movement and Socialist
       Change, in (eds) Miliband and Saville, Socialist
       Register 1983.

55.   For a general discussion of community adult education
       see K Ward, Community Adult Education: its Potential
       and Limitations, in (eds) J A Jowitt and R Taylor, The
       Politics of Adult Education, Occasional Papers, No 5,
       Bradford, 1985.

       For an examination of four models of community education
       (ie. Community Organisation, Community Development,
       Community Action, and Social Action) see T Lovett, C
       Clarke, and A Kilmurray, Adult Education and Community
       Action, Croom Helm, 1983, Chapter 3.

Chapter 2

RESPONSES TO UNEMPLOYMENT

Without any doubt unemployment is a major issue throughout the late twentieth century industrialised world. High levels of unemployment have characterised all major capitalist economies since the mid-1970s: and all major political parties are agreed that the phenomenon of unemployment is not only a centrally important political issue but raises also most profound economic, social and moral questions. In Britain, of course, the problem has been particularly acute, and it is no exaggeration to claim that unemployment is generally held to be the single most important social and political issue in the 1980s.

There has been a considerable amount of educational, training and 'therapeutic' activity undertaken with unemployed people in Britain (in addition, of course, to other areas of provision). Whilst much of this has come through the statutory agencies, there has been a significant amount of work undertaken by the voluntary sector too.

Within the specific field of AE, provision for the unemployed has received considerable attention, and a modest but significant level of additional funding, during the 1980s. In this context it is important to note that the bulk of Pioneer Work activity - the central concern of this book - has been devoted to developing work with the unemployed. Whilst this has been focussed, rightly and naturally, upon the needs and problems of the unemployed in the immediate vicinity - urban West Yorkshire - it has also been linked to national initiatives and developments (described and analysed in Chapters 3 and 4). Appropriate educational provision for unemployed adults, then, has been the central thrust of Pioneer Work's concerns. In this chapter, the national context within which these initiatives have developed is explored and analysed briefly, and the problems confronting adult educators wishing to develop appropriate provision are discussed.

The 1930s and the 1980s

The starting point must be the comparison with the 1930s.   In
many ways there are close parallels at all levels between the
unemployment situations in Britain in the 1930s and the 1980s.
Unemployment in both decades was a chronic problem.   By 1931
there were 687,500 long-term unemployed out of a total of 2.7
million.   Whilst there had been persistent unemployment
throughout the 1920s, it was not until the early 1930s that
the structural nature of unemployment, and its importance as a
major national problem, was generally recognised.   As in the
1980s, regional variations were pronounced, with North East
and North West England, South Wales and Clydeside the worst
affected areas; and manual workers in the traditional heavy
industries comprised the overwhelming majority of   the
unemployed.
     A variety of institutions, both statutory and voluntary,
became involved in work with the unemployed in the 1930s.
Churches, charitable bodies, voluntary organisations, local
and central government, and more particularly a variety of
adult educators, responded to unemployment.(1)
     By the early 1930s, clubs for the unemployed were being
established in many parts of the country.   These were often
supported, or indeed initiated, by churches and 'Mayors'
Funds'.   They were most commonly located in church halls.
Deliberately or otherwise, the churches helped shift the focus
of responses to unemployment away from political concern
towards recreational and leisure pursuits.
     Voluntary organisations seemed to share the   same
perspectives.   In 1930 a national conference concerned with
promoting work with the unemployed was organised by the
British Association of Residential Settlements, the YMCA and
TOC H Centres.(2)   In 1932 a conference called by the British
Institute of Adult Education led to the establishment of a
Central Advisory Council for Unemployed Workers; and in 1933,
this developed into a National Committee for the United
Kingdom associated with the National Council of Social
Service.   This Committee subsequently received funds from the
newly appointed Commissioners for Special Areas and the
proportion of clubs with an occupational base and   an
educational programme increased.
     It was mainly the case, however, that 'the majority of
unemployed club members always used them for recreational
purposes.   George Stevens, who worked as an organiser with
National Council of Social Service wrote in 1938 that "75% of
the membership of unemployed clubs regard it as a place in
which to be idle...."'.(3) Numerically, at least, the growth
of the clubs was significant.   Over 2,300 were known to the
NCSS in May 1934 and they were used by 250,000 people.
     These   developments were supported by a number   of

educational agencies.   The British Library organised a
National Book Appeal for the unemployed, residential colleges
organised   courses   for   the   unemployed,   and   the   local
authorities,   in   many   areas,   in   addition   to   providing
facilities   for   the   young   unemployed,   gave   increasing
assistance through classes provided in unemployed clubs, or
attempted to bring the unemployed into their further education
institutions.

      The Responsible Bodies (ie. the Workers' Educational
Association - WEA - and the University Extramural Departments)
were   also   involved in pioneering work with   the   unemployed.
With financial support from the Pilgrim Trust, the WEA
appointed tutor-organisers for work with the unemployed, and
organised classes for the unemployed clubs in many areas.   It
has been argued that the involvement of the extramural
departments   and   the   WEA   in   providing   classes   for   the
unemployed 'frequently, wittingly or unwittingly nudged adult
education away from political concern towards recreational
activities, and diverted the attention of the unemployed from
the   field   of   political   action   to   the   palliatives   of
recreational and leisure pursuits'.(4) This argument would
seem to have been supported in official circles, judging by a
Board of Education pamphlet on the educational problems of the
South Wales coalfields: 'With so much unemployment, it is
more than ever necessary to make proper provision for ...
hobbies and recreational activities of all kinds and the
cultural use of leisure'.(5)

      As in the 1980s, therefore, there was a wide variety of
providing bodies in the 1930s.   A key difference, however, is
that   whereas   in   the   1930s   there   was   a   prominent   and
influential organisation representing the unemployed - the
National   Unemployed   Workers'   Movement   (NUWM)   - no   such
organisation has existed in the 1980s.   The NUWM was a
militant left-wing movement, led by Communist Party members or
sympathisers,   most   notably   Wal   Hannington,   the   National
Organiser.   After the 1926 General Strike the TUC broke off
its joint activities with the NUWM, but both organisations
were   active   in   the   1930s,   and,   with   their   different
ideological   orientations,   were   responsible   for   a   strong
'social purpose orientation' within educational provision for
the unemployed. By contrast, despite persistently high levels
of unemployment, the labour movement of the 1980s has not
created a mass, national movement of unemployed people: nor
has there been an emphasis upon social purpose adult
education.   In the 1930s the cause of the unemployed was seen,
by the general public as well as by the labour movement, as an
integral part of the working class movement. The Jarrow March
of 1934 symbolised this connection, and has passed into the
nation's folklore.   Despite attempts by both the TUC, and the
far left groups, to organise similar demonstrations in the

1980s, there has been little public impact: and, indeed, relatively little public support.

Among the reasons for this lack of a political profile may be the relative heterogeneity of the unemployed of the 1980s, in terms of occupational and geographical location, and the existence of a substantial 'black economy'. More important, probably, is the fact that 'the majority of the hard-core unemployed are unskilled or semi-skilled manual workers, many of whom were never in unions nor had any contact with the Labour Movement when they were in work'(6) (authors' emphasis). Thus the privatised, atomised and consumerist culture of the 1980s, and the substantial weakening of the collectivist working-class culture of the pre-war period,(7) have had a profound effect on the context within which unemployment exists, and the attitudinal profile of the unemployed population.

Finally, of course, there is a marked contrast between the skeletal, 'means tested', and wholly inadequate welfare provision of the 1930s, and the more highly developed, albeit still inadequate, welfare state system of the post-war period. However inadequate in numerous ways the welfare state system of the 1980s may be held to be in relation to the unemployed, there is no doubt that the benefits system provides, for the majority of the unemployed, a protection against absolute poverty and destitution, and therefore a disincentive for political agitation.

Whatever the reasons, though, the important point in the context of our analysis of the educational provision is that, in the 1980s, the orientation towards 'social purpose' adult education has been largely absent. It is to an examination in more detail of the educational response to unemployment in the 1980s, and the priorities, motivations and objectives underlying this response, that attention is now turned.

Responses to Unemployment in the 1980s

There are at least two aspects of unemployment in Britain in the 1980s about which there is virtually universal agreement: unemployment is a long-term, fundamental problem; and it is a high priority political issue. Thus the Manpower Services Commission (MSC) stated in 1985 that with unemployment in 1984 at 1.2 million and 'still rising, ... the best assumption for planning purposes is for a continuing high level of unemployment throughout the period (1985-89) and for a level of long-term unemployment remaining at around the one million mark'.(8) And, although the British economy is particularly badly affected, this is agreed to be a problem endemic in all contemporary capitalist industrial societies. Thus the OECD in 1983 estimated that the western nations

would have to create 20,000 more jobs than they are
losing, every day for five years, if unemployment is to
return to its 1979 level ... About 35 million people are
jobless in the western industrialised countries
(including Japan). There are around 20 million on the
dole in Western Europe alone.(9)

Politically, there is agreement from all quarters that
unemployment will remain the priority issue in British
politics, at least in the short to medium term.(10)

No government, and indeed no political ideology, has a
clear, confident or simple 'answer' to the problem of
unemployment, however. Whilst the parties of the moderate
left (ie. the Labour and Alliance parties) call for a
measure of reflation and public sector investment to reduce
unemployment and provide some stimulus to economic as well
as social regeneration, none claims that unemployment can be
wholly 'cured'. Indeed, in Britain as elsewhere in Western
Europe, there has been a somewhat desperate investment in
short-term programmes designed to reduce the numbers
unemployed by virtually any means, whilst leaving the
economic infrastructure largely untouched. 'The get-them-
off-the-register impulse has spanned work-sharing
initiatives like early retirement. The give-them-something-
to-do concern has underpinned huge training and job creation
programmes ...'.(11)

Statistics and Definitions

Before analysing the various responses in more detail,
the problem of the definition of unemployment, and the
important issues relating to gender, and class, within the
context of unemployment, must be explored, and the wider
ideological ramifications noted.

According to official government figures the unemployment
total throughout 1985 remained around 3.2-3.3 million.(12) In
January 1986 the Department of Employment announced that a new
all-time record total of 3,407,729 unemployed had been reached.

Two preliminary points about the official statistics must
be noted, however. First, there have been criticisms from a
number of sources that the figures are a considerable
underestimate of the real unemployment total.(13) According
to 'Labour Research', the record jobless total of September
1982, officially put at 3,343,000 was, in reality nearer 5
million. Second, and perhaps more importantly, the basis for
calculating the figures was changed by the Government in late
1982 to include in the jobless total only those claiming
unemployment benefit. Thus, the 1986 total does not include
all those who used to be registered for work but who did not
claim benefit. That change alone cut the unemployment total

by 246,000.(14)   And the figures would look even worse if unemployed men over 60 had not been removed from the official statistics in April 1983.   (Men over 60 received enhanced benefit payments in return for having agreed to be removed from the register of those seeking employment.)

The Unemployment Unit , the independent research and lobbying group, claimed that on the old basis of counting, the January 1986 total would have been 3,801,000. Moreover, the effects of the change in the method of calculating the statistics has been to underestimate substantially the number of long-term unemployed (it has been argued, by as much as 300,000(15)).   It therefore seems reasonable to claim that the official figures underestimate to an extent the seriousness of the problem of unemployment. This is a contentious area, however, as arguments relating to statistical material almost always are.   But such complex arguments should not be allowed to obscure the central point: whatever the basis of calculation for the figures, the problem of unemployment is of major proportions; and, secondly, the official figures are fundamentally 'homo-centric'. Generalisations about unemployment have been made primarily from the experience of adult male workers.   Excluded from the official statistics are large groups of women: in particular married women who have been in full-time employment but have not paid the full national insurance stamp, homeworkers (the majority of whom are women), and temporary and seasonal workers and part-time workers, many of whom are women.

This seemingly administrative omission of women reflects a set of political and social assumptions about the unemployed, about work, and about a hierarchy of workers, which ensures that some categories of people who are not in paid employment appear in the statistics, while others do not. A broader definition would therefore seem to be required. Hayes and Nutman define unemployment as 'a state of worklessness experienced by people who see themselves or are seen by others as potential members of the work force'.(16) Work, usually, means paid employment: and the only resource most people have to sell is their labour power, and to do so, usually to an employer, has become 'the normal and legitimate way of life, and of supporting oneself and any family'.(17)

Some political dimensions

Underlying this whole discussion, of course, is the fundamental assumption, common to all industrial capitalist societies, that wage labour is the 'natural' economic order, and that paid work is good, both of, and in, itself. This is a contentious assumption, as socialists and other progressives have pointed out insistently, as it attempts to make permanent and beyond criticism, what are held to be essentially contingent capitalist economic relationships.

The domination of the economic ruling class, within a society characterised by class conflict, has resulted, so socialists believe, in the common acceptance of a 'culture of capitalism'. Amongst other things, this has put a high value on paid work per se: the best known articulation of this view being the so-called 'Protestant work ethic'. Proponents of such a view - which has been dominant in most capitalist societies in various forms for more than a hundred years - hold that work must be 'methodical, disciplined, rational and uniform',(18) and that it is a duty to gain through work, profits and skills which can be reinvested to create more work.

The value placed in this way upon the labour process is at one remove from directly material considerations and has a strong ethical, normative resonance in contemporary society. Even at a time of record unemployment such attitudinal factors are of profound importance. A recent survey, for example, found that there was 'no real evidence to support the belief that unemployment causes people to lose the will to work'. On the contrary, all the evidence supports Marsden's conclusions that

> so strong are the pressures and informal sanctions
> supporting work in our society that some of the workless
> cling to the desire to work to a much greater degree than
> our society has a right to expect in view of what they
> had experienced through work and unemployment.(19)

To place the analysis of unemployment within this wider context highlights a series of complex political and ideological questions. For those who adhere to the socio-economic system and its values, such problems are not of a high order, at least at the theoretical level. Thus, unemployment is a 'technical' problem (albeit with negative, costly and problematic side effects) which can be solved through appropriate economic measures and the inculcation of appropriate values and attitudes. (Which economic measures and which values and attitudes are in fact appropriate is, of course, a matter of some considerable political debate and difficulty, as can be seen from the sharp internal differences which characterised the fissures in the Conservative party in the 1980s.)

However, the problems created for the left are profound indeed. Reformist socialist parties in general (ie. non Communist and non-Marxist socialist parties) in the West have always been committed to full employment, maximum remuneration for the wage labour force, and industrial growth within a mixed economy structure. Such policies have applied particularly perhaps to the British Labour party, which has always been long on pragmatism and short on socialist theory, compared with its continental counterparts.(20) The Labour Party has thus been centrally committed to a wage labour economy: indeed, its whole rationale and historical genesis has lain to a large extent within a trade union movement whose very being was, and is, defined by the parameters, practices and assumptions of industrial capitalism and the wage labour system. In other words, in this context Labour is fully committed to the work ethic and the structure of both a labour process, and by implication a value system, based upon the inherent worth of 'paid work'.(21)

A similarly fundamental and historically based aspect of the left's belief system which is relevant here, is its adherence to a traditional definition of 'working class', and a focus - in terms of both theory and practice - on the defence of that class above all else. Mention has already been made of the 'gender bias' inherent in views of unemployment: and, in Chapter 1, the whole question of disadvantaged sections of the population and the existence of a 'double bind' for such groups, was explored. But it needs re-emphasising here that the whole thrust of the labour movement has been towards the employed, manual, male, white working class. Whilst there has been generalised sympathy for the plight of the other disadvantaged sections of the population there has been little serious attention paid in either theoretical or practical terms, to the recognition by the labour movement of such people being part of the working class. From the time of Marx onwards there has been a de facto downgrading, if not dismissal, of the 'lumpen proletariat'.

Within this framework the unemployed have no place. For Marx, of course, the 'reserve army of labour' was an important concept analytically. But the 'real' working class was composed of those engaged in class conflict by virtue of their position within the productive system.

Such attitudes have dominated labour movement thinking in the nineteenth and twentieth centuries. As will be seen in Chapter 5, trade unions are as yet unable to find either the structures or the ideological framework to cope with the needs of their unemployed members. Are unemployed trade unionists any longer real members of the union - can they be? And, indeed, can they really be seen as working-class? On the other hand, there is an obvious heterogeneity amongst the unemployed as a whole: in no way are they a potentially unified group.(22) There is an ambiguity over such issues, which questions the whole basis of labour movement perspectives.

Yet there are numerous analysts and critics who are not prepared any longer to view the unemployed as 'merely' a casualty of capitalism, an example of the social detritus on the edge of the capitalist system. For several decades neo-

Marxists and others have been questioning, in various ways, the centrality afforded to the traditional working class within socialist politics. Marcuse in particular has argued that new focal points for resistance to capitalism must be found - amongst the ethnic minorities, amongst alienated youth, the unemployed and so on.(23)

More recently there has been a substantial questioning of the very work ethic itself, and the wage labour system which underlies it; and, indeed, of the whole philosophy of industrialism and man's conquest of nature, of which Marx no less than the capitalists was the advocate. The Greens have become a major political force and are at the forefront of such questioning:(24) and their ideas are beginning to make themselves felt within the wider political sphere, not least in Britain.(25)

Feminists, too, have criticised strongly the hitherto prevailing assumption on the left that the labour process is confined to <u>wage</u> labour - and thus predominantly to male, manual workers. What is needed is an acknowledgement that human labour, and human exploitation under capitalism, is an inherent part of almost <u>all</u> social and economic relationships, and that that exploitation takes a variety of forms in the differing contexts.

Such arguments are connected to the wider analyses of those who have questioned the future of work, as conventionally defined. The sharp division between employed and unemployed, work and non-work would thus evaporate as attention was focussed upon the <u>needs</u> of the economy and society at any given time: and the concept of a genuine social income would become applicable. This would not be seen in traditional British income maintenance terms, which treats categories of people as recipients of compensation or allowances - this is fundamentally a 'social problems' approach which explains unemployment in terms of the characteristics of the individuals or groups in question. Social income can be described as the right to an income independent of a job, to meet the needs of the citizen rather than the worker. As Gorz states,

it is no longer work and workers that must be paid, but life and citizens. Since people's labour is ceasing to be the main source of wealth, their needs can only be realised, and products distributed, if the means of payment are unrelated to the amount of labour required by production.(26)

In this context, then, there would be no such thing as the current negatively defined concept of unemployment; rather, there would be different phases of activity, and different types of activity which people would engage in at various points in their lives.

In this section, which began with a discussion of the definitions of unemployment and the problems inherent therein, we have touched subsequently upon some fundamental political and ideological issues. This study is not the context in which to pursue these fully (though some aspects of this discussion are returned to in the final chapter). Rather, the intention has been to show that unemployment is not just 'another problem' to be tackled within existing structures, assumptions and practices. It is a centrally important and problematic development of modern society, destined to be a dominant factor in political as well as economic debate for the foreseeable future. And, most important of all, it raises a series of fundamental questions - as least for those on the left - both about the nature of socialist analyses of existing society, and about the orientation and structure of the society that, it is hoped, will replace it. Thus, the issue of unemployment itself illustrates that new ways of thinking about economic structure and the future of work are urgently needed. The old 40/40/40 idea - that the main purpose in life is to work 40 hours a week, for 40 weeks of the year, for 40 years - has been permanently undermined. But nobody is yet sure what to put in its place.

Educational Responses to Unemployment

Given these theoretical and conceptual uncertainties and ambiguities over the nature of unemployment and its societal and political implications, it would be unreasonable to expect educational practitioners (with minimal resources) to have produced a coherent national framework of provision for the unemployed. Nevertheless, significant efforts have been made and the remainder of this chapter is devoted to a contextual survey of such provision in order to provide a general framework within which the microcosmic practice of Pioneer Work can be analysed in subsequent chapters. Before examining specific educational responses, it is relevant to outline very briefly a variety of other responses to unemployment in the 1980s.

The Manpower Services Commission

In Britain, the MSC has emerged as the major institutional response made by government to unemployment. The MSC was established initially as a 'quango' by the Labour Government in 1973 to monitor the effectiveness of the labour market and the supply of jobs. A separate unit, the Training Services Agency (TSA) was established to review and finance new job-training ventures. The TSA soon became a unit within the MSC where both jobs and training were monitored. The MSC grew from a staff of 12 and a budget of £125.4 million in 1974 to a staff of more than 22,000 in 1984 and a budget of £1,767.8 million.(27)

Expenditure planned for 1985/86 is £2.3 billion. This represents a threefold increase over the 1979/80 expenditure and double the 1981/82 level. This is due mainly to the rapid expansion of the expenditure on youth programmes and on temporary employment measures, particularly the Community Programme. In 1984/85, the Youth Training Scheme (YTS) had 375,000 entrants and the Community Programme (CP) 130,000.

The MSC claims that there will be an extra 100,000 filled places on the CP by May 1986 (taking the projected total to 230,000) and plans were also made in 1985 for a two year, instead of the current one year, YTS.

It is not relevant to provide a detailed critique of the MSC and its programmes - this is available elsewhere - but a number of significant points needs to be highlighted.(28)

One obvious advantage for government is that the MSC programmes kept more than half a million people off the dole queues in 1984/85 since participants are not included in the unemployment totals. However, the overwhelming emphasis within MSC programmes is towards young unemployed people: for the majority of long-term unemployed adults the MSC has little to offer, and this will continue to be the case throughout the later 1980s, even though provision is being expanded.

The orientation of all MSC programming is towards vocational training. Its whole rationale is based upon the assumption that unemployment can be cured (or at least reduced to a minimal level) by matching up, through training and re-training courses, the needs of industry and commerce with the skills of the labour force. Thus the MSC fundamentally depoliticises unemployment and defines it in technical and organisational terms. In arguing, for example, that the major problem of youth unemployment is one of 'mismatch' between young workers' capacities and aptitudes and those characteristics required by employers, the MSC analysis obscures the causes of unemployment and redefines it in a technical manner. (And in this, it should be noted, it is in the tradition of the consensual, managerial approach to politics and issues, which characterised the 1950s and 1960s. Political and economic problems were seen generally as technical, requiring organisational, logistic and managerial - rather than ideological - decisions and skills.) Naturally, from this perspective, the orientation is wholly towards 'training' as opposed to 'education'. The MSC's documents in the early 1980s clearly equated 'education' with 'training' in order to meet the supposed needs of employers and industry.(29) In fact, education is rarely mentioned in the documents; certainly there is no discussion about education developing an individual's awareness about self and society,

37

still less about the need for collective, social purpose
education. Moreover, the MSC stresses the necessity of
certain attitudes and behaviour towards work. There is no
reference to people's own interests and choice in educational
and training matters.

Similarly, the MSC has exercised, in some respects, a
social control function. By taking almost 400,000 young
people off the streets, for example, and placing them in an
environment where they experience work discipline, the MSC is
not only introducing young people to potentially useful skills
and knowledge: it is also introducing an element of
institutional discipline and control.(30) Whether or not
this is desirable is of course another question: what is
beyond dispute is that such functions are important
considerations when decisions on future development and
financing of the MSC are undertaken.(31)

There are of course numerous examples of the MSC, through
one or other of its programmes, contributing significantly to
both educational and community development. And such
contributions should be neither ignored nor dismissed.
However, these are essentially ancillary by-products of the
MSC's central role, which has been to act as the primary
agency through which government has attempted to re-assert
capitalist values and discipline upon the young unemployed;
and, in the quickest and the cheapest way, reduce the number
of registered unemployed by a series of short-term, ad hoc
programmes, whilst interfering neither with the economic
infrastructures nor with the dominant value system.

The Local State

In recent years, many local councils have developed a wide
range of economic measures and structures which attempt to
deal with some of the problems of unemployment.(32) Economic
Investment Boards, Departments of Industrial Development and
Employment, as well as 'Unemployment Committees', have been
established. The initiatives which have grown out of these
developments include support for small firms and cooperatives,
as well as the attempt in some areas to develop imaginative
local job creation schemes.

These are obviously not a solution to mass unemployment;
and at one level, have simply meant increasing numbers of
councils competing for declining amounts of mobile capital.
But, overall, many of the schemes undertaken have led to new
approaches, stressing both the opportunities for local
people's initiatives, and the desirability of socially useful
employment (eg. insulation schemes, combined heat and power
schemes).

With the abolition of the Metropolitan County Councils in
1986 such initiatives may be severely threatened.

Nevertheless, schemes operating on a modest scale thus far in the 1980s have demonstrated the value of experimenting with models of development in the field of work with the unemployed, which provide alternatives to the 'orthodox' approach of the MSC.

The Churches and Voluntary Organisations

The churches have developed various initiatives nationally and locally around unemployment in the 1980s, just as they did in the 1930s.

In 1981 a national project called 'Church Action with the Unemployed' was started. The objective of this ecumenical initiative is 'to provide a resource for members of local churches, enabling them to work with increasing numbers of unemployed people'.(33) Initially, 25,000 clergy were circulated, and subsequently 200,000 leaflets on such issues as coping with unemployment, and information for unemployed young people and adults, were circulated. Small grants were also available for a limited number of local projects.

At a local level churches often provide premises or support for community organisations, many of which are concerned about unemployment. This support involves counselling and information for unemployed people and, frequently, use of the MSC to finance specific programmes such as YTS or CP.

In some areas, networks of community and voluntary groups have formed around the issue of unemployment. For example, in Devon and Cornwall, churches and local groups formed an umbrella organisation to spread information and coordinate local projects about unemployment.

At a national level, voluntary organisations, sometimes in conjunction with church leaders, have been attempting to generate further debate around unemployment. For example, in July 1985 the National Council for Voluntary Organisations produced a discussion document which suggested a 'new opportunities' programme for all long-term unemployed involving a personal development programme consisting of part-time education and community work. This programme would be 'a means of breaking out of the cycle of decline caused by long-term unemployment'.(34) At a local level, voluntary organisations have initiated a wide variety of schemes for unemployed people, sometimes in partnership with local authorities. These include skills workshops, drop-in centres, community enterprises, cooperatives and skills and learning exchanges.(35)

As with the churches, there is a considerable amount of activity but, not surprisingly perhaps, some confusion, or at least ambiguity, about the perspectives and objectives. Do they reflect moral concern for the unemployed and attempt to

raise the level of awareness about unemployment generally, or
are they attempts to involve the unemployed themselves in the
development of self-help networks? If the latter, what are
the objectives of such networks? And what is the place of
education, either for individual fulfilment or collective
social purpose, within this framework? All these are
fundamental questions, and apply with equal force to the
provision made by the educational institutions themselves.

The TUC

There are now more than 200 Unemployed Workers' Centres which
come under the umbrella of the TUC Services for the
Unemployed. These centres have grown at a rapid rate since
the TUC issued guidelines for them in January 1981. Their
work is examined in Chapter 5(36) but it is relevant here to
highlight some central issues.
    The TUC guidelines vested control in a Management
Committee consisting of 'equal numbers of representatives of
the trade union movement nominated through the TUC Regional
Council, and the local authority'. Almost as an after-
thought, was added: 'it will also be important to include
representatives of the unemployed'.(37) It should be noted,
however, that an examination over time of the development of
the centres in various regions indicates that by 1985, in
contrast to earlier years, more unemployed people themselves
were becoming involved.(38)
    From 1981 to 1983 the majority of centres was funded by
the ubiquitous MSC. In 1985 approximately 42% of them were
financed in this way. These centres, then, have often been
subject to the MSC's political restrictions, which has
prevented them from campaigning on contentious issues.

Adult Education Responses

In the context of this study it is within the field of AE that
the major interest lies. What has been the response of the AE
service to mounting unemployment?
    During the 1980s, there has been a proliferation of
schemes, courses and activities for unemployed people in many
parts of the country organised by a wide range of adult
education agencies and voluntary organisations.(39)
    It is perhaps surprising that such a comparatively wide
range of educational provision, albeit often ad hoc,
uncoordinated, and capable of catering for only a small
fraction of the unemployed, actually exists at all in the
current political and educational climate, when the primary,
secondary and tertiary sectors of the education service have
had major cutbacks, and are in general disarray.(40)
    Adult Education - the 'Poor Cousin' - has been affected

very adversely indeed by the overall cutbacks in education. And these effects have been felt in all AE sectors: LEAs (by far the largest providers of non-vocational AE), the University Adult Education (UAE) departments, and the Workers' Educational Association (WEA).(41)

There is no doubt that the quantity, quality and type of provision varies enormously both across and within all regions, but there has certainly been a proliferation of activity for unemployed people which is seen both in 'mainstream' programmes as well as in the development of special projects. At one level, many agencies have reduced or waived fees for unemployed people involved in the mainstream programme. Some UAE departments offer limited free entry, some WEA Districts advertise fee concessions at the discretion of their branches, and some voluntary bodies make similar concessions; but all are obviously limited in what they can do, given the severe cutbacks. In recent years, the Open University has had a special fund to assist its unemployed students. Local authorities vary enormously in their policies over this but many provide free enrolment, or at least reduced rates, for unemployed people. Many LEAs extend these arrangements to the dependents of the unemployed and others widen eligibility to all those in receipt of any form of welfare benefit.

In practice, it is often difficult to distinguish between special programmes for the unemployed, and mainstream programmes which have often been adapted and modified to meet changing needs and requirements. It is normal practice, for example, for LEAs to provide basic education free, and it is probable that the majority of people using this service are unemployed, overwhelmingly so in day-time provision. In addition to this, however, the national Adult Literacy and Basic Skills Unit (ALBSU) has funded, between 1982 and 1984, nine 'special development projects' aimed specifically at unemployed people.

The same development has occurred with 'Second Chance' education. Since about 1970, many LEAs and UAE departments and WEAs have organised such courses as 'Second Chance', 'Return to Learn', 'New Horizons' and 'New Opportunities'. These have been aimed broadly at adults who had not previously had the opportunity to realise their full educational potential, and who may wish to return to study as mature students either at FE or adult college level, or within the HE institutional structure. (Sometimes these courses have been aimed specifically at women, and they have been held normally in the day-time.) Although not initially designed for the unemployed, many students on them fall within this category. In addition, such courses have sometimes been integrated into special projects with the unemployed.

Special projects for work with the unemployed have

usually developed with special funding (as, for example, the ALBSU projects mentioned above). Some WEA Districts and UAE departments (for example, the WEA Northern District and the Universities of Leeds and Surrey) have received additional DES funding for two or three years to develop specific projects.

McDonald summarised the aims of programmes specifically designed for the unemployed in the following ways:

> These may aim to provide ... basic education, ESL, second-chance, and in-fill (to existing courses). They may be aimed at increasing employability, at job-seeking, at self-employment. They may be concerned with helping people to formulate their educational needs. They may be concerned with helping people to face up to unemployment and make choices for themselves, including the acceptance of alternatives to employment. They may be intended to help people to be more aware of their own interests and abilities with a view to taking the first steps towards any of these possibilities.(42)

Overall, it is clear that two parallel developments have been taking place in AE for the unemployed. Adult educators in all sectors have attempted to make access to existing facilities easier; and/or special programmes have been developed. McDonald comments that in the course of her enquiry, 'there was much evidence of concern for the needs of special groups and much imaginative development of outreach and provision to satisfy them'.(43)

The combination of these factors - increasing evidence from projects and reports about the educational needs of the adult unemployed, allied to increasing concern generally in education about the financial and ideological predominance of the MSC - led the DES to take some initiative.

Thus, in spite of continuing major cutbacks affecting all adult education agencies, it was announced in Parliament on 5 March 1984 that a three year DES initiative costing £2.5 million would be launched to improve educational opportunities for unemployed adults.

The main elements in this DES initiative, subsequently entitled REPLAN, were: (i) the appointment of a team of eight regional field officers and a national coordinator; (ii) a programme of projects which aims to develop local educational provision for unemployed adults; (iii) a series of staff development workshops organised by the Regional Advisory Councils for Further Education. The National Institute for Adult and Continuing Education (NIACE) was made responsible for the management of (i) and (iii), while the Further Education Unit (FEU) (the FEU is an 'independent body funded by the DES with a remit to promote, encourage and develop the efficient provision of further education in the

UK'(44)) became the agent for the management of a programme of curriculum development projects which aim to develop, evaluate and disseminate good practice. In addition to these programmes, Education Support Grants were provided for a number of local authorities to plan and coordinate provision in their areas for the adult unemployed.

During 1985, the FEU managed a programme of 30 development projects, while NIACE was supporting 44 projects by the summer of 1985. The operation of two of the NIACE-funded projects with which Pioneer Work has been concerned is examined in some detail in Chapter 4, but it is relevant in this general context to highlight a number of points about the REPLAN initiative.

Given the major crisis of unemployment, a national initiative costing £2.5 million over three years can hardly be regarded as a major, significant long-term response. It could also be argued that REPLAN does not even provide new or additional funding for adult education. The resources have been made available from cuts imposed on UAE and the WEA generally.

It does, however, reflect long overdue concern that 'something must be done' educationally for unemployed adults (many of whom will never work regularly again) over and above the MSC temporary work schemes.

A three year temporary programme can be seen as a token gesture. Since the 1960s, successive governments have developed a large range of temporary, inadequately funded, pilot projects in response to emerging problems.(45) Examples include the Educational Priority Areas, Urban Aid, the Community Development Projects, and the Inner-City programme. REPLAN is but the latest example of this trend in British social policy.

Like many of its predecessors, it is primarily a 'top-down' approach, funded, planned and controlled by a central government department. For example, in the first batch of projects managed by NIACE, only 7 out of 44 were voluntary sector initiatives. Like previous pilot projects, it reflects increasing centralisation in the form of definition of priorities by a central funding agency. It has been argued, however, that the 'problems of special funding would appear to arise less from its centrality than from its short-term nature'.(46) There is also the possibility that REPLAN – together with all special projects – may simply develop ghetto initiatives for unemployed people which are inappropriate and inadequate since the unemployed are not a homogeneous group. They can then become tokenistic institutional responses to unemployment which do not influence or change mainstream programmes, and provide no long-term benefits for unemployed people themselves.

In spite of these criticisms and serious limitations,

however, there is the possibility that REPLAN and other special projects may have a useful demonstrative effect. If projects are carefully monitored, they can contribute to the emerging debate about long-term adult unemployment and the most appropriate forms of publicly funded intervention (whether this be in educational or other fields). If a broad definition of unemployed people (including the unregistered unemployed, particularly women) is adopted, then the danger of ghetto initiatives can be avoided. Such projects can also offer an alternative to the exclusively vocational approach to adult unemployment which is exemplified in the statements and programmes of the MSC.

Overall, then, REPLAN could prove to be a useful catalyst, demonstrating examples of 'good practice' in this new and important area of AE development and, hopefully, presaging the allocation of substantial funding to enable major programmes of appropriate provision to be undertaken subsequently.

Unemployment in West Yorkshire

Finally, within this contextual overview, it is important to describe briefly the regional situation within which the Pioneer Work programme takes place. The first general point to note is that, as in the 1930s, the North, South Wales, Scotland and Northern Ireland suffer considerably higher levels of unemployment than the South, South East and South West of England.(47) Moreover, there are even greater disparities in the proportions of the labour force in particular areas which are long-term unemployed.(48)

It is also important to note the differences within regions, and even between districts in the same town or city, as well as rapidly changing levels of unemployment in specific areas over short periods of time. In Hackney, for example, unemployment in the mid-1970s was near the national average, but by 1981 it was 50% above the average, even though it was located in the region with the lowest level of unemployment.

In West Yorkshire the number of unemployed people, at 14.6%, whilst not the highest in Britain, conforms to the general pattern of there being higher unemployment in Northern regions.

Since the nineteenth century, the area has been dependent upon a number of traditional industries such as engineering, textiles and coal mining. The engineering industry has suffered particularly in cities like Leeds and Bradford because of the decline in manufacturing industry during the recession. For example, from 1974 to 1980, at least 12,000 engineering jobs were lost in Leeds. Bradford lost 5,000 jobs between 1976 and 1980 in its ten largest manufacturing firms, 2,000 jobs being lost from the closure of Thorn Electrics alone.(50)

Similarly, the textiles industry, which previously accounted for two-thirds of all jobs, output and investment in the area, has experienced a large decline. The post-war decline of the industry generally has been due mainly to competition from man-made fibres and import penetration of the clothing industry, but was accelerated in the 1970s by additional factors, which included membership of the EEC and the impact of new technology. Textile workers, then, have been made redundant because of a combination of slackening demand, and increasing mechanisation, the latter accelerated by the Department of Industry incentives to update machinery and increase productivity. The process of rationalisation and consequent closures reduced the textile workforce in Bradford from 73,000 in 1961 to 29,000 in 1977. (In January 1980, 900 workers were made redundant from one company, Associated Weavers.)

The loss of employment in the clothing industry has had particular effects on the employment prospects for women. Since the 1950s, employment in the industry has been halved, so that in some parts of the region, unemployment is almost double the county average. Many smaller employers have closed because they have been unable to compete with larger operations, especially with the move to invest in new forms of technology requiring large injections of capital. Other, large manufacturers have switched from production to the more profitable retail side of the industry.

Although the balance of West Yorkshire's industrial structure has gradually been shifting towards service industries, the employment provided has not been sufficient, and/or of the type, to counteract the job losses in the traditional industries, or to allow for any expansion in the labour market. In fact, even in the service sector there have been significant job losses.(51) In the office sector, the desire to increase productivity and profitability has encouraged the rapid introduction of new technology to replace jobs. In the public sector, a similar effect has been achieved through strict financial guidelines and general cutbacks in public expenditure.

Overall, it is clear that the impact of rapid industrial and technological change, leading to major job losses, has been felt throughout West Yorkshire.

The following table illustrates the severe scale of redundancies in recent years.(52)

	Bradford	Leeds	West Yorkshire
Jan - June 1979	636	1,659	3,521
Jan - June 1980	2,074	1,940	7,469
Jan - Dec 1980	3,704	5,369	15,588

1980 was the peak year for redundancies, but, in 1984, there were still twice as many confirmed redundancies as in 1977 in Yorkshire and Humberside. 81 firms notified 3,426 redundancies in Leeds in 1984. The rate of closures and redundancies has slowed since 1981 but this is mainly because there is a much smaller manufacturing sector in the area after the previous years of dramatic decline.(53)

The end result of this process of continuous decline is seen in local unemployment rates. Many inner-city wards in Leeds and Bradford have 'official' unemployment rates of well over 20%.

> Long-term unemployment in Leeds stands at record levels. Over 17,000 are officially recognised as having been out of work over 12 months, 40% of the unemployment total. Changes in methods of counting and unregistered unemployment mean the real figure is probably higher than 25,000 ... the plight of those suffering long-term unemployment is desperate. Half of those out of work over 30 have been jobless for over a year. 25% of the official count, 10,000 people in Leeds, have been out of work longer than two years. For tens of thousands in Leeds, unemployment means continued misery, poverty and despair. To them, unemployment has taken on the status of a jail sentence and the prospects grow worse.(54)

Moreover, as has been noted earlier, whilst unemployment affects all sections of the community, the large majority is working-class. Thus Department of Employment statistics show that in 1982, for example, 60% of the unemployed had previously been general labourers or other manual workers (compared with 9% managerial and professional and 13% clerical workers).(55)

Conclusion

It is within this context of industrial decline, and serious and persistent unemployment, that AE in West Yorkshire, in its various organisational forms, has tried to formulate provision appropriate to the needs of the local communities. Given both the preponderance of working-class, socially and educationally disadvantaged people amongst the unemployed, and the liberal, social purpose ethic which informs its provision, Pioneer Work has concentrated its efforts very largely on these groups. The remainder of this book is devoted to describing and analysing these attempts and drawing some conclusions as to future practice from the experience of the three years of Pioneer Work undertaken thus far.

REFERENCES

1. See H Marks, Unemployment and Adult Education in the 1930s, Studies in Adult Education, Vol 14, September 1982.

2. See J Allaway, The Educational Centres Movement, NIAE and ECA, 1977, pp 27 - 30.

3. G Stevens, Education in the Unemployed Centres - An Inside View, Year Book of Education 1938, cited in Marks, Unemployed and Adult Education in the 1930s, p 4

4. R Fieldhouse, The Ideology of English Responsible Body Adult Education 1925 - 1950, PhD thesis, unpublished, University of Leeds, 1984, p 113.

5. Educational Problems of the South Wales Coalfield, Board of Education: Education Pamphlet No 88, HMSO, 1931, p 173, cited in Marks, Unemployment and Adult Education in the 1930s, p 4.

6. Robert Taylor, The Observer, 25 August 1985.

7. For a discussion of this development and its implications, see Richard Taylor, 'The End of the Party?': the working class, Labourism and socialist change in Britain since 1945, in (ed) L Spencer, Working Class Culture in Post War Britain, Manchester University Press (in press).

8. Corporate Plan 1985-1989, MSC, 1985, p 6.

9. D Thomas, Taking the Measure of Unemployment, New Society, 16 May 1985, p 223.

10. See, for example, ibid.; Taylor, 'The Observer'; and the Manifestos of all the major political parties for the 1983 General Election, and their subsequent statements on economic and social policy in the 1980s.

11. D Thomas, Learning about Job Creation, New Society, 23 May 1985, p 262.

12. Employment Gazette, January - December 1985, Department of Employment.

13. See, for example: Unemployment, the Fight for TUC Alternatives, TUC, 1981; (eds) L Burghes and R Lister, Poverty Pamphlet No 53, CPAG, 1981; F Showler and A Sinfield, The Workless State, Martin Robertson, 1981; and

A Sinfield, <u>What Unemployment Means</u>, Martin Robertson, 1981.

It should be noted, however, that, from the right, have come counter-claims, from Sir Michael Edwards, for example, that, largely because of the 'black economy', official unemployment figures are gross <u>over</u>-estimates.

14. Employment Gazette, November 1982, Department of Employment.

15. J Hughes, The Long Term Unemployed, unpublished paper, 1984.

16. J Hayes and P Nutman, <u>Understanding the Unemployed</u>, Tavistock, 1981, p 2.

17. Showler and Sinfield, The Workless State, p 122.

18. Hayes and Nutman, Understanding the Unemployed, p 3.

19. R Brown <u>et al</u>, Changing attitudes to Unemployment?, Research Paper No 40, Department of Unemployment, 1983, p 35. (The passage cited is from D Marsden and E Duff, <u>Workless: Some Unemployed Men and Their Families</u>, Penguin, 1975, pp 263-4.)

20. See, for example, Ralph Miliband's now classic analysis of the Labour Party, <u>Parliamentary Socialism</u>, second edition, Merlin Press, 1973.

21. And it is significant, too, that such beliefs and attitudes are by no means confined to the centre and right of the party: the whole Marxist tradition is imbued with the same convictions.

22. Although it should be borne in mind that the large majority are manual working-class in background. In 1982, unskilled and semi-skilled unemployed totalled approximately 60% of the unemployed. Employment Gazette, Department of Employment, October 1982.

23. See H Marcuse, <u>One Dimensional Man</u>, Routledge and Kegan Paul, 1964.

24. See, for example, Embrace the Earth: a Green View of Peace, CND publication, 1983; and the publications of the Green Party (formerly the Ecology Party), and of Socialist Environment and Resources Association (SERA).

25. See R Taylor, Green Politics and the Peace Movement, in (eds) D Coates, G Johnston, and R Bush, A Socialist Anatomy of Britain, Polity Press, (Basil Blackwell), 1985, pp 160-170.

26. A Gorz, Paths to Paradise: on the Liberation from Work, Pluto Press, 1985.

27. Annual Report 1983/84, MSC, 1984, Table 6.1 and 6.4.

28. For factual information about MSC, see Corporate Plan 1985-1989, MSC, 1985. For critical analyses, see H Salmon, Unemployment, Government Schemes and Alternatives, ACW, 1983; and, by the same author, Unemployment: Two Nations, ACW, 1984.

29. See, for example, A New Training Initiative: a Consultative document, MSC, May 1981; A New Training Initiative, an agenda for action, MSC, December 1981.

30. Trade Union groups have also argued that the schemes provide cheap labour and therefore indirectly lead to job substitution. (See, for example, A Trade Union Response to YOPs and the NTI, Sheffield Trades Council, 1982; and D Carter and I Stewart, YOP, Youth Training and the MSC: the need for a new Trade Union Response, TGWU Region No 6, 1983).

31. More specifically, the MSC has attempted to control its programmes politically. For example, Technical Colleges involved in youth programmes were warned in 1982 that courses could be closed if they included material on political or related activities. TUC Centres for the Unemployed using MSC funds have been informed that they must not engage in campaign activities: this includes the display of posters or pamphlets which question government policy or urge changes to existing government programmes. Centres at Sheffield, Newcastle and Bristol had their funds withdrawn for refusing to follow the MSC's guidelines.

32. See, for example, Jobs for a Change, GLC, 1983.

33. Church Action with the Unemployed, Publicity leaflet, 1983.

34. See P Ashby, The Long-term Unemployed - Action for a Forgotten Million, NCVO, 1985.

35. See Salmon, Unemployment, Government Schemes and Alternatives, pp 43 - 7.

36. These Centres have been analysed in some detail in K Forrester and K Ward, Servicing the TUC Centres against Unemployment, TUC, 1985.

37. Unemployed Workers' Centres, TUC Guidelines, TUC, 1981.

38. K Forrester and K Ward, Serving the TUC Centres Against Unemployment.

39. See Education for Unemployed Adults, ACACE, 1982; J McDonald, Education for Unemployed Adults: Problems and Good Practice, DES, 1984; A H Charnley, U K McGivney, and D J Sims, Education for the Adult Unemployed, NIACE and REPLAN, 1985.

40. In 1975, educational spending accounted for 6.25% of the national product and had risen 30% in real terms in the previous six years. By 1982 it constituted just under 5.25% of the national product and had fallen by 3% in real terms compared with the mid-1970s. Over the period 1983-84 to 1986-87 it is planned to cut real spending on education by more than 10%. The Higher Education sector is also scheduled for further major cutbacks, following the 1981 University 'cuts', according to the Government's 1985 Green Paper on Higher Education.

41. In the LEA sector, for example, where only 1% of national education expenditure is allocated to AE, cuts have been felt disproportionately in AE. Thus, in 1979, LEA fees for AE classes rose by an average of 37% and enrolments fell by 11%. (Source: Continuing Education: From Policies to Practice, ACACE, 1982.)

42. McDonald, Education for Unemployed Adults, p 22.

43. Ibid, p 26.

44. FEU Focus No 4, August 1984.

45. For a detailed discussion of this trend in social policy, see, K Ward, A Case Study in Community Action, M Phil thesis, unpublished, University of Bradford, 1979.

46. McDonald, Education for Unemployed Adults, p 32.

47. The following table, taken from official statistics, illustrates the inequalities in the geographical distribution of unemployment.

June 1985	South-East	9.6%
	East Anglia	10.3%
	South West	11.3%
	Yorkshire & Humberside	14.6%
	West Midlands	15.1%
	Scotland	15.3%
	North West	15.9%
	Wales	16.3%
	North	18.5%
	Northern Ireland	20.9%

Source: Employment Gazette. Vol 93, No 7, July 1985. Synopsis of Table 2-3.

48.
Region or Country	Long-Term Unemployment as % of total unemployment October 1983	
	Male	Female
Northern Ireland	51	28
Great Britain	41	26
Northern Region	45	29
Wales	43	27
Scotland	42	27
South East	35	23

Source: Extracted from Employment Gazette Vol 91, No 12, December 1983, Tables 2.2, 2.3 and 2.6 (regions).

49. See P Harrison, Inside the Inner City, Penguin, 1983.

50. Source: The Economic and Social Crisis in West Yorkshire, Leeds TUCRIC, 1981.

51. For example, in March 1981, Grattans' warehouses announced 500 redundancies brought about by the firm's computerisation programme.

52. Source: Economic Trends, No 23, November 1984, p 65, West Yorkshire County Council.

53. It should also be noted that redundancy figures are not comprehensive since employers are required to notify only impending redundancies involving ten or more workers.

54. Leeds Trades Council Unemployed Centre, Annual Report 1984-85, p 17.

55. Employment Gazette, Department of Employment, October 1982.

Chapter 3

A COMMUNITY-BASED UNIVERSITY ADULT EDUCATION PROJECT

Origins

Since its creation in 1946 the Department of Adult and Continuing Education at the University of Leeds (hereafter, the Leeds Department) has had a particular and continuing concern with the extension of adult education opportunities to the educationally underprivileged in general, and the working class in particular. Thus, both the founding professor and head of department, Sidney Raybould, and the Yorkshire North District of the WEA with which the Department has always worked closely, had a central commitment to the development of liberal education for working-class adults. And among the prominent members of staff in the 1950s and early 1960s were such people as E P Thompson and J F C Harrison, two of the most notable exponents and practitioners of working-class adult education.(1)

The work of the Leeds Department has always been centred on the sustained (usually three year) adult class aimed particularly at those who have had no previous experience of higher education. The Department has a long and successful record in this area, especially in historical and local studies, from the 1950s onwards. Of particular significance, however, is the equally longstanding commitment to industrial studies sustained course provision, both day release and evening, for trade unionists. From the early 1950s the Leeds Department has organised courses with many of the major trade unions in its extramural area (the miners, the steelworkers, the textile workers, public sector unions etc.) and, since the late 1960s, also with the TUC.

The intention throughout has been to combine course content relevant to shop stewards and union activists, with a commitment to critical, analytical and open-ended exploration of industrial studies. The methodological centre of the approach has been to regard industrial studies as an 'area study' within which the trade union and labour movements are the reference point, but the exploration of their relationships with the wider society, as analysed through the various relevant disciplines, has been the overriding concern. The industrial studies provision has thus conformed to the 'education for social purpose' orientation of the radical liberal tradition, and has been concerned with widening the perspectives of trade unionists and encouraging rigorous academic study.(2)

Whilst the industrial studies programme has been the bedrock of the Leeds Department's provision for working-class adults, there has also developed since the mid-1970s a complementary concern with community adult education. After detailed discussions within the Department it was agreed in 1976 that a vacancy be filled by a lecturer in social science with specific responsibility for the development of community adult education in Bradford. A significant programme of community adult education work in the Bradford area was developed by the appointee, Jean Gardiner, with the support of a group of full-time staff colleagues. Of particular note was the varied programme of work with women, ranging from estate-based discussion group courses with working-class women stemming from initial contact at 'mother-and-toddler' groups, through to sustained New Opportunites for Women (NOW) courses held at various locations, including the University's centre. Several successful courses were also held in conjunction with Asian women's groups, and a wide range of contacts established with both voluntary and statutory agencies. In 1979 an official DES inspection of this whole area of work was carried out, and the subsequent report was extremely favourable.(3) Indeed, HMI has been a constant and much valued support in the whole development of community adult education, and, later, of the Pioneer Work section.

Finally, in addition to the community adult education appointment in Bradford, the establishment in the Department of a community work lectureship in 1975 had enabled the development of extensive links with tenants' groups, advice centres and community centres in Leeds.

By the late 1970s, therefore, a well-established, though very small, community adult education presence had been established in the Department.

All in all, then, the Leeds Department had a successful 'track record' on working-class liberal adult education by the start of the 1980s. In 1981 the University Senate initiated a fundamental review of the Department's finances, structure and provision.(4) Whilst this review was in progress the Department decided, for quite unconnected reasons, to approach the DES to fund a special experimental post to develop work with the unemployed. Following discussions between the DES, HMI and the Leeds Department, it was agreed that special funding should be provided, initially for three years, for a lectureship to develop work with the unemployed. 90% of the funding came from the DES, and 10% from the University – in reality from Departmental funds. The post was advertised through the normal University channels, and Kevin Ward, who had previously been the community work lecturer in the Department, was appointed in September 1982 to a fixed-term post.

When the University Senate group reported on the Department, it recommended, amongst other things, that community adult education with disadvantaged sections of the population, stressing the importance of educational innovation, experimentation and research, should become an established feature of the Department's work. Thus, in the autumn of 1982, the Pioneer Work section was established, initially with three full-time staff members (Richard Taylor, a member of staff in the Department of Adult and Continuing Education, joining with Jean Gardiner and Kevin Ward) but totalling the equivalent of only two Pioneer Work posts. Arrangements were also made for there to be funds set aside for the employment of part-time organising tutors (see below).

Objectives and Structure of Pioneer Work

The primary aims of the Pioneer Work section were, as they remain: to construct educationally innovative structures and curricula for the development of working-class adult education; to select specific 'target groups' within the community for which such provision can be made and to devise programmes specifically designed to meet their needs; to build a network of inter-agency links, across a very wide field, so that, as course programmes develop, a proportion of the University's provision can be seen as 'pump-priming' activity covering the initial phase, with other agencies taking over responsibility for the work once it is established; and, finally and crucially, the monitoring and analysis of the project utilising a comparative methodology, involving both the different contexts of the Leeds and Bradford situations and the socio-political and educational evidence concerning the 'success levels' of the various approaches adopted.

To achieve these objectives it was decided from the outset that a team structure was essential. Two Pioneer Work teams were established, one in Leeds and the other in Bradford, with liaison being undertaken by two full-time staff (Taylor and Ward). The teams were composed of Group 1 and Group 2 tutors: that is, full-time staff (Group 1) and the part-time organising tutors (Group 2) referred to above. These latter were paid on the part-time tutors' rate for seven hours teaching/counselling/organising per week for 40 weeks p.a. Several aspects of their role have been of central importance in the development of Pioneer Work. Most important of all, perhaps, is the simple fact that Pioneer Work could not have functioned viably without their involvement in the development and organisational groundwork required to establish a Pioneer Work programme. The very high level of commitment, expertise and sensitivity required has been forthcoming in almost all cases, and the 'Group 2s' have been an integral part of both teams. They have, though, worked under extremely difficult conditions. Without exception they have worked way beyond the seven hours per week for which they were paid (on average at least three times this amount). And, because of funding insecurity, there could be no guarantee of continued employment as a 'Group 2' beyond one academic session (and, on occasion, the arrangement had to be for considerably shorter periods). Moreover, because 'Group 2s' are formally engaged, as far as the University is concerned, on the same basis as any other part-time tutor, there has been none of the benefits of full-time employment: no holiday or sick pay, no N.I. or Superannuation rights, and no formal status within the Department. Finally, 'Group 2s', in the nature of Pioneer Work, are working as isolated individuals, despite the team approach, and do not enjoy the institutional backing of the University in their day-to-day work. Given the extreme difficulty of this type of high-risk, developmental work, this is an intolerably stressful working context in the longer term. An important principle, however, had been established. Part-time tutors were to be paid, however minimally, for organising and contact work, as well as for teaching.

The numbers of 'Group 2s' working at any given time have varied, but, on average, there have been two in each of the Leeds and Bradford teams. Over the three years of Pioneer Work's existence some ten 'Group 2' tutors have been involved at one time or another. The high turnover of 'Group 2' staff has resulted from a combination of the unsatisfactory nature of the structure, as indicated above, and the high quality of those involved, which has enabled most of them to obtain full-time educational posts elsewhere. One ex-'Group 2', for example, is a full-time employee of Bradford Metropolitan District Council, responsible for the allocation of approximately £1m. p.a. from the European Social Fund for development and training for unemployed adults; two other ex-'Group 2s' have obtained full-time lecturing posts in community adult education.

Such a high turnover has obviously affected adversely the continuity and coherence of the project teams in both cities. And yet, as has been said, without the 'Group 2' system, the whole Pioneer Work structure would not have been viable. At one level, the problem has been one of funding: trying to get 'a quart out of a pint pot'. There is further discussion of this, in relation to funding strategies, in the concluding chapter.

The 'Group 2' system was not the only complication in the Pioneer Work team structure. From the outset the two teams have operated very differently. The Leeds team, through all the staffing changes, has had a coherence and focus, concentrating on work with the unemployed, though this has included some important developments in women's education and with ethnic minority provision. The disadvantage, in broad terms, has been the lack of a wide-ranging Pioneer Work coverage. There has been no work with the retired, for example. On the other hand, in Bradford, the team has suffered from too much heterogeneity, with too few appropriate resources being available for developing the work with the unemployed. Moreover, the absence of a full-time member of staff devoting energy entirely to developing, co-ordinating and teaching within the provision for the unemployed has been a major handicap. And the difficulties of operating in Bradford, with no real physical base (no offices etc), and with administrative services and information located in the Department at Leeds, have been very considerable. On the credit side, though, Bradford has seen significant developments in women's education, some minor though potentially important beginnings with the Asian community, and, perhaps most noteworthy of all, the development of a strong, innovative and expanding programme of work with retired working-class people. (Early in the life of Pioneer Work - the winter of 1982 - Jill Liddington was appointed to a half-time vacancy on the staff of the Department and took responsibility for developing this work in Bradford.) All these areas of work are discussed in some detail in subsequent chapters.

Despite these general problems the team approach has worked reasonably well. A collective, and as far as is possible, democratic and informal, team approach is essential if the endemic isolation and problematic nature of the Pioneer Work tasks are to be overcome. Similarly, only through this collective approach can agreement be reached amicably over funding allocations when finance is scarce. A high price has been paid for these advantages, however. There have been lengthy and frequent meetings. The Leeds and Bradford teams meet frequently, each meeting usually lasting half a day. In addition, there have been regular joint team meetings. As the overall staffing size of Pioneer Work has expanded (see below), so it has been increasingly necessary to have regular meetings of all full-time Pioneer Work staff (to discuss policy, funding, staffing and related issues). There have also been numerous sub-group meetings between staff concerned with particular aspects of the work. In addition, there are regular meetings between the Pioneer Work teams and the 'Group 3' tutors (ie. those tutors who teach particular, individual courses, have no organising work, but are responsible to either a 'Group 1' or 'Group 2' tutor).

The workload of meetings within the Pioneer Work structure, leaving aside the committee structure within the Department and the University as it affects Pioneer Work, is thus very considerable. Moreover, the nature of Pioneer Work itself necessitates a large number of meetings with individuals and agencies with which developmental courses are being planned, taught and monitored. The other central problem in the 'internal structure' of Pioneer Work results from the inherently inequitable status and remuneration of different members of the team. Although operating on a co-operative and 'equal' basis, the Pioneer Work section is part of a traditionally hierarchical Departmental decision-making structure where the Co-ordinator is, in the last resort, responsible to the Head of Department and, where DES resources are concerned, to the Director of Extramural Studies, for policy priorities and financial expenditure. In practice, because working relationships at all these levels are harmonious, this has not been a major problem. But, potentially, the structure is highly problematic.

More serious have been the discrepancies within the Pioneer Work teams. Essentially, the problem has resided in the disparity between full-time Departmental staff, on the one hand ('Group 1' tutors), and part-time staff ('Group 2 and 3' tutors). There is an obvious and major difference in wage levels. But this is exacerbated by two further inequalities: the lack of both job security and job status. The University has no contractual obligation to such part-time tutors who are paid entirely on a piece-work, hourly rate basis.

Inevitably, despite generally good working relationships, these differences create tensions. One of the long-term goals of Pioneer Work must be to rectify, or at the very least ameliorate, some of these anomalies.

The other central aspect of Pioneer Work structure concerns its relations with the Department, the DES, the University, and, as Pioneer Work has expanded, with the various outside agencies that have funded particular aspects of Pioneer Work activity. This latter aspect is discussed briefly below in the context of the general development of outside agency involvement: here, concentration is upon the other areas mentioned.

The core funding for Pioneer Work has come through the overall DES grant aid to the Department, with the addition of the special funding for the three year temporary post occupied by Kevin Ward (and subsequently extended for a further two years when Kevin Ward was appointed in 1983 to a full-time tenured lectureship in the Department, working with Pioneer Work). It was agreed within the Leeds Department that a maximum of 20% of the DES grant to the Department should be allocated to Pioneer Work in any given year, for part-time

tutor programming costs (including 'Group 2' tutor costs).
This excluded full-time staffing costs but, again, it was
agreed that 20% of full-time staffing should be the
provisional ceiling for Pioneer Work involvement in the longer
term.*

Given the interests of the DES in this innovative work,
and its direct concern through special funding of the
temporary post, and the interests of both the University and
the Department in this new and rapidly developing sector, it
was agreed to establish a Supervisory Group, to oversee both
the policy and practice of Pioneer Work.(5)

Supervisory Group Committee minutes and reports (which
constitute a detailed survey and analysis of the Pioneer Work
programme in each year) are subsequently circulated to
Departmental staff meetings and, on occasion, to the
University's Adult and Continuing Education Committee which
oversees all Departmental provision and activity, and reports
directly to the Board of the Faculty of Education, and General
Purposes Committee (a sub-committee of Senate).

Pioneer Work then has been highly accountable both to
funding bodies and to the organisational structure of the
University, and staff have had to produce detailed and
continuing evidence of their activities. This is in marked
contrast to the work of many university academics and adult
educators in other settings.

Research and Evaluation

From the earliest planning stages, staff were agreed that
close monitoring and evaluation was essential. Indeed, as a
section of a university department, a major part of the
justification for Pioneer Work lay in its strong research
emphasis. More positively, it was felt that staff had a

---

*This original agreement has been complicated by two factors:

(a) the increase in outside funding (ie. non-DES
mainstream grant) has meant that Pioneer Work may
increase as a proportion of total Adult Education work in
the Department to more than 20%, whilst using less than
20% of DES mainstream grant. The position since 1983 has
thus been that the 20% of mainstream grant agreement
remains in force, but that an ad hoc agreement on the
total percentage of Pioneer Work, however funded, within
the Adult Education provision is negotiated each year;

and (b) the 'new formula' for grant aid has changed the
basis of funding for Pioneer Work, as it has the basis of
all other DES funded provision (see below).

major responsibility for research for several reasons, apart from institutional necessity:

i) the results could contribute generally to the ongoing debate about working-class and community-based adult education, and specifically to the emerging debate about unemployment.

ii) similarly, experimentation in programming and provision for other disadvantaged adults, if properly monitored and analysed, would contribute to other major areas of debate and development within adult education - education for retired and elderly people, women's education, and ethnic minority education.

iii) a key aspect of Pioneer Work is educational innovation, in the sense of constructing experimental approaches, delivery systems and curriculum content designed to meet the needs of disadvantaged adults. Again, if such innovation is monitored accurately and analytically, the resulting evidence is instructive for adult educators elsewhere.

iv) given that a large part of Pioneer Work (ie. work with unemployed people) had received special funding from the DES, close monitoring and evaluation was essential for the dissemination of experience and results.

v) without research, there is no basis for critical reflection both before, during, and after, particular phases of work.

In practice, research and monitoring is often ignored by adult educators. This means that valuable lessons from hard-won practical experiences are being lost; moreover, this lack of research information contributes to the perpetuation of a low profile, under-resourced, and poorly regarded adult education service.

In Leeds, an action-research model for Pioneer Work (which is discussed below) was adopted from the outset. This involved all full and part-time staff in continuous monitoring and evaluation. In addition, the DES agreed to fund a Research Project from 1984-86 (see Chapter 8) employing a part-time research assistant. Focussed on work with unemployed people, this has concentrated on both user and tutor experiences of courses which have been organised. This detailed examination of users' views is particularly important as part of a conscious move away from the all too common assumption of 'superior knowledge' on the part of adult education providers and researchers.

A framework of analysis was needed for Pioneer Work which would incorporate information about a wide variety of courses, and who attended them, and an evaluation, not just of the courses themselves, but also of the processes which led (or, just as importantly, failed to lead) to them. This information and the subsequent analysis depended primarily and fundamentally on the views of users.

The research, then, had to be an integral part of the provision, if this was to be developed. Thus an action-research framework has been used in which the research has had to adapt to the environment of Pioneer Work, and disrupt the programme provision as little as possible.

In recent years, there has been extensive academic debate about the potential and the problems associated with adopting an action-research framework.(6)

Some of these issues are discussed in more detail in Chapter 8, but it should be noted that this framework does not involve the simple testing of pre-determined a priori hypotheses. It emphasises, instead, the development of three phases which are inter-related. These are initiation, contact and development, and implementation. In educational work with unemployed people and others, the first two phases should be present throughout. In Pioneer Work they took up much time, particularly in the first six months. The implementation phase (in this case, the development of classes and courses with working-class groups) obviously and crucially depends on the success of the earlier phases. It developed much sooner in Pioneer Work than would normally be anticipated, because of contacts and previous experiences of the staff involved. It should not be assumed, however, that the implementation phase implies the abrupt ending of the two earlier phases. Because of the dynamic inter-relationship of these phases in an action-research project, the initiation and development work continues throughout: in practical terms, when some initiatives fail, others must be developed if the varied approaches and categories of courses are to be monitored consistently and evaluated; also, if initiatives succeed, then the contact and development phase must be continued for further planning.

There are three aspects of research which underlie each of these phases:

i) Process-orientated research: this emphasises the collection of relevant quantitative and qualitative information about initiatives which are being taken. Quantitative data in Pioneer Work is available through detailed registers and reports which all tutors must provide for each course. Registers include questions on users' sex, age, educational background and other relevant details. There is, then, a great deal of information, both about the different types of courses which have been organised, and about the characteristics of people who have attended.

Essential though this information is, it does not provide insight into the processes which led to successful or, just as importantly, failed initiatives and courses; nor does it provide insight into the user's thoughts, feelings and consciousness, or how she/he might judge success or failure, importance or unimportance.

The Pioneer Work research, therefore, has attempted to combine quantitative data with qualitative research; this consists of detailed monthly reports from part-time 'Group 2' tutors, as well as reports from and meetings with 'Group 3' tutors. Records have also been kept of formal inter-agency meetings and more informal contacts and approaches. Discussions and evaluation between organisers, tutors and participants are the most important element in this continuous action-research process.

ii) Historical research: this emphasises concern with the development of events through time. Action-research in this project is not concerned with examining an educational initiative in a static way at one particular time: rather, it examines adult education initiatives over a period, and takes into account a range of factors which inhibits or encourages these initiatives, including local authority policies and practices, and the resources available to, and the attitudes of, possible participants at the local level.

One simple example about the need for exploration over a period of time is the analysis of the four approaches which is provided later in this chapter. An analysis of these different approaches over a three year period is obviously more valuable than analysis from one year.

iii) Case-study research: this emphasises the use of a small set of examples, which, when examined over a period of time as outlined above, can provide the basis for generalisation.(7)

A major task in Pioneer Work throughout the three years, but particularly in the first year, was the analysis of questions surrounding the initiation and contact and development phases referred to above. In practice, could liberal adult education actually be developed with, for example, groups of unemployed people and older people? If so, in what ways? How could groups and individuals be contacted and become interested? How could inter-agency

61

links be established to facilitate this work?

It was only when these contextual phases were successful (ie. when different types of courses were actually established in various settings) that further detailed educational questions could be examined. What happens to students on different kinds of courses? What do they see as the uses or value, if any, of this and other kinds of adult education? Do they continue in education after these courses and, if so, in what way? Or, do these courses help in other ways or have other - perhaps unintended - consequences? What were the outcomes as seen by both tutors and students?

Overall, then, attempts have been made to monitor and evaluate systematically a number of educational initiatives by utilising quantitative and qualitative information. The first stages focussed on how various categories of courses were organised via different approaches. Later stages are focussed on tutors' and students' perceptions of the processes and learning outcomes of courses.

The collection of information depends on the co-operation and involvement of tutors and students. Research is not being carried out on passive objects; rather, attempts are made to demystify research and use it as a tool with tutors and students for critical reflection, as well as to satisfy political necessity (eg. with funding bodies). A description of how this was done with tutors on one of the NIACE/REPLAN projects is provided in Chapter 4.

Funding

The sums of money allocated from DES grant have varied since 1982/3. Broadly, the overall allocation per year has averaged out at approximately £20,000 for part-time tutor costs, with small ancillary grants for photocopying, teaching aids etc., and much larger components from outside funding agencies (see below). (In addition, there was in 1982-3 additional earmarked funding of £9,000 from the DES for the development of Pioneer Work). The full-time staff costs are subsumed in the overall staffing of the Department. Staffing levels overall in the Department have varied considerably since the late 1970s, partly because of the relentless succession of UGC and DES 'cuts', but also because of a large number of retirements. At the time of writing (late 1985) there are 27 full-time equivalent academic posts of which $3\frac{1}{2}$ are devoted to Pioneer Work. In addition, teaching contributions from other members of full-time staff total approximately a further half post.

The allocation from DES grant has been barely adequate to provide a viable programme base for Pioneer Work. Moreover, because the funding situation of the Department, through no fault of its own, has been so uncertain, even chaotic, at the beginning of each financial year, proper planning has been impossible. Almost every year an initial cut in Pioneer Work's allocation in the autumn has been followed in the spring by a sudden release of additional funds. Such funding uncertainties, added to the uncertainty over the continuation of fixed-term posts, are a chronic departmental problem; but, for Pioneer Work, they threaten overall viability.

This is not the place to enter into the details of the iniquities and irrationalities of the 'new formula' for DES grant aid to 'Responsible Bodies' (ie. University Adult Education Departments and the Workers' Educational Association). But reference must be made to some of the specific ways in which this affects Pioneer Work provision. From the outset all Pioneer Work classes have been provided free of charge. This was established as an initial principle to which no exception would be made. It was agreed that both on principle - because of the serious social and educational disadvantage which existed for all Pioneer Work students - and in practice - because students could not afford any class fees and would not attend if they were levied - this was an absolute requirement. Under the 'new formula', fee remissions from the DES for various categories of disadvantaged students can be made only on the assumption that a charge of 20p per hour has been levied. This may, in the longer term, create serious problems for Pioneer Work.

Far more serious, however, is the overall thrust of the 'new formula'. Grant in future is to be paid on output measured in effective student hours (ESHs). (Although there are qualifications and 'weightings' to this system, they have only marginal effect on the basic criterion.) This has several implications, all seriously deleterious as far as Pioneer Work is concerned. The best way to maximise ESHs is to provide short, undemanding courses with a guaranteed appeal, which will recruit large numbers. The cheapest way to staff the programme is to rely on relatively low paid part-time tutors, who have no job security etc., with a small full-time staff of UAE organisers and entrepreneurs. The less time spent on experimental, time-consuming and 'high risk' educational development the better: no ESH credit is given for organising and developmental work, nor is there any credit for research, monitoring, evaluation etc.

Pioneer Work is, of course, inherently high risk, experimental, time-consuming in terms both of pre-course organisational and developmental work, and of in-course monitoring, evaluation and consultation; and it places a very strong emphasis upon research.

Under the 'new formula', therefore, Pioneer Work represents a drain on Departmental resources and, prima facie, there is a strong case for reducing its funding base. Of course, not only are there strong arguments in principle

63

against such a course of action, there are also strong pragmatic, 'political' reasons for continuing with and expanding Pioneer Work. These are reviewed in the final chapter. But here it is important to note the serious problems presented by the 'new formula' for Pioneer Work's continued operation.

Outside Funding and Inter-agency Co-operation

Inter-agency co-operation has always been a central operating principle of Pioneer Work. In the chapters that follow numerous examples of inter-agency work will be examined. Indeed, virtually all Pioneer Work provision has been made on a co-operative, inter-agency basis. In many cases, only locally based agencies (principally voluntary groups) have the requisite local network knowledge and expertise to enable Pioneer Work to make appropriate provision. In many other situations only other institutions and providers have the appropriate expertise and staff to enable Pioneer Work to construct provision (for example, Local Education Authority co-operation in skills and leisure education).

It has also been a major objective of Pioneer Work to hand over to other more appropriate agencies a proportion of its provision once the innovative first stage has been accomplished and the work established. This was quite clearly stated in the Senate report at the outset, and underlines the criterion of educational innovation. In broad terms, to date about one quarter of all Pioneer Work provision has been handed over in this way. The agencies involved have varied widely - from the LEAs and WEA through to Unemployment Centres, welfare organisations and so on. Equally important has been Pioneer Work's objective of making financial and organisational links with appropriate outside bodies. Again, later chapters will give details of the various schemes in this category that have been developed with Pioneer Work since 1982. Here, some general points should be noted.

There have been the following outside funded schemes operating since 1982: the secondment, for two years to the Leeds team, of an experienced LEA adult education worker; the REPLAN grant to Pioneer Work, jointly with Harehills Housing Aid, for a two year post (plus ancillary costs), to develop work with Asian women; the REPLAN grant to Leeds LEA, jointly with Pioneer Work, to develop City Centre work with the unemployed; the grant from the DES to finance a research project, initially for one year and subsequently extended to two, to analyse the effects on both users and tutors, and the curriculum issues arising from the programme of work with the unemployed from 1984 to 1986; and a grant from Bradford Metropolitan District Council in 1984/5 to develop work with the unemployed within the Metropolitan District.

These relationships have been immensely valuable in a number of ways. They have provided much needed additions to the finances and staffing levels of the teams in both Leeds and Bradford, and, consequently, they have extended the scope and variety of the work undertaken and broadened the experiential basis of the staff concerned. (For example, the BMD grant enabled the Bradford team to employ an Asian 'Group 2' tutor in 1984/5 and thus make a useful contribution to ethnic minority provison.) Such schemes have fulfilled a vital political role too: they have given Pioneer Work credibility and reputation with the University, and have shown that, in terms of educational research as well as educational provision, Pioneer Work is regarded by influential outside institutions as having something of value to contribute. Indicative of the national prominence of Pioneer Work, and in particular of the work with the unemployed, have been: the growth of consultancy work in 1984 and 1985; the links with Ruskin College, Oxford; the visit by Noel Thompson, Under-Secretary at the DES, in 1984; and the prominence of the 'Leeds model' in the Universities Council for Adult and Continuing Education report on work with the unemployed, presented in 1985. (Taylor and Ward were members of the six-person UCACE working party producing the report.)

Outside funding arrangements have led to major problems, however. The complexity and uniqueness of each arrangement has created considerable extra administrative, supervisory (and clerical) work for Pioneer Work full-time staff. Moreover, the problems of negotiating suitable arrangements with a somewhat inflexible, bureaucratic and conservative university administration have been time-consuming, frustrating and often unproductive. Perhaps most important of all, such funding is almost invariably short-term (from one to three years), thereby necessitating perpetual renegotiation of contracts and funding. Not only is this immensely time-consuming, but it also results in a critical lack of continuity in areas of work which above all others require a commitment of resources, both financial and personal, over time to build confidence and viable educational provision.

Retionale for University Involvement

Despite all the problems and complexities outlined above, it is, in our view, evident that Pioneer Work has been fulfilling an important role. Whatever the reasons, and whatever the projected 'cures', there can be no doubt that ours has long been and remains a grossly unequal society, as was argued in Chapter 1. Amongst the large numbers of socially and educationally disadvantaged in our society there is not only great material need, but great educational need too. Of this, also, there can be no doubt. But why should the university, as opposed to other agencies (the LEAs in particular) which are more appropriate for and expert in 'basic education', be concerned with such work? Surely, it could be argued, university adult education is quite properly becoming more concerned with very different adult educational concerns: high-level and intensive post-experience and professional education. And, given these trends, it is surely doubly questionable for the university to be involved in schemes of the Pioneer Work type. However urgent the social, political and educational need may be, this basic, almost remedial, education is not the function of the university whose role, by definition, is concerned with the highest levels of academic attainment and research.

This, in our view, is a wholly mistaken argument. Although universities were established as elite academic institutions and have their central rationale in a necessarily elitist concept of the attainment of academic excellence in various ways, there is also an important sense in which they are, or should be, serving the communities within which they exist. This has been increasingly the case since the 1950s with the massive expansion of publicly funded higher education. Universities are 'encouraged' by both government and other bodies to build links with the industrial, commercial and professional communities. And, to an extent, they have been successful in achieving these objectives. But there is also a crucial need for universities to interact with, and provide educational services for, the wider, majority community. It is here that UAE Departments have their central role - as a bridgehead between the university and the community. A significant part of that role must be the provision of appropriate educational services to those in the community who have not had access previously to higher education. This is a difficult but important task, requiring professional expertise and commitment. A Pioneer Work approach provides the framework from within which at least a proportion of the university's very considerable reservoir of academic expertise can be put to the service of those 'disadvantaged' sections of the community. Moreover, UAE Departments have a unique concern with the liberal, critical, open-ended approach to adult education which has much to offer of relevance and benefit to disadvantaged sections of the community, and complements the more vocationally and leisure oriented concerns of other agencies.

Above all, however, universities are uniquely qualified to provide the research expertise which this new area of community-based adult education must have if it is to develop rationally and efficiently. Universities are distinguished from other institutions of post-school education in a number of ways, but, most centrally of all, by their special commitment to research.

One danger in community adult education is to respond randomly, and in ad hoc terms, to expressed need, with no coherence or evaluation of results. In order to use scarce resources effectively the evaluation of experimental provision is essential. The dissemination of examples of 'good practice' is as important as the provision itself, especially in new and developing areas of work. It is for this reason that Pioneer Work, encouraged by both the DES and the University, has given such a high priority to the research and monitoring role.

For all these reasons, therefore, university involvement of this kind is not only justifiable but essential if such work is to develop coherently and successfully in the AE sector as a whole.

In the remainder of this chapter a brief overview of the programme and 'practice' of Pioneer Work in its first three years of existence is given, as an introduction to the more detailed analyses of the different aspects of provision provided in subsequent chapters.

An Overview of Pioneer Work Provision 1982–85

The Background

'But how did you start in practice?' is a question which some adult educators have put to Pioneer Work staff since the work started in 1982.

Unlike the Open University's 'In and Out of Unemployment' project which developed a 'top-down' approach, Pioneer Work attempted to build on a wide range of experience and contacts at the local level. Collectively, staff had considerable experience of university adult education, community work, work with women and trade unions, and involvement in voluntary sector activities. It was from this basis of experience and 'network knowledge' that Pioneer Work grew.(8)

It was explained earlier that Pioneer Work provision has focussed upon work with four groups: unemployed adults; retired people; women; and black groups. Later chapters examine in more detail these different, albeit overlapping, areas of work, but it is important to note here the approaches which were used initially.

The work could have been developed in a whole variety of ways. Resources, for example, could have been concentrated on one large council estate. In order to utilise fully the many and varied contacts which had been made in both Leeds and Bradford, however, it was decided to adopt four particular approaches. These avoided the dangers of treating any of the priority groups as homogeneous blocks, and also provided the basis for subsequent analysis.

These approaches can be described as:

i) the Community approach: ie. utilising and extending a
network of contacts through community groups, small
voluntary bodies, tenants' associations and
neighbourhood groups.

ii) the Institutional approach: ie. working with other
educational and related bodies (eg. LEAs, WEA,) on an
inter-agency basis. The aim was to maximise scarce
resources and avoid overlap and duplication.

iii) the Organisational approach: ie. working in close co-
operation with organisations specifically concerned
with the unemployed. These include TUC Centres Against
Unemployment, Drop-in Centres, and other 'out-of-work'
centres.

iv) the Trade Union approach: ie. the development of
contacts at different levels within trade unions (eg.
full-time officials, education officers, shop stewards,
branch members) to raise the issue of unemployment and
explore the feasibility of educational provision for
unemployed members.

The Community and Institutional approaches are examined
in detail in Chapter 4, and the Trade Union and the
Organisational approaches are analysed in Chapter 5.

The Provision

In less than three years, 343 Pioneer Work courses have been
organised with working-class groups in Leeds and Bradford.
These include courses with unemployed people, the retired and
black groups. Special provision was also made for women.
Most of this provision has been in the form of short courses
lasting 10-12 weeks (ie. one two-hour meeting per week) but
course length varied, from 4 week introductory courses, to
some lasting more than 20 weeks. There has also been a
considerable number of day-schools. All courses were free of
charge. The total number of students who attended two or more
sessions was 3,969 and, on average, 9 people attended each
course. In practice, however, some groups were smaller with
6-7 members while others had 20 or more attending.
Most of the courses were with unemployed people: in
1983/4, for example, these made up 75% of total provision.
Such statistics are important, but, in practice, the situation
is more complex. Because of the broad definition of
unemployment which was adopted in Pioneer Work many of the
participants at these 'unemployed' courses are unregistered

women, and some (albeit a minority) are black. Similarly, in courses for women, many are unemployed, and may also be black.

There is, then, a deliberate overlapping of audiences which avoids ghettoisation, but at the same time, special provision has also been necessary. Thus there have been, for example, courses specifically aimed at unemployed people through unemployed centres, and special courses for women.

Reference was made earlier to the four approaches which Pioneer Work adopted, viz: Community, Institutional, Organisational and Trade Union. These have been monitored over the three years and Table 1 shows the percentage of classes which were organised via each approach in Years 1 and 3.

TABLE 1   percentage of classes by approach

	1982/3	1984/5
Community	26%	47%
Institutional	34%	26%
Organisational	37%	27%
Trade Union	3%	–

The table (and the subsequent case studies in Chapters 4 and 5) indicates that over a period of three years, contacts have been not only initiated via three approaches, but also maintained, and used as a continuing basis for organising a range of courses with a wide variety of working-class groups. The statistical failure of the Trade Union approach is examined in detail in Chapter 5.

The Community approach, which involves working with community groups and centres, tenants' associations and neighbourhood groups, has proved the most successful way of providing educational opportunities with groups who have minimal and often negative formal educational experiences. From a detailed sample of the first year's work, it was shown that 90% of people attending courses via this approach had only basic education (ie. had left school at the minimum age) and only 6% had any experience of higher education.(9) These figures were broadly confirmed by the second year's overall statistics where 87% had no experience of higher education. This approach, examined over time, also proved successful in attracting women - many of whom would not have attended classes advertised for 'the unemployed'. In the first year's sample, 47.3% from this approach were women. In the second year, it was 70%; this increase was also the result of more courses being organised specifically with women.

It was for a combination of these reasons that this approach was deliberately extended in 1984/5 to make up 47% of total provision.

The Institutional approach has involved working with the LEAs and the WEA on a co-operative basis. This inter-agency approach has proved crucial in avoiding overlaps and duplication, and has maximised scarce resources. It has also involved the beginnings of linked and staged provision. For example, by working with various sympathetic local authority adult education centres in different parts of the cities, Pioneer Work has provided liberal adult education, while the local authority has organised qualification-based classes and also basic education courses in literacy and numeracy. In general, the aim has been to complement and extend the work of the LEAs, by adding a liberal dimension, and by experimenting with innovative models of provision. For example, work initiated in Bradford in 1985 with Urdu language and culture classes in close cooperation with Bradford and Ilkley Community College, resulted subsequently in the college taking the course and students on to the mainstream college programme for higher level work.

In addition to working with specifically educational institutions, Pioneer Work has also co-operated with other agencies, which, whilst not having a primarily educational role, have been anxious to develop an educational perspective, particularly for unemployed people. Thus, courses have been developed jointly with Technology and Skills Centres, Libraries, the Probation Service, Social Services, the Health Authority, and with some churches.

Courses organised via this approach dropped from 34% of total provision in the first year to 26% in the third year. This is mainly accounted for by the number of courses which were taken over by other agencies, and was part of a deliberate Pioneer Work policy.

The Organisational approach involved working with a number of drop-in centres and organisations for the unemployed in Leeds and Bradford as well as with organisations working specifically with older people, black groups and women. These included two TUC Centres Against Unemployment. (There are now 210 such centres in the country.)

Given that one prerequisite for Pioneer Work was to make contact with unemployed and other priority groups and individuals, it was clearly very important to establish close liaison and co-ordination with these types of organisations. It was encouraging to note, therefore, that 37% of total provision came about via this approach in the first year. By the third year, this had dropped to 27%. As with the Institutional approach, this drop is mainly accounted for by a number of courses which were taken over by other agencies. For example, Pioneer Work organised courses at the Leeds Centre Against Unemployment when it first opened. Once an educational presence has been established and courses

organised, the LEA was persuaded to fund courses there. By
1985, the LEA was funding more courses than Pioneer Work at
the Centre.
It is not surprising that those recruited for courses
held at such centres contained a very high proportion of the
registered unemployed. In the first year, 82% of participants
via this approach, and in the second year almost 90% of people
attending courses at the Leeds Centre, were registered
unemployed - and 60% of these were long-term unemployed. The
obverse of this, however, also needs examining : many
unregistered unemployed, particularly women, do not attend
such centres. For example, in the second year of the project
when an educational presence had been firmly established in a
number of these centres, only 30% were women. This compares
unfavourably with an overall female participation rate of 49%
for all classes that year, and a 70% rate for classes from the
Community approach.
Statistics about the participation of women have been
referred to in the approaches which are outlined above. A
more detailed analysis of work with women is provided in
Chapter 6, but it is worth noting here the dramatic increase
in courses with women over the three years.

TABLE 2   Women's courses as percentage
                              of total provision

1982/3   :   12%
1983/4   :   20%
1984/5   :   30%

This increase from 12% to 30% is not the full picture.
In addition to these courses specifically for women, (eg.
Women's Health, and Opportunities for Women) many women
attended other Pioneer Work courses. The success of the
Community approach in attracting women over the three years
obviously accounts in part for the increasing number of
women's courses, but there is also the issue of using scarce
resources for this area of work as part of a deliberate
policy. Pressure from experienced full-time and part-time
women tutors in Pioneer Work has ensured that work in this
area (both for specific provision and for increased female
participation in all courses) has been given high priority.
It should be clear from the statistics which have been
provided in this chapter that a great deal of information has
been compiled about how courses are organised and what type of
people attend them: male/female, age, educational background,
unemployed etc. There is, however, no information available
at all about the ethnic composition of participants. Given
that Pioneer Work aims to work with black people in addition
to other groups, this is a surprising omission. On the one

hand, ethnic monitoring is crucial if agencies are to evaluate their work critically. From this point of view, Pioneer Work staff have felt that it is important; in practice, however, some individual participants and tutors are opposed to questions about ethnicity being included on a register. This issue has not as yet been resolved.

One major problem has been that all the DES funded Pioneer Work staff are white. A male Asian tutor was appointed part-time in 1984/5 with a grant from Bradford Metropolitan District Council; and one of the NIACE funded part-time lecturers is an Asian woman. The NIACE/REPLAN project is specifically, albeit not exclusively, focussed on work with Asian women. Also, much of the Bradford Metropolitan District Council grant was used both to employ black tutors and also direct courses specifically towards black people. It is mainly because of these special grants that 21% of total provision in 1984/5 was either organised and taught by a black tutor and/or mainly directed towards black people.

Nevertheless, two short-term, under-staffed and minimally funded projects are inadequate for the major development of this difficult area of work. Moreover, there are dangers, of course, in focussing on special projects; these can hide the extent to which these issues are not confronted in the rest of the programme, and lead to the ghetto approach which Pioneer Work staff have been so anxious to avoid in working with unemployed people and women.

If black members of staff were appointed and involved in the overall programme, then the dangers of the ghetto approach could at least be minimised. In 1984/5 two temporary half-time University lecturing posts became available. Pioneer Work received University approval for one of these posts to be concerned with 'ethnic minority' work. This would have created an opening for a black staff member to be involved with the overall programme. In the event the University appointing committee decided that a white person should be offered this post. The issues this raises about the University as an institution in the context of community-based work with black groups are explored in Chapter 9. It is important to refer to this here, however, since it was a significant factor which inhibited a particular area of work from being developed fully and effectively.

Professional Consultancy Work

The vast majority of Pioneer Work courses have been aimed, successfully, at people who had no experience of tertiary education. A small number of courses in 1983/4, however, and a large number the following year, were organised for professional workers from statutory and voluntary agencies.

These recruited large numbers and proved very popular. They included regional and national courses for TUC Centre workers, day courses for community workers, and involvement in the REPLAN Regional Staff Development Programme. If resources were available, this second level work could be increased dramatically. Though only a small proportion of the work overall, such provision is of considerable importance. One of the key roles of good UAE practice has been the education, induction and training of professionals engaged in a wide variety of industrial, social service, and educational occupations. Those involved have ranged from shop stewards and other union activists on day release courses, to social workers and adult educators. Throughout, though, the intention has been the same: to provide a thoroughly professional and 'vocational' programme, appropriate to the group in question, within the context of a critical, open-ended liberal approach. The essence of the approach is thus to combine the vocational and the liberal, the 'practice' and the 'theory', and the 'experience' and the 'education'.(10)

When it is done well, this approach can provide invaluable induction - via the education of key groups of educators and trainers - into 'good practice'. In the case of this aspect of Pioneer Work, it is of particular importance that those engaged in the field should be able to benefit from such provision. In that sense, therefore, this part of the Pioneer Work programme, disseminating 'good practice' to other professionals, is of significance.

Types of Courses

A very wide variety of courses was organised, but for monitoring and comparative purposes they were categorised as follows: (the categorisation here excludes the programme of work with the retired which was rather different in kind and which is analysed in some detail in Chapter 7).

A. Welfare rights, social policy and unemployment-related classes
B. General and educational counselling and discussion groups
C. Subject courses (economics, psychology, sociology)
D. Interest courses (music, video, photography)
E. Courses specifically related to local issues and/or expressed need ('Organising in the Community', 'Know the System','You and the Police')
F. Women's courses.

In practice, many courses fall into several categories and the categories proved inadequate over time. For example, as noted above, professional, consultancy work courses were developed in the second and third years, and do not fall under any of these headings. New technology and computing courses were developed in the second year - these are categorised as D (Interest courses), although they could equally be categorised as C (Subject courses); the same point applies to local history classes. In spite of these limitations, however, it is useful to compare the course categories for Years 1 and 3.

TABLE 3	percentage of courses by category	
	1982/3	1984/5
A	26%	13%
B	23%	7%
C	10%	–
D	20%	33%
E	9%	17%
F	12%	30%

Table 3 shows that there was a 50% decrease from Year 1 to 3 in Category A (welfare rights courses etc). It is worth examining the reasons for this.

In the second year, it was decided not to replicate all the welfare rights courses. Instead, building on the extensive contacts which had been established, an ambitious inter-agency 20 week course (one half-day per week) on advice work and welfare rights was organised. It attracted 21 students, all of whom were workers or volunteers involved with the unemployed in community centres or through community and advice groups throughout Leeds. In this case, then, Pioneer Work's resources were used for consolidation and concentration; one longer, more advanced course, aimed at key individuals was organised, rather than the previous relatively widespread provision of courses.

This course was then successfully handed over to a city-wide group of advice workers, who received funding from the British Council of Churches to run a similar course in 1984/5. This successful handover, however, illustrates the necessity of monitoring over time: no funding was available for this course in 1985/6, and it is possible that what appears to have been a successful handover may in fact become a failed initiative when examined over a longer period.

Counselling and discussion groups (Category B) fell from 23% to 7%: this illustrates the simple finding that people are more attracted towards specific courses which they are initially interested in, or which are directly relevant to them, rather than open-ended discussion groups. The increasing proportion of Interest courses (up from 20% to 33% over the 3 years), and courses related to local issues or expressed need (up from 9% to 17%), illustrates the same point.

A more detailed exploration of course content, and what types of courses were organised through different approaches, is provided in the following chapter.

The fundamental Pioneer Work approach, then, has been based upon developing innovative and appropriate educational provision for working-class groups on an inter-agency, community basis. The next chapter explores in some detail, through a case study approach, the ways in which the provision has been made, and the problems and achievements experienced.

REFERENCES

1. See E P Thompson, The Making of the English Working Class, Penguin, 1963; and J F C Harrison, Learning and Living 1750-1960, Routledge and Kegan Paul, 1963.

2. For more detailed analysis of both the radical liberal tradition in UAE, and the specific orientation of industrial studies provision within this context, see R Taylor, K Rockhill and R Fieldhouse, University Adult Education in Education in England and the USA: a reappraisal of the liberal tradition, Croom Helm, 1985, Chapters 2, 5 and 8.

3. For details see HMI Survey of Adult Education for the Disadvantaged, DES, 1978; and for a general survey of Jean Gardiner's work over this period see her Community Adult Education Report 1976-1980, published by the Department of Adult and Continuing Education, University of Leeds, 1981.

4. The report recommended a series of wide-ranging reforms over and above the Pioneer Work developments which are the focus of attention here. The report, which was implemented with modifications, after discussion, combined with a succession of UGC 'cuts' and the DES 'new formula' for the allocation of grant aid, resulted in a radical change in orientation and a diminution in size in the Department by the later 1980s.

5. The membership of the Supervisory Group was: the head of the Department of Adult and Continuing Education (chair), HMI (representing the DES), chairman of the School of Education (representing the University), the Director of Extramural Studies, the Co-ordinator of Pioneer Work, and the Academic Adviser (responsible for Departmental/WEA liaison).

6. A Rapoport, The Dilemmas in Action-Research, Human Relations, vol 23, No 6, pp 489-513, 1975; H Homstein, and B Bunker et al, Social Intervention - A Behavioural Science Approach, Free Press, New York, 1970; (eds) L Zurcher and C Bonjean, Planned Social Intervention -

An Interdisciplinary Anthology, Chandler Publishing
Company, USA, 1971; C H Weiss, Evaluating Action
Programmes, Boston, Mass., USA, 1974; P Marris and
M Rein, Dilemmas of Social Reform, Routledge and Kegan
Paul, 1967; M Key, P Hudson and J Armstrong, Evaluation
Theory and Community Work, YVFF, 1978; R Lees and
G Smith, Action Research in Community Development,
Routledge and Kegan Paul, 1975; N Bailey et al,
Resourcing Communities, Evaluating the Experience of
Six Area Resource Centres, PCL, 1980.

7. For a detailed discussion of the methodological issues
    of the case study format, see K Ward, A Case Study in
    Community Action, M Phil thesis, unpublished, University
    of Bradford, 1979.

8. It is not being implied that community-based projects
    need years of preparatory work. What is clear is that
    staff must have time to initiate relevant contacts and
    establish legitimacy at the planning stages of any
    project. It is obviously impossible to say precisely
    how long this takes because local circumstances vary
    greatly, but a period of six months would seem to be the
    minimum. This point also has resource implications as
    experience elsewhere shows.

9. For further details see K Ward, Beyond Tokenism -
    Unemployed Adults and Education, November 1983,
    Department of Adult and Continuing Education, University
    of Leeds, Chapters 2 and 3.

10. For a more detailed discussion of this argument in the
    context of trade union and social work education, see R
    Taylor and K Ward, Extramural Work: different settings,
    common themes, Adult Education, vol 54, No 1, June 1981,
    pp 12-18.

Chapter 4

UNEMPLOYED IN THE COMMUNITY

Introduction

'Nowt's changed round here - but we must be the best educated group of tenants in the city'.

This quotation from a tenant on a large council estate epitomises both the potential and the limitations of working-class adult education, particularly with unemployed people. It raises fundamental questions about the effects and outcomes of adult education initiatives, which will be returned to later in this chapter. It assumes, however, that adult education with working- class groups has actually taken place, and so the first question must be how initiatives were started and what developed as a result.

These questions are examined in this chapter in the context of work with the unemployed. The four approaches which were used are outlined in Chapter 3 and illustrate the fact that a broad definition of unemployment was adopted to include the unregistered unemployed - particularly women. Leaving aside the Trade Union approach and the Organisational approach which are examined in Chapter 5, the Community and the Institutional approaches provide important lessons for the development of work with the unemployed 'in the community'.

The Community Approach

This approach, which involves working with community groups and centres, tenants' associations and neighbourhood groups, led to 26% of total provision in the first year and 47% in the third year. It depends crucially on detailed contacts and credibility with a wide range of local groups. It is interesting to note that people contacted via this approach were much more interested in education which they themselves saw as relevant to their circumstances and needs - the only category of course they were not interested in was 'subject' courses. This is hardly surprising given the educational background of participants in this approach: 90% in the first year had left school at the minimum age, and the overall statistics for the second year showed that 87% had no experience of higher education. Reference is also made in Chapter 3 to the high proportion of women who attended these courses 'in the community' - 47.3% in the first year and 70% in the second year.

In general, only those with a relatively high level of education develop an interest in the major subject areas (whether arts, science or social studies). The approach used here therefore was to construct issue-based, rather than subject or discipline-based, courses which would lead into discussion and analysis of wider issues.

A wide variety of courses was organised including: Welfare Rights, Organising in the Community, Housing, Video in the Community, Alternative Health, Women and the Media and 'Is There Life After Housework?'. The following case study describes how a range of courses was developed in one area and what the outcomes were.

Case Study I: Halton Moor Tenants and The Community Discussion Group

In one area of two large council estates with high unemployment rates, the project had links with a local community worker and several members of a small tenants' association. These estates mainly consisted of 1930s built houses interspersed with post-war blocks of flats. In 1982 there were no adult education courses locally which these tenants saw as relevant to their circumstances and needs. By July 1985, ten courses had been organised. All were attended by people who had left school at the minimum age and had no previous experience of adult education. These courses included Welfare Rights, Organising in the Community, How Community Groups Work, Know the System, and Getting it Across - Print and Display.

There is nothing unique in how these courses were organised and taught. Many adult educators now have experience in 'outreach work' and 'community adult education', but case studies in detail, and particularly those relating to work with unemployed adults, are still scarce. It is for this reason that this case study is included.

The crucial starting point was that possible plans were developed from the earliest stage with several tenants. None was interested in adult education, and they felt no-one would come to courses relating to unemployment, unless people were offered jobs. They were, however, obviously interested in issues which directly affected them such as welfare rights, housing problems in the area, and the work of the small tenants' group. The tenants and the project then jointly planned and organised two courses on the basis of these issues: Welfare Rights, and Organising in the Community. The former was held in one of the tenants' sitting-rooms and the

78

latter in a local community centre. It took several months to plan and jointly organise these two courses. This planning process with potential or core members of a proposed course is fundamental to its success or failure.

Welfare Rights   The Welfare Rights course, which was attended by nine women and one man, was not formally advertised at all.   People were notified in one part of an estate purely by word of mouth.   There were five regular attenders from the street in which the course was held.   The participants all understood that the course was not a CAB-type training course, but was intended to discuss critically a number of social policy/welfare rights issues which directly related to their experiences (eg. the introduction of the Housing Benefits scheme at that time) in the context of an introductory framework about the whole benefit system and its relationship to the Welfare State structure.   At the end of the course, tenants felt they had increased their personal knowledge and understanding, and it also helped them, when other people from the estate had queries about welfare rights.   They saw themselves as a link to the experienced advice workers at a neighbouring Information Centre.   One of those who attended has since become a full-time volunteer at this centre.

Organising in The Community   Three members of this group also helped plan the Organising in the Community course. Unlike the Welfare Rights course, this was advertised, but only locally on the estates.   At a general level, the aim was to look at how local groups can influence, and are influenced by, the local authority.   This involved discussion of political and organisational issues in the local state, within the historical context of post-war administration in Leeds City Council.   From a detailed review which was carried out with twelve people who attended, it is clear that the course strengthened, or in some cases created, interest in, and understanding of various forms of community activity.

The course was a combination of visiting speakers, carefully-selected tutor inputs with handouts, and discussion.   The speakers included the local Housing Manager, and the new chairman of the Housing committee, the day after he had been appointed.   The tenants were impressed by the fact that 'educational courses' could cover such topics, call on relevant high-profile speakers if they were carefully planned, and provide a forum for the discussion of a wide range of topics.

Just as important as the specific topics which were discussed, was the fact that the course helped demystify, and indeed opened up the idea of adult education in an area where traditional attitudes to education range from awe to apathy. It was, however, a concept of adult education which was based on joint planning and control by the users; these issues were explicitly discussed with course members.

79

The Community Discussion Group   After this course, the group felt there was a basis for continuity and called itself the Community Discussion Group (CDG). This was, in part, an attempt deliberately to avoid the use of the word 'education', which it was felt would deter many people, but was also intended to make a distinction between this type of group, and the action groups in the area (although in practice there was overlapping participation).

Organising in the Community and at Home   The next course, three months later, was Organising in the Community and at Home. The same joint planning process was undertaken and this course had six members who had attended the earlier courses and six newcomers. Several sessions critically reviewed developments which had been examined in the previous course (eg. changes in local housing policy and practice) as well as providing introductory sessions on other issues which group members themselves identified as important, ie. bringing up children and women's health.

One unintended consequence of the session on women's health was that an independent self-programming women's health group developed in the area, and continued to meet regularly on an informal basis for several years. Although women's health groups are common in many areas, they do not often develop independently on council estates.

How Community Groups Work   At that stage, joint planning for another course was inhibited by difficulties within the tenants' association. Several members had left disillusioned and there were arguments between remaining members. This serious, but common, problem in community work was turned to educational advantage. Because the CDG and the project were seen as supportive, but outside the local arguments, there was enthusiasm for a course on How Community Groups Work. Case studies were provided about experiences elsewhere, and relevant, detailed handouts given each week as a lead into experiential discussion. According to the local community worker this course clarified and strengthened community activism in the area.

By autumn 1984, courses had been running for two years and an adult education presence clearly established in the area. Indeed, the core members of the CDG expected and demanded provision to continue on topics and issues decided by them.

Know The System   New members had joined an additional tenants' group in the area and the planning group felt that an updated course on 'Knowing the System' would be of benefit both to core members and new members. The planning group wanted a course which examined how decisions were taken at the local level linked to an examination of the role of councillors and officers. Information was also requested about Councils' budgets and finances in the context of rate-capping and the abolition of the Metropolitan County Councils.

This course proved the most difficult to prepare. The tutor involved had taught social policy at postgraduate level, but the preparation of relevant materials and handouts for this course, which also drew on participants' own experiences and considerable local knowledge, was extremely time-consuming. The course eventually consisted of a quiz about local government finance and responsibilities, detailed handouts, videos, speakers and discussion. From reviews subsequently carried out with the group, it seems that the mix of teaching methods used proved valuable. Group discussion, and the manner in which the quiz encouraged active learning rather than passive acceptance, were particularly mentioned. It is difficult to find documented case studies of other adult education courses with unemployed people and working-class groups which discussed in detail such issues as the abolition of the metropolitan counties and its effect on their area.

The Exhibition The tenants were increasingly regarding education as a crucial support and an underpinning for their community activities. This became particularly evident in 1985 when they used several courses as a base, to plan and prepare a major exhibition about what they regarded as the inadequate state of repair, and dangerous structural condition, of a block of flats in their area.

Three courses ran concurrently: video, photography and 'Getting it Across - Print and Display'. The video and photography courses were funded by the LEA: having been unable to establish a systematic educational presence in the area, LEA adult education staff were more than willing to cooperate on a joint basis. These courses were used to collect visual information about conditions in their area. The 'Getting it Across' course involved the writing-up of relevant information for the exhibition - this included history, information on housing conditions elsewhere, survey material collected by tenants, technical reports on the flats, and recommendations.

The exhibition, which had taken four months to prepare, received widespread press and TV coverage. It consisted of large display boards, photographs, and a video about the flats called 'Yesterday's Dream - Today's Nightmare'.

As a result of the publicity, the tenants showed the exhibition and the video at the Civic Hall, and were subsequently invited to show it to the Housing Minister at Westminster, accompanied by their MP and the Chairman of the Housing committee - apparently the first tenants' group to show a video to a Minister at Westminster about conditions on their estate.

Relevant and Purposeful Education - Educational Continuity

After the exhibition, it seemed that adult education could hardly be more relevant and purposeful. It is clear from the description of all the courses, however, that explicit attempts were made to relate educational provision to a range of issues which participants themselves defined as relevant to their needs and circumstances.

The courses were neither advertised nor imposed from an outside agency. Systematic and detailed joint planning and publicity was initiated by the project with local people. The content of the courses indicates that 'relevance' was gradually extended and broadened to include a wide range of issues (from women's health, to conflicts within groups, to the relationship between central and local government).

The course contents also illustrate the simple fact that experimentation and innovation are needed in course design: this was particularly the case with the experientially based 'How Community Groups Work' course and the 'Know the System' course.

The outcome of these courses, according to the participants themselves, has been threefold: it has strengthened community activity in various ways; it has dramatically increased the self-confidence and knowledge base of a number of participants; and it has provided a solid basis for educational continuity and progression. This does not mean, in this example, applying for a university place or other qualification-based courses, but rather the continuation of critical, liberal adult education. Moreover, this continuation, which consists of a core group of 5-6 people who have attended most courses, plus new participants, depends fundamentally on their wish for it to continue. It is a small example of educational provision which is controlled by users but resourced by adult education professionals.

The Limitations It should be clear from the descriptions above that the project regards the work with the Halton Moor tenants as a significant success, and a vindication of the community approach over a period of time. It should be pointed out, however, that although Pioneer Work initiated contacts with a local community worker and local tenants, and then systematically maintained them over time, the adult education work could not have started or continued without the support of the community worker and local tenants. In other words, Pioneer Work depends essentially on these existing or embryonic contacts, and if they do not exist, then adult education initiatives in general and Pioneer Work in particular would be even more limited than they are at present. Pioneer Work cannot pretend to have extensive community work resources to develop initial contacts on estates.

Another issue is the dividing line between the roles of the adult educator and the community activist. In practice, this dividing line was easy to define with the Halton Moor tenants. The value of the adult educator for them was as someone who was outside the local politics, and inter-group relationships. Once trust had been established, and it became clear that the tutor supported their activities and aims, there was no problem with the dividing line. Indeed, the tenants would have regarded it as condescending and patronising if the tutor, Kevin Ward, had imposed himself on them at their action meetings and in negotiations with local politicians.

A final broader issue is the relationship between adult education and social change. It is not relevant to explore this issue in detail here, but it was referred to in the quotation at the beginning of this chapter: 'Nowt's changed round here - but we must be the best educated group of tenants in the city'. This quotation is from one of the Halton Moor tenants who has been a regular attender at all of the courses outlined in the case study. From no previous experience or interest in adult education, he then expected too much from it. At least his concept of adult education was a liberatory one: he neither expected nor wanted a job, qualification, or training, nor did he regard adult education as something useful just to fill in his enforced leisure time. Rather, he expected it to contribute to a greater understanding of his own living conditions and local issues, and also to lead to social change: the latter aim, obviously, it cannot fulfil.

The Halton Moor case study illustrates how courses can be developed in the community for unemployed people, including unregistered unemployed, who have not previously had any experience of or interest in adult education. Moreover, it is a critical liberal adult education related to their needs and circumstances which has created interest. These types of courses, developed at Halton Moor and elsewhere by community workers and outreach adult educators, could be termed 'education for everyday living'.

In the words of a DES representative who visited the estate and met the tenants: 'It's something which could happen on every council estate in the country'. Perhaps the outcomes envisaged by the DES if this were to happen would differ in some respects from the objectives of tenants such as Fred Medd, quoted earlier: but all are agreed that such educational programmes could provide a crucial additional dimension to the lives of people in such communities.

Case Study II: Some Failed Initiatives

The criterion of success via the Community approach on the Halton Moor case study was the establishment of a critical liberal adult education presence. It is interesting to compare this with other initiatives which failed to do that.

In one inner-city area, the project did not have the detailed contacts which were built up over time with the Halton Moor tenants, but a similar process was adopted. Meetings were held with an LEA adult education worker and members of a local community centre management committee who were anxious to 'do something' for the unemployed. After several detailed meetings with this group, it was decided to advertise a Drop-in facility (the centre has a cafe attached to it), use of the centre's workshops, and advice/discussion groups. The advertising for this was very extensive in the area. Most of the houses and local shops were leafleted and there was publicity on the local radio. In the event, this initiative failed to recruit a regular core group. Two individuals attended regularly and a number of other people occasionally dropped in, but they just as quickly 'dropped out' once they had received the advice they had initially come for.

There are several reasons for this failure. Referring to 'Discussion Groups' explicitly was too vague, generalised and open-ended, in a context where, apart from recreational activities, there was no educational presence. Also, although careful links were established with the community centre management committee, the project did not realise until later, not having worked with them before, that they were narrowly based in the area and in fact did not have the extensive detailed contacts which they themselves thought they had. This meant that, unlike the Halton Moor example, there were no effective and positive 'word of mouth' networks to advertise and explain about the initiative. In the event, even extensive leafleting proved unsuccessful.

Besides their narrow base, the managment committee was also handicapped by the lack of any community work support, which was available with the Halton Moor tenants. In organising courses in the community, it is always explained that, although the project can help with publicity about courses, and talk to interested people, it cannot function without an active partnership. This, backed up by community work support, was present at Halton Moor but conspicuously lacking in this example.

In spite of these problems, this initiative did have some unintended consequences. A number of retired people - there is a significant number in that area - responded to the advertising, and a regular Senior Citizens' Club was established. The community centre had been trying to establish such a group, and was delighted with this development.

The following report illustrates another initiative which failed and the reasons for this failure.

'No problems. An ideal location for a Pioneer Work project. A virgin estate, educationally speaking, with just over 3,000 people of whom 18% of men and 12% of women were unemployed. There were few shops, an infrequent bus service into town, one-third of households with kids, and no community facilities until now. What was obviously needed was an adult education project.

I'd done my homework - contacted the doctor, health visitor, local social services office, a recently appointed local education outreach worker, "mums-and-tots" groups, a vicar and a community association representative. I'd arranged for the new community building to be specially opened and for the estate to be leafleted.

We had set up links with the continuing education office to take over the course on "parents, children and families" if we successfully developed it first. A creche worker had been lined up.

Therefore I can't understand why it's ten past one and I'm sitting alone with my tea, sugar and milk when the class was due to start at one.

In the end I have one customer, the stalwart of the "mums-and-tots" group and her child and we have a useful half-hour exchange.

Week 2 - it's the same sorry tale. I decide to try some door-to-door knocking - back to the grassroots. However, houses are either empty, inhabited by retired people or guarded by large, unfriendly dogs. All the families with young kids must live on the other side of the estate.

I call it a day. So why didn't it work?

1. There was no core community group. Hence there was no network to spread the word and more importantly no way of knowing whether the course was actually what was needed.

2. There was no community worker to help bring a group together.

3. There was until that month no community centre where people could meet and hence no tradition of education work.

4. Key agencies failed to deliver specific clients who might have been interested'.

The Institutional Approach

The first part of this chapter has examined the potential and the limitations of developing adult education for unemployed people in specific geographical areas, by working with, and through, community and tenants' groups, and community centres.

It is now necessary to contrast this Community approach

85

with the Institutional Approach as a method of organising courses for unemployed people.

This involves working with other educational and related bodies (eg. LEAs, WEA) on an inter-agency, co-operative basis. It has maximised scarce resources and avoided overlap and duplication.

Reference was made in Chapter 3 to the fact that relationships with the LEAs in Leeds and Bradford have been a key aspect of this approach, but that the project has also co-operated with other agencies, which, while not having a primarily educational role, have been anxious to develop an educational perspective, particularly for unemployed people. These have included Technology and Skills Centres, libraries, the Probation Service, Bradford Playhouse and some churches. Examples of courses include a New Directions course at a library, Rock n' Roll, Women's Diet and Health, with the Probation Service, and Women and the Media, and Say It With Video, with Bradford Playhouse.

The Community and Institutional approaches are being examined separately because there are major differences between organising courses primarily with locally controlled community centres and neighbourhood groups, and courses with LEA centres and other institutions or agencies. In practice, a wide range of courses has been organised via each approach.

The Institutional approach led to 34% of overall provision in the first year and 26% in the third year (Table 1, Chapter 3). The overall statistics from the second and third years broadly confirm the results of a sample which was carried out in the first year (see Appendix I).

The sample showed that this approach attracted 55% women; 65% of participants were registered unemployed and 56% were long-term unemployed. These figures indicate that an encouraging number of the long-term unemployed are attracted to day-time courses. This approach was also successful in attracting large numbers of people with only basic educational backgrounds: 80% had no experience of higher education and 69% had left school at the minimum age. It is interesting to note, however, that 20% had experience of higher education, while only 6% of those in the Community approach came into this category.

These statistics illustrate the major difference between the Community and Institutional approaches. Even when advertised, courses with neighbourhood groups and local community centres in working-class areas rarely attract people with experience of higher education. The Community approach, then, as illustrated by the statistics, and by the Halton Moor case study cited earlier in this chapter, attracts an almost exclusively working-class clientele. LEA centres, however, even those based in inner-city areas, already have some sort of educational presence or image, which naturally attracts a proportion of people with experience of tertiary education. Also, partnership with some agencies (eg. the Playhouse in Bradford) clearly means that the audience will be educationally mixed. Even though the project is interested primarily in courses with educationally disadvantaged unemployed people, it would be unnecessarily restrictive and artificial to exclude the minority with experience of higher education. These issues, however, illustrate the necessity for careful monitoring of all courses which are organised.

The LEAs The Institutional approach depends primarily on close relationships with the LEAs, although this is much more difficult in practice in Bradford, where, until 1984/5 there had been virtually no adult education area-based staff and structure. From the outset, attempts were made to avoid potential conflict and competition between this new university project and local authority adult education staff. To ensure close working, an experienced LEA staff member in Leeds was seconded to the project for the first two years. He successfully developed the beginnings of linked provision by using both LEA funds (for basic courses), and project resources for a range of liberal adult education courses (including Welfare Rights, Discussion Groups, and Educational Counselling and Study Techniques). Also, for the first two years, it was explicitly agreed by Pioneer Work and the LEA in Leeds, that one of the project's part-time organising tutors should be an LEA part-time Head of Centre. This ensured that a wide variety of joint courses was organised (again, deliberately maximising scarce resources by utilising both project and LEA resources). This relationship, however, just like course provision, needs careful monitoring. It was described earlier how the Institutional approach dropped from 34% to 26% of total provision over the three years, mainly because a number of courses were deliberately handed over to the LEA. This 'handover' objective is an important one because some courses are more appropriately organised in the long term by agencies other than Pioneer Work. In 1983-84 an increasing number of courses for women was organised. These included two successful courses entitled: 'Is There Life After Housework?' and 'There is Life After Housework'. These had been organised with an inner-city community centre and had recruited women who did not have any previous experience of higher education. The LEA agreed to fund these courses for Autumn 1984. Pioneer Work regarded this handover as a success because it seemed to ensure long-term continuity for women in that area, and it also showed how Pioneer Work could influence the type of courses funded by the LEA. In the event, according to reports from that area one year later, this handover was not successful. The LEA did fund the course and provide a tutor but unfortunately the processes developed by the project (eg.

detailed pre-course negotiations) did not take place; it also seems possible that the LEA tutor was not appropriate for this group of working-class women. This example illustrates the necessity of monitoring this handover function over a period of time. Pioneer Work now feels obliged to organise courses at that location once again.

It is mentioned above that the Institutional approach involves working with other agencies as well as with LEAs. The case study below briefly illustrates this.

Sweet Street Technology Centre

This centre organises full-time courses but was anxious that its facilities should be available for unemployed people. In Summer 1983, agreement was reached between Pioneer Work and staff at the Technology Centre that a two year programme of free courses for the unemployed in new technology and computers be organised.

After two years, twelve successful courses have been organised. The relationship between the two agencies illustrates the value of joint working and collaboration. Sweet Street provided free use of their extensive facilities while Pioneer Work paid for tutors' fees (this amounted to £2660 over the two years). Advertising was done by both agencies and, unlike that for courses in the community, was extensive throughout the city, including job centres.

The courses were free and had to be held in the evenings since the facilities were not available during the day. Most other courses for unemployed people were held during the day.

The aim of these courses was to increase familiarity with computers and develop an awareness of their impact on modern life. This aim is consistent with one of the overall aims of Pioneer Work - the development of a critical awareness related to particular topics. Thus, the aim was not simply to learn practically how to use the equipment, but also to analyse critically the different usages of computers.

The courses in the first year were mainly basic and introductory, but in the second year there was evidence of educational continuity and progression. Groups of students who had attended basic short courses made demands for more advanced courses: these 'intermediate' courses were organised in the second year and attended by earlier students : there was, then, a deliberate follow-on. Three students from these intermediate courses are subsequently attending full-time day courses at the centre.

It is interesting to note that the expectations and anticipated outcomes as seen by students on these courses are markedly different from other courses. In the second year it became clear that students hoped the courses would either lead on to more specific 'training' (which it did for the three students above) and/or increase their job prospects. This is the only category of course in our work with the unemployed where this job orientation became significant. It is different in character, then, from survival and coping courses, or the types of courses which were referred to in the Halton Moor case study.

Now that a successful educational presence has been developed with unemployed people at the Technology Centre, it is hoped to persuade the local authority to fund these courses on a long-term basis.

The relationship with the Technology Centre is a good example of the Institutional approach, illustrating, as it does, the maximisation of scarce resources and the provision of linked and staged educational continuity and progression. It is an example of the 'pioneer' role of the University in developing new areas of work, some of which are more appropriately funded in the long-term by other agencies.

The Constraints of Short-term External Funding
The REPLAN/NIACE Projects and the Bradford Council Grant

Reference was made in Chapters 2 and 3 to two projects which were funded for two years by REPLAN/NIACE in Leeds, and a special grant for work with the unemployed for one year which was provided by Bradford Metropolitan District Council.

Within Pioneer Work, it had been agreed to use the Bradford grant mainly (albeit not exclusively) for work with black 'unemployed' groups, and this was also the focus for one of the NIACE projects.

These extra resources obviously enabled more community-based courses for unemployed people to be developed, but they also raise a number of issues about working with black groups, and a number of problems and constraints related to short-term external funding.

The Bradford Council Grant

This grant, for one year, was used to employ two part-time organising tutors, and also to recruit specialist tutors for particular courses.

Before the grant was even approved, considerable Pioneer Work staff time had been spent on drafting the application, meeting council officials and subsequently writing three redrafts of the application. When it proved successful, there was the usual process of job descriptions, advertising (including Asian language papers) and appointing.

An Asian tutor was appointed: several months later, when he was offered employment elsewhere, he left the project. As was noted in Chapter 3, this illustrates a general problem for short-term projects, and particularly those who employ part-time staff: any alternative employment with better conditions and greater security will obviously be accepted. As will be seen later, exactly the same thing happened with both NIACE projects.

A second Asian tutor was appointed but there were only eight months of the grant left. At that stage, it was debatable whether it was right to expect a possibly inexperienced person to develop new courses with black groups. In the event, some important initiatives were taken which led to a number of courses being organised. This was fortuitous for Pioneer Work, but only happened because of the ability, commitment and energy of the 'replacement' tutor.

The courses which developed included Urdu Literacy, New Technology and Computer Appreciation, West Indian Art and Culture, Black People in Society, An Introduction to Indian Classical Music, African History, Basketry, and Parents and Schools.

The processes for organising these courses were similar to those outlined in the Halton Moor case study. The tutor first had to spend a considerable time talking to potential users - in a number of cases this was to users of several Asian community centres. Unlike Halton Moor, there were no action groups in some of these areas, so it was not possible initially to develop courses such as Organising in the Community; neither was there interest in courses explicitly related to unemployment. There was enthusiasm, however, for courses which related to people's particular culture such as the ones outlined above. As discussions developed over several months, interest was also expressed in other topics such as New Technology, and Schools and Children.

Amongst Asian parents in Bradford there was interest and concern about education, as evidenced by the Honeyford controversy.* In this context the tutor was able to organise two successful bilingual courses for Pakistani and Bengali parents in different schools.

The problems of an eight month project became particularly evident as all these courses were organised. Not only did the tutor have to do outreach, gauge potential interest, find suitable tutors and organise the courses: from the earliest stage, he also had to plan for the possible continuity or handover of the course if another agency seemed more appropriate. With the Urdu Literacy and the New Technology and Computers classes, he received an undertaking from the local college for continuity.

The varied tasks listed above illustrate the complex and

---

* Honeyford was a Bradford Headteacher who was suspended for alleged failure to implement the Council's anti-racist policies. The case received extensive local and national publicity in 1985/6.

broadened role of an organising tutor. One of Pioneer Work's general problems is finding suitable tutors for community-based courses. This is particularly problematic for a project staffed exclusively by white people, in working with black groups. Materials are often not available in the necessary languages; specialist tutors rarely speak the appropriate languages, and are often lacking in cultural awareness. These issues of recruitment and support for tutors with black groups also became evident with one of the NIACE projects. At the time of writing, it is fair to state that Pioneer Work is grappling with, rather than resolving, these crucial issues.

The Bradford Council grant, then, illustrated the acute problems of short-term funding. Valuable developments occurred in this instance, but the Pioneer Work staff have mixed views about whether, in general, the necessary input both for initiating extra funding (time-consuming grant applications and meetings) and then utilising it most effectively (regular support and progress meetings with part-time staff and monitoring of work) justifies the outcome in the long term.

The REPLAN/NIACE Projects

When the REPLAN/NIACE programme was announced, it was felt within the Project that there was no alternative but to apply for funding - given that staff had argued to the DES(1) that special funding was desperately needed.

Two joint applications were drafted somewhat hastily and both were approved. It is worth noting that new sources of funding are often known about only by professional workers: voluntary organisations and community groups, at whom these projects are often aimed, are not in a position to respond rapidly. It was for this reason that Pioneer Work staff resisted the temptation to expand their own programme directly, and instead developed two new projects with other groups.

The City Centre Project

One project was organised jointly with the Continuing Education Service of the Leeds Authority, and also involved the local TUC Centre Against Unemployment. (For further detail on these centres, see Chapter 5.) This project, initially agreed for two years, started in September 1984 with two half-time workers and finance to employ other tutors (a budget of approximately £17,000 p.a.). Located in the city centre of Leeds, the aim has been to make contact with and develop relevant educational provision for 'those long-term adult unemployed whose life experience (homelessness, institutionalisation and isolation) prevent them from having a realistic expectation of early re-entry to employment or mainstream education or training'.(2)

This project, then, is focussed on the long-term unemployed, but particularly those in a specific geographical area, the city centre, and those who use the variety of hostels in Leeds. It should be clear that this particular audience is difficult to reach and presents major challenges for adult educators. Applications for the posts of project workers showed that there were very few people within the region with direct, relevant experience of working with the long-term unemployed, or of developing educational provision within hostel accommodation.

When two workers were eventually appointed, one left after several months: like the Asian tutor at Bradford, she was offered a full-time post elsewhere. Several months were lost in readvertising and reappointing.

After nine months work, however, 17 courses have been organised for different, usually small, groups of long-term unemployed people in hostels, day-centres, the Resettlement Unit and the Centre Against Unemployment. These can be categorised in three ways:

> Survival and coping courses (eg. Welfare Rights, Look After Yourself, DIY)
> Interest and Leisure courses (eg. Art, Music, Video, Hairdressing)
> Alternatives to Employment (eg. 'Setting Up Shop': a course on co-ops and self-help).

These courses and the processes which led up to them have been carefully monitored. The workers agreed to a detailed monitoring and evaluation framework (see 'Note on Monitoring and Evaluation Framework', appended to this chapter). Monitoring and evaluation is something which most adult educators agree with in principle, but often fail to do anything systematic about in practice. The workers in this project had not been accustomed to it, but in spite of the chore of providing detailed monthly reports, they already feel that it is valuable in identifying learning points and pinpointing general issues.

The workers are asked to do <u>pre-course monitoring</u> (ie. the processes and the contacts which lead to potential courses); <u>course monitoring</u> (this includes a statement of intent about the aims, objectives and context of courses, details about participants, and tutor reports and course evaluation); and <u>post-course and continued monitoring</u> (what happens to participants after courses and general assessment of future priorities).

Some general issues have already emerged after nine months work:(3)

(i)   heightened expectations and short-term funding. Some of the initial courses were necessarily short and experimental; when they proved successful, they raised within groups of students, expectations which sometimes could not be fulfilled.   However rigorous the contract between the project and the individual/ groups, inevitably there have been occasions when people have been frustrated that no real ongoing educational provision has been made.   This has implications not only for the project in determining its focus and use of resources, but also (given that the project is administered by the LEA) for mainstream local authority budgets, and raises the question of the relationship between short-term funded projects and mainstream funding.

(ii) The dangers of the ghetto effect.   Establishing a short-term funded project for the unemployed can be 'ghettoising', and have a dysfunctional effect upon mainstream provision.   Evidence already exists that mainstream providers, rather than critically examining their work and considering ways in which access for the adult unemployed can be improved, are falling back on the view that this work and that need is being provided for outside the main arena.

Similar issues have already emerged in the second REPLAN/NIACE project in Leeds which received funding.

Harehills Housing Aid/Salah Kainder

Harehills is an inner-city area of Leeds in which seven languages beside English are commonly spoken.   Pioneer Work had organised several Welfare Rights and Housing courses in the area in conjunction with an independent voluntary advice agency which had been operating in the area for ten years: Harehills Housing Aid/Salah Kainder (HHA).

The REPLAN/NIACE programme provided the opportunity to extend this type of programme.   It was also felt strongly within Pioneer Work that voluntary agencies, such as HHA, should have information about, and be in a position to respond to, new programmes.   This was clearly not the case with the first round of applications under the NIACE programme.

The establishment of inter-agency co-operation and joint working with statutory and voluntary bodies is an objective of Pioneer Work which has been emphasised both in this chapter, and in Chapter 3.   It was for this reason that a joint application from HHA and Pioneer Work was made.

The project was approved in the summer of 1984.   Funding (similar to the City Centre project) was agreed for two years.

Two half-time workers were to be appointed with additional funding for specialist tutors. In the event, the project did not start fully until March 1985. It is relevant to examine briefly the reasons for this delay.

One reason was the problem of clarifying with the University administration the precise meaning of a joint project. These issues were referred to in Chapter 3. Here, it is important to emphasise that these problems were so serious that, at one stage, HHA almost withdrew from the project because of what was seen as the insensitive and bureaucratic attitude of the University authorities, over which Pioneer Work had no control.

The other reason for delay related to the needs of the project. The project could have started much sooner had white people been appointed. The Management Committee, however, for reasons of both principle and practice, decided an Asian appointment, to at least one of the posts, was crucial. Eventually one Asian woman and one white woman were appointed, but the delays caused the project to lose several thousand pounds which had been granted for 1984/85.

The project is only in its early stages but a number of issues which relate to the constraints of short-term funding and work with black groups has already been identified. After five months, the Asian worker was offered and accepted a permanent full-time job elsewhere. Continuity of staffing, then, has been a problem both with the two NIACE projects and the short-term Bradford grant.

The courses organised at HHA to date include Nutritional and Health Issues, with a Bengali Women's Group, Welfare and Housing Rights with a Caribbean 'Mums-and-Tots' Group, a Rights course in Bengali, for a Bengali Men's Group, and 'Starting a Playgroup', and Understanding Computers, with Asian women.

It is not normal practice for a significant proportion of Asian women to become involved in anything other than family or domestic activities (although it should be noted that the label 'Asian' does not denote homogeneity any more than 'unemployed' does). The workers have been attempting to reach such people and give them access to courses.

The choice of buildings is also important, as some are acceptable to various communities and women may come to them, whilst others are not. It is essential to offer Asian women from such backgrounds 'women only' classes with women tutors. The provision of creches has also been important as most of the women attending courses have young children.

The courses have been taught in various languages. The Asian worker has taught in Punjabi, but for other classes interpreters have been used and this presents major educational and organisational problems. Also, teaching materials are rarely available in relevant languages, and the workers are having to develop their own, which in itself is a major task.

Another issue is the vastly differing educational backgrounds of students within a single group. Many groups comprise people who are not literate in any language and have little experience of education, and people who have high qualifications from abroad which are not recognised in this country, and who are perhaps not fully proficient in English. These differences create varied needs for teaching materials and styles, and also different expectations of what education should be like.

As with the City Centre project and the work in Bradford, early attention has had to be given to the issue of continuity after the short-term project finishes. The City Centre project is facing the problem of integration into mainstream LEA programmes and budgets, and the same problem will be faced by HHA. However, another extremely difficult but potential avenue for continuity lies in establishing over the life of the project an educational presence with independent voluntary organisations, which might continue educational activities after the project ends. These include a proposed Asian Women's Centre, and the Sikh Temple, but for this to be possible, close complementary working is essential with LEA workers and others involved in the area.

The total funding which Pioneer Work helped secure for the work in Bradford, and the two NIACE projects, amounts to almost £94,000 over a three year period. It should be clear from the description of each that similar issues, albeit in different contexts, are being raised.

Continuity of staffing has been a major problem for the three projects. At the time of writing, one (the Harehills project) is still facing the major problem of replacing a key Asian woman worker as soon as possible. Short-term funding both creates this problem (staff will obviously leave for jobs with greater security) and exacerbates it during the project (vacancies have to be filled as soon as possible, leading to the danger of inappropriate appointments).

The work in Bradford and at Harehills illustrates the issues for education providers of working with black groups, while the City Centre project shows the potential of concentrating on specific groups of long-term unemployed people. They show, too, the importance of selecting specific audiences and targets: not only is it inappropriate to aim just for 'the unemployed' (they are not homogeneous); it is also inappropriate to aim just for 'Asian women' or 'long-term unemployed' since these also are not homogeneous categories.

The Bradford case study raised the question of whether the input (staff time over grant applications, supporting part-time staff and monitoring projects) justified the outcome. It could be argued that one year grants are probably inappropriate, and may even be harmful for the development of community-based provision with people who have not experienced adult education previously. Projects also need more than two or three years' funding to develop this work adequately. The three examples described in this section show that valuable lessons based on careful monitoring are emerging, but that ultimately long-term resource questions will have to be confronted by agencies such as NIACE which administer short-term programmes for central government.

Conclusion

The descriptions of the Community and Institutional approaches together with the case studies indicate ways in which unemployed people in the community, both registered and unregistered, can be involved in adult education. The majority of people contacted had no previous experience of adult education, and had left school at the minimum leaving age.

This section examines a number of issues which are crucial for the development of this kind of work. These are:

Free and flexible provision
Processes for course organisation
Educational innovation and progression, and handover to other agencies
Work with black groups
Tutor identification and support
Essential resources.

Work with women, and action-research and monitoring are equally important issues, but these are examined in more detail in subsequent chapters.

Free and Flexible Provision

All Pioneer Work courses have been free, as noted in Chapter 3, and this is essential if provision is to be developed with working-class unemployed people. Free provision also removes the barrier of detailed and bureaucratic registration processes which may deter some people.

There must also be flexibility over both location and timing. Only the professional, continuing education courses (eg. those with community workers) have been held in the University. All the others have been held in a variety of community locations: council tenants' sitting-rooms, community centres, LEA buildings, and churches. Courses have been held at different times of the day to fit in with the needs of the particular group. In addition, there has been experimentation and flexibility over publicity. Sometimes thousands of leaflets and posters have been distributed advertising courses, and publicity secured through the local media. In some of these cases, other agencies (eg. LEAs, the Probation Service) have met these costs. On other occasions there has been minimal formal advertising and publicity has been mainly through local networks. The success of this latter approach depends crucially on an intimate knowledge of, and acceptance by, these networks. There are strong indications, however, that this latter approach can often be the most effective.(4)

A minority of courses was advertised specifically for unemployed people: most did not explicitly refer to unemployed people but, in part, because they were usually held in the day-time, they did in fact attract almost exclusively the unemployed.

Processes for Course Organisation

The case studies which are outlined earlier in this chapter, including both the successful and the 'failed' ones, indicated the processes which are essential for successful course development.

Detailed pre-course negotiations are necessary with an existing, or at least potential, core group of users. Failing that, there should at least be joint working with an agency or workers who have guaranteed contacts and knowledge either of a particular geographical area, or of the potential of particular topics (eg. community workers, LEA workers, health workers, probation officers, New Technology staff, etc). Without these detailed pre-course contacts and discussions, it is unlikely that courses will succeed, since few adult education workers and projects have sufficient resources for initial in-depth outreach or contact work.

Educational Innovation and Progression, and Handover to Other Agencies

As was noted in Chapter 3, an essential part of a university adult education role is educational experimentation and innovation. It has thus been regarded as entirely valid for the project to develop courses such as 'It's only rock 'n roll', Organising in the Community, Know the System, and a range of video and photography courses. As the Halton Moor case study illustrates, several new issue-based courses were devised and used successfully.

However, this experimentation is only valid if a number of criteria is met. The research and monitoring role must be rigorously applied. This includes joint assessment with users about organisational and curriculum strengths and weaknesses. Secondly, the course context and the teaching approach must be essentially within the liberal adult education framework. In general, it must be concerned with individual and group development, rather than vocational, training, or qualification orientations. Similarly, whilst such courses may be concerned, especially in the early stages, with leisure, recreation or skills acquisition there should also be a broader element. The course must involve some attempt at reviewing alternative analyses, and explorations of the subject matter within a wider context. The following examples illustrate this crucially important point.

Various courses such as Rock 'n Roll, Video, and Photography can be taught in a narrowly instrumental and technical way, or the technical information can be integrated within a critical analysis of the social contexts, purposes and implications of the development of such technical skills.

The Rock 'n Roll course included an examination of the following issues:

Local music and its historical context; what are the opportunities for cultural expression today?

Women and popular music: sexual stereotyping (with practical examples): the management and exploitation of sexual difference.

The economic construction of the popular music industry and the importance of new technology.

The tutor organised the free use of professional studios for several sessions, and the group wrote and produced two songs which were taped and taken away by participants as a tangible result of the course. This course, then, was an excellent combination of theory, practice, discussion and action.

A media course at a community centre was described in the following way:

Course aim: To look at how various media treat community issues such as environmental conditions or unemployment and critically to assess how media can best be used in the community context. Course format: The class will be actively encouraged to research, script, shoot and edit a short video presentation on the local area. Around this central resource, discussion will take place on issues of: media bias; the notion of stereotypes; editorial

'balance'; 'subjective' versus 'objective' presentation.
If appropriate, 'professional' productions in the form of
documentary or news programmes will be used and
discussed. Although there will not be an emphasis on
technical expertise, it will be necessary and useful to
consider some aspects of the way in which technical
limitations and possibilities influence the meaning of
the finished product. As an integral part of the class,
there will be a day-school which will explore the
possibilities of using various media (in addition to
video) for communication. Thus, through discussion,
examples and some 'hands-on' experience, the class will
look at the implications of photography, posters,
community newspapers, slides, slide-tape, etc.

The third factor relating to experimentation is that
continuity or a longer-term outcome should be attempted.
The Halton Moor and the Technology Centre case studies
earlier in this chapter are examples of Pioneer Work
initiating short courses, but then continuing them for several
years. At the Technology Centre, continuity involved linked
and staged progression and then a minority of students going
on to full-time courses. Attempts are now being made to hand
over the courses to the local authority. At Halton Moor,
there has been educational progression and continuity through
examination of a range of relevant community issues.
The case study from Bradford illustrates how several
courses (Urdu Literacy and Computer Appreciation) were handed
over to the local college. On the other hand, the NIACE City
Centre project illustrates the problems for short-term
projects of receiving mainstream budget priority. This, then,
inhibits educational continuity.
At one community centre, a group of women attended a
successful Women and Health course. Once an educational
presence had been established and legitimised, most of the
women then attended a Women and Media course.
This handover function, however, is not always as
successful in the long term as it appears initially. A
women's course ('Is There Life After Housework?') was
successfully handed over to the LEA, but because of a failure
to implement detailed pre-course negotiations, and the use of
an inappropriate tutor, the course was not a success.
Reference was made in Chapter 3 to the development of a
large number of Welfare Rights courses in the first year, but
concentration in the second year on a longer, more advanced
course aimed at key volunteers and workers. This course was
then successfully handed over to a city-wide group of advice
workers, who received charitable funding for this course to
run in 1984/85, the third year of Pioneer Work. This

seemingly neat progression, however, illustrates, as the example above does also, the necessity of monitoring over time. No funding was available for this course in 1985/86.

Thus, successful handovers may become failed initiatives, or at the very least present organisational and financial problems for Pioneer Work.

Work with Black Groups

Criticisms were made earlier in this chapter and in Chapter 3 about what could be termed Pioneer Work's 'ghettoisation' of work with black groups. It was explained that 21% of total provision in 1984/85 consisted of courses which were either organised and taught by a black tutor and/or mainly directed towards black people; but that this was mainly because of special, external, funding (from Bradford Council and from NIACE) and did not represent a major commitment from the mainstream Pioneer Work budget.

The problems of developing such work with full-time staff within the wider university context relate in part to the irrelevance and inadequacy of many of the traditional university criteria for appointment. These issues are discussed in Chapter 9, but it is important to note here that there is a series of obvious problems inherent in this work if there are only white members of staff. Black members of staff would obviously speak the necessary languages and could develop appropriate contacts more easily. In their absence, it takes longer to organise this kind of work and it costs more. For example, publicity is expensive because leaflets and information must be printed in various languages. Because relevant materials are rarely available in different languages, translating must be done. It is particularly difficult to find specialist tutors with bilingual skills, and thus interpreters, as well as tutors, must be paid for classes.

On average, this kind of work costs at least twice as much as other community-based adult education. From experiences with Harehills Housing Aid, Pioneer Work is arguing for more funding from NIACE for precisely these reasons.

A number of educational problems has also been highlighted. If an interpreter is being used, it is difficult for the tutor to gauge accurately student reaction. Also, discussion is made more difficult, and the temptation is for the tutor to develop a simplistic, didactic style.

Another issue which is common in community-based provision, but which is particularly difficult in this context, is the vastly differing educational background of students in a single group. There may be people not literate in any language, people with high qualifications from abroad but with no proficiency in English, and people with no qualifications but moderate English. These differences create varied needs for teaching materials and styles, and also different educational expectations.

Tutor Identification and Support

It might be thought that Pioneer Work, as a section of a University Adult Education Department, would have access to a wide range of tutors from within the University who could contribute to a programme with unemployed people.

There are two principal reasons why this has not happened. It should be clear from this chapter that the courses which have developed have not, in the main, been traditional subject or discipline-based courses. Rather, they have been issue-based and have developed from detailed negotiations with groups. It has not, then, been possible simply to slot appropriate subject lecturers into particular courses. Even if this had been possible, there would then have been another set of problems. Many university lecturers do not have any experience in teaching adults, beyond their formal undergraduate teaching. Adult education experience beyond the university walls is comparatively rare, and particularly so with groups of working-class unemployed people who have not themselves had any experience in adult education.

The identification of appropriate tutors has been a problem: it has been overcome, mainly, in an ad hoc fashion. Because of extensive contacts in Leeds and Bradford, Pioneer Work has been able to identify and use tutors who, in addition to appropriate academic criteria, have relevant community-based experience combined with knowledge of particular areas (eg.Women's Health). In many instances, these tutors either survive on part-time work or have themselves been unemployed. This latter point is important, since such a tutor can more naturally empathise with groups than other tutors. Identifying tutors for black groups is, of course, particularly difficult for providing bodies staffed exclusively by white tutors. Overall, there is an urgent need for more systematic ways of identifying and supporting tutors. However, this is very difficult in a context where part-time tutors are often, for obvious reasons, almost as transient and as temporary as the members of some groups.

Pioneer Work has organised meetings of part-time tutors which have demonstrated the range of issues which have been covered (from Women's Health to New Technology to Local History); these have been invaluable in sharing experiences, but have been notoriously difficult to organise regularly. This is mainly because Pioneer Work cannot pay part-time tutors for attending meetings and there is a limit to how much unpaid extra work they can undertake. Other meetings have been held with particular topic tutors - eg. meetings with tutors from women's courses or media courses (video, photography etc) have been held to review progress.

Overall, then, the project has been fortunate in utilising its pre-existing network of contacts to identify appropriate tutors. It has not succeeded, however, in establishing mechanisms which can identify, train and then support an integrated and reasonably long-term team of tutors.

Essential Resources

Many projects naturally argue that they are inadequately resourced. However, given both the volume and the nature of the work which has been referred to in this chapter, it is clear that this is a problem so acute for Pioneer Work that it threatens the long-term viability of the work.

The pre-course processes and negotiations, tutor identification and support, monitoring and evaluation, and the securing of external funding, as well as the maintenance of existing funding, all point to the need for secure, long-term financial arrangements. At the time of writing, this has not been secured, although negotiations are in progress with the relevant funding agencies. These resource questions, however, must be resolved if this work is to be maintained in the long term. These questions are re-examined in the final chapter.

REFERENCES

1.   See K Ward, Beyond Tokenism - Unemployed Adults and Education, Department of Adult and Continuing Education, University of Leeds, November 1983.

2.   Application to NIACE, 1984.

3.   Project Report to NIACE, September 1984 - May 1985.

4.   For further discussion of this point, see K Ward, Outreach in Practice: Some Examples of Community-based Projects, REPLAN Review, DES, 1986.

APPENDIX I

NIACE PROJECT   **December 1984**

NOTE ON MONITORING AND EVALUATION FRAMEWORK

Introduction: Monitoring and evaluation are essential for two reasons:

as a tool for critical reflection during and after phases of work, and as a public relations necessity for funding bodies etc. It is an aspect of work which adult educators should be involved in, but, in practice, often ignore. The framework outlined below is a simple and unoriginal attempt to ensure that effective monitoring procedures are built into the NIACE project from the outset.

1. **Pre-course monitoring:** In the initial stages of the project most of the workers' time will be spent on liaison work - contacting other agencies, workers, examining existing provision etc. Monthly reports from the workers should indicate (on the basis of daily and weekly logs which they will be expected to keep) precisely how much of their time has been spent on such activity, and with whom (eg. senior worker, part-time tutor, customer of existing provision etc). This report (each worker to have at least half a day free towards the end of each month to write this) should also include an initial analysis of the effectiveness of such work (eg. 40 hours spent talking to staff of other agencies which led to two tentative suggestions for courses, may be over-emphasising the agency contacts).

   As the project develops, workers will begin to form ideas for course development. These ideas must be referred to in the monthly reports, and the aims of potential courses explored. eg. sewing in x location; suggestion came from discussions with x users.

   Aim = purely recreational **or**
   Aim (based on discussions with users) = initially recreational but eventually oriented towards a Women and Health informal discussion group.

2. **Course monitoring:** Before courses develop, workers will be responsible for recruiting tutors who agree with and are committed to course monitoring procedures. This includes:

   (i) A Statement of intent: the worker and/or the tutor must provide a statement of intent and a syllabus in writing before any course starts. This is to ensure that the worker and the tutor are clear in advance about what they are trying to do and why. (This information is needed even if in practice the aims of the course and its details change as it develops).

   (ii) Course Register: each tutor must provide a register for the worker(s) with details of participants' age, sex, educational background etc. This information obviously depends on absolute trust between users and tutor, but is essential information for the project.

(iii) Course Report: Each tutor must provide a detailed report at the end of each course and comment on location/setting for the course, course content and potential outcomes of the course based on users' views.

3. **Continued monitoring:** As the project develops, the monthly reports should refer to all the courses which the worker is organising, comment on their progress and also examine any 'teaching' which the worker herself is involved in. Assessment must also be made of other tasks (eg. if a disproportionate amount of time is spent on individual counselling and/or doing outreach work in cafes etc, how effective is such work for the amount of time spent on it?).

4. **In-depth Interviews:** The aim of this project is to develop relevant educational provision for and with what will inevitably be a tiny proportion of the unemployed in Leeds. Ultimately, their views are more important than ours. As the project develops, therefore, it may well be essential to develop in-depth interviews with a sample of users (another project is already doing this and has devised appropriate questionnaires). The workers will not have time to do this so some resources must be set aside for it.

Chapter 5

EDUCATIONAL INITIATIVES WITH TRADE UNIONS AND THE TUC CENTRES AGAINST UNEMPLOYMENT

Introduction

This chapter examines a number of initiatives which have been taken by Pioneer Work to develop educational provision around unemployment with two trade unions and with the TUC Centres Against Unemployment.

The report of the Advisory Council for Adult and Continuing Education, 'Education for Unemployed Adults', indicated the urgent need of attempting to 'try out ways of responding' to local needs.(1)

Given both the development of the TUC Centres in the early 1980s, and the long-established and extensive Industrial Studies programme for trade unionists which is organised in West Yorkshire by the University of Leeds Department of Adult and Continuing Education, it seemed appropriate to include work with trade unions and the Centres as important categories.

Trade unions have a greater density of membership in Britain than in many other countries.(2) Given the extensive resources which are available, any decisions reached by trade unions about unemployment are of considerable importance. The historic links with a major political party reinforce the general importance of such decisions.(3)

Before examining the initiatives which were taken by Pioneer Work, it is important to outline trade union policy towards the unemployed.

Trade Union Policy towards the Unemployed

Following a resolution from the 1980 Annual Trades Union Congress, a special Consultative Conference was called 'to consider ways by which the interests of the non-employed could be represented'.(4) In moving the resolution, Clive Jenkins expressed some of the trade union concern and fears behind the rising number of those out of work, and also, in the first substantial loss of members in trade unions affiliated to the

TUC since the 1930s. 'The Government would like to drive a wedge between those who are in work and those who are not ... We must ensure that we establish a community of interest between all those who have to work for their livelihood and those who want to do so', he reported to delegates. Another speaker forcefully expressed an additional fear when warning delegates that the 'National Front are waiting in the by-roads, ready and willing to take advantage of this situation'.(5)

In November 1980, the Consultative Conference recommended a strategy based on two major innovations: the development of trade union retention policies, and the establishment of Unemployed Workers' Centres (UWCs) nationally.

The Conference

> revealed a wide consensus that unions should continue to develop their organisations and services for the retention of unemployed members and where appropriate, the recruitment of unemployed people. The Conference urged that unemployed workers centres (UWCs) should be established with trade union backing to advise, assist and involve the unemployed, and that the TUC should provide overall coordination for the work of trade union bodies in relation to these developments. It decided that the approach should be as simple and flexible as possible.(6)

On the aims and objectives of the centres, the report continued, 'the centres should provide unemployed people with information and advice about opportunities and assistance for training, mobility and generally on help available to the unemployed ... They should also provide a focal point in the community where unemployed people could make contact with each other'.(7)

TUC Regional Councils were to be responsible for the establishment of the Centres, working through the local Trades Council. Voluntary, part-time regional organisers (Services for the Unemployed) were envisaged, working in coordination with a national TUC officer (Services for the Unemployed).

Progress since 1981 in the establishment of the Centres has been rapid; by May 1981 over 50, by 1983 over 180, and by 1984 over 200 Centres had been established.(8)

In spite of this rapid development, or perhaps partially because of it, the Centres have encountered major problems. First, there has been some ambiguity over the role and objectives of the Centres, as defined by the TUC. That this is recognised by the TUC itself (or at least the Organisation and Industrial Relations Department of the TUC which is responsible for the Centres) is suggested in the first Bulletin for the Centres which mentions the need 'to strike a balance between the need for Centres to be effective from the Movement's point of view, and the need for public funds' accountability'.(9)   The 'public funds' referred to were provided by the Manpower Services Commission (MSC) which between 1981-83 provided most of the funds for the Centres.(10) As a recent survey mentioned, the major problem of MSC funding is the limitation 'on political activity within, and by a Centre.   Sheffield and Newcastle, for example, have both had their grants withdrawn after failing to observe the MSC guidelines'.(11)

Another major problem which Centres have encountered is their relative isolation from local trade union activity and from local political organisations. Despite the consolidation of UWCs throughout the last year or so, and emerging evidence of extensive activity within and, to a more limited extent, outside the Centres,(12) problems remain.   As some Centres note, we 'can hardly report the visit of a single trade union officer over the last year',(13) and the Leeds Centre reports 'a complete lack of knowledge of the Centre and its work by many workplace organisations'.(14) And these are by no means isolated examples.

These major problems, however, should not detract from significant achievements which have been made in many Centres. Particular mention should be made of the advice facilities which are heavily utilised in many areas, and indeed threaten to dominate and monopolise resources in some Centres.(15)

Educational Initiatives: Some Case Studies

Four examples of educational initiatives which Pioneer Work has taken are outlined below.   Two involve working with individual trade unions, one is concerned with educational provision for users at a Centre, and the final example refers to regional and national courses for Centre workers and activists.

The description of the examples is followed by an analysis of four major issues.   These are: curriculum aims and objectives;   establishing links with trade unions; educational approaches;   and finally, monitoring the effectiveness of the initiatives.

Example One: The Amalgamated Union of Engineering Workers (AUEW), Leeds District

In September 1982 Pioneer Work approached the Leeds District Secretary and Committee of the AUEW to explore the possibilities of an educational project involving unemployed AUEW members.   Not only had there been a large number of factory closures in the Leeds engineering industry in recent years, but the Department had existing educational links with

107

the union through its industrial studies day release provision for engineering workers. Tutors were familiar, for example, with the union's local struggles and had contact with certain individuals within the union. The AUEW, in short, seemed an appropriate trade union to explore the possibilities of a 'pilot project' involving unemployed members.(16)

It took three months of detailed negotiations between Pioneer Work and the District Committee before a joint partnership was established to develop the initiative. The union paid for publicity and administration as well as providing use of its premises when free courses for AUEW unemployed members were advertised, but Pioneer Work was responsible for organising and running the group which eventually developed.

From January to July 1983, weekly two hour meetings were held at AUEW House, in the centre of the city.

Educationally, the project attempted:

to develop unemployment as a concrete local issue and not an abstract, national problem centring on percentages and figures;

to encourage activity by the unemployed group utilising its collective experience;

to contribute towards defining unemployment as an issue within the AUEW;

and to provide a collective evaluation of the psychological and social change issues arising from the experience of unemployment.

Attendance at the classes varied between five and thirty, with a core group of 12. A programme for the classes was negotiated with students and reflected their immediate concerns: eg. welfare rights, the personal and social experiences of unemployment, through to evaluative discussions of the structure of the union, union provision for the unemployed and recommendations of change. Visits and outside speakers (eg. from the Alternative Technology Centre) were arranged.

After six months, attempts were made to transfer the classes to the TUC centre nearby. But, in the event, the group was discontinued.

Example Two: A 'White-collar' Trade Union

This second example of work with a local trade union around the issue of unemployment was started in early 1985. The approach adopted in this 'white-collar' example is to work primarily with employed trade unionists around unemployment issues. A residential weekend school is planned for early 1986 for employed branch members of the union. Unemployed union members will have an important education role in the school. The difference between the AUEW example and the 'white-collar' example has resulted from an appreciation, within the Pioneer Work group, of the complexities and difficulties of trade unions implementing retention policies. These points are further developed below.

Example Three: Educational Provision for Users at an Unemployed Workers' Centre

More substantial provision, organised over a longer period of time, has developed from the third and fourth examples.

The Leeds Centre Against Unemployment was established in 1982 with one worker paid for by the local authority, and several MSC workers.

Although Pioneer Work, together with a wide range of other organisations, had been involved initially in the planning for the Centre, it was obviously dependent on the Centre attracting unemployed people in order to develop educational provision. Informal discussions started with a small group of unemployed users, and from this base a discussion group and a Welfare Rights group started meeting regularly. It took more than six months to establish this initial educational presence. After one year, twelve courses had been organised, and the local authority persuaded to fund courses at the Centre from its mainstream budget, in conjunction with Pioneer Work. After three years, it is clear that education at the Centre has become one of its main attractions: more than 25 courses are now organised there each year. Initially, establishing an educational presence at the Centre was a major success, as was the handover of several courses to the local authority, but a number of more problematic political and organisational issues referred to earlier in this chapter, underlie this development.

All courses are free and a creche has been provided: there are no restrictive enrolment procedures, and people have joined courses whenever they wish. In 1983/4 almost 90% of people attending courses at the Leeds Centre were registered unemployed - and 60% of these were long-term unemployed. However, as was mentioned in Chapter 3, many unregistered unemployed (particularly women) do not use such centres. It is for this reason that special attention has been given to creche provision and a number of 'women only' courses.

In the first two years, the courses which were organised could be categorised mainly as 'survival/coping' courses and 'interest' courses. The former included Welfare Rights, Survival on the Dole, and Dressmaking; the latter,

Photography, Video, Art, Music, and Local History.

Example Four: Regional and National Courses for TUC Centre Workers and Activists

The two hundred and ten TUC Centres Against Unemployment, although they face major problems which are referred to elsewhere in this chapter, represent the largest single network of responses to unemployment which has been made in this country. It is for this reason that the TUC Centres are now beginning to attract attention from organisations and groups elsewhere in Europe and in the USA. It seemed important, therefore, to secure access to, and involvement with, this network officially through the TUC rather than act independently in organising courses for Centre workers.

In September 1983, 30 workers from Centres in Yorkshire and Humberside attended a three day workshop which was organised by Pioneer Work together with the National TUC Officer responsible for the Centres and the Regional TUC.(17) Since then, there have been annual three day workshops for new workers (and, increasingly, unemployed users) with a Recall Day some three months later to evaluate developments. This is followed, within the year, by a two day 'advanced' workshop aimed at participants from the earlier course. The objective is to provide a number of educational opportunities throughout the year for Centre workers.

Arising from the experience gained from these workshops and discussions developed by the participants, the Department initiated the first national residential schools for Centre workers and users involving participants from all nine TUC regions. These residential weeks, held twice annually, have been organised in conjunction with Ruskin College, Oxford, and with the national TUC officer (Services for the Unemployed). The first national course, held in July 1984, was funded by the Fire Brigades Union, and subsequent courses have also been funded by trade unions nationally.

Three of the four examples outlined above are still continuing, and inevitably, changing.

Nevertheless, it is worth abstracting some general points for consideration, in the hope that others involved in this area of work can benefit from the lessons, mistakes and reflections generated by the four case studies. As mentioned earlier, this discussion will be structured around consideration of four areas.

Curricular Aims and Objectives

A G Watts provides a useful chart of the four alternative curricular aims relating to the issue of unemployment (figure 1). As the author indicates, the four identified aims and

seven outlined objectives are not mutually exclusive and might
be better represented as a continuum, although there is some
tension between the categories. Likewise, the four case
studies briefly outlined above will not, and perhaps should
not, settle neatly and comfortably into any clearly
conceptualised categories concerning broad curricular aims.

Figure 1: Four alternative curricular aims relating to the
issue of unemployment.

	Focussing on society	Focussing on individuals
Change	Social Change	Individual Change
	1.contextual awareness	2.employability skills 3.alternative opport- unity awareness 4.opportunity creation skills
Status quo	Social Control 5.adaptability awareness	Individual Coping 6.survival skills 7.leisure skills

(adapted from A G Watts, Education, Unemployment and the
Future of Work, Open University Press, 1983,p88).

Nevertheless, such a graphic display of 'ideal typical'
aims helps focus discussion around important issues.
Interestingly, the UCACE 'Working Party on Education for the
Unemployed' identifies four objectives not greatly dissimilar
to those of Watts. These are:

education for re-employment and career change (perhaps
corresponding to 'social control' in figure 1);

education designed to open up access to further
education, eg. 'Return to Learn' courses which raise
personal confidence and increase awareness of personal
potential and of opportunities (perhaps similar to the
'individual change' category);

education to help the unemployed to adapt to their
changed condition (eg. welfare rights, how to cope on a
low income, personal fulfilment and filling enforced
leisure time) Watts' 'individual coping' aim;

and education for collective social and political purposes (eg. social and political analysis of, and responses to, unemployment) the 'social change' option in figure 1.(18)

As might be expected, educational provision by Pioneer Work involving trade unions and the unemployed has tended to focus around Watts' 'social change' dimension.

Thus one of the AUEW course aims was 'to contribute towards defining unemployment as an issue within the AUEW'. Likewise, the first three day workshop for regional TUC workers and users had small group activities structured around building links between the UWC and other organisations , such as church groups, tenants, trade unions etc. The one-week residential courses perhaps most clearly reveal the 'social change' focus through those sessions which examine the 'economics of unemployment', 'history and unemployment' and the provision of a 'contextual awareness' (as Watts terms it) of the present reform of the social security regulations. In other words, through choosing to work through trade unions, there was always likely to be a focus on 'social change'.

However, it would be misleading to characterise the curricular aims exclusively on this 'collective-social change' level. There was the awareness of possible dangers when an exclusive focus on macro issues informs the timetable. All the examples, except the 'white-collar' one have the explicit educational objective of overcoming feelings of isolation, fragmentation, and lack of confidence often experienced by participants on the courses. This is attempted in various ways: by the simple means of providing people with the opportunity to meet and exchange experiences, to 'provide a collective evaluation of the psychological and social change issues arising from the experience of unemployment' (as the report on the AUEW example mentioned), and through the attempt to develop unemployment as a concrete local issue and not simply a national abstract problem centring on percentages and figures.

The link between the two objectives of 'social change' and personal development, is provided in the attempt to arrive at concrete plans of future activity (eg. in relationship to clarifying roles within the UWC, in attempting to encourage greater union branch activity over a particular unemployment issue, in building links with other organisations and in raising additional finance). There are no prescribed types of activity which flow from the courses - individual trade unions and UWCs present too various a range of complexities, constitutions and objectives for this to be possible, even if desired. Rather, the educational work on the courses provides the opportunity for reflection on the purpose, direction and activities currently being pursued (or not pursued, as the case may be) by course participants within their organisation, informed by an increased awareness of some wider social, political and historical factors accounting for and shaping the present situation. As will be mentioned briefly later, the monitoring/research function aims to evaluate the usefulness of the courses in regard to this 'activity' factor.

Educational Approaches

From the comments above, a number of questions may immediately be raised. Who decides on the curriculum? How structured or formal is the learning process? Given the diversity of background experience and ability, where is the starting point? How were the courses established and why were they developed in particular ways?

There will be further questions that could be added to this list. Without pretending to provide a sufficiently detailed response to the few questions listed above, the comments below will provide additional information concerning some of the choices, dilemmas and concerns that have shaped this area of work.

Irrespective of the particular case study – the AUEW, the white-collar example or the UWCs – the syllabus is the result of an ongoing process of negotiation. In the first three day workshop for the UWC workers, for example, the syllabus was the result of three meetings over a period of two months, involving representatives from various UWCs. As the report from the workshop explained, 'we feel it is politically and educationally important for the Centre workers themselves to be directly and fully involved in the planning discussions for such initiatives'.(19) Since this first workshop, the syllabus has benefited from and been strengthened by the detailed evaluative sessions with participants. Attention, for example, has moved away from internal problems and confusions within the Centres when they were first established, to a greater concentration on building relationships with other organisations and voluntary groups.

Likewise, the residential weekend planned in the near future in the white-collar example, has been the subject of discussion in the Divisional support group for some months.

Despite these efforts of ensuring that the course reflects the collective needs of the participants, the teaching methods additionally encourage and permit a re-negotiation of the syllabus during the course. These teaching methods were mainly experimental, structured around small group activities with plenary report back sessions. It was felt that such an approach encouraged maximum involvement, allowed possible feelings of educational apprehension to be overcome within a more intimate and supportive structure, and encouraged the development of learning from one another. These comments characterise the AUEW and UWC's courses to a greater extent than the white-collar illustration. After the proposed weekend school, the main educational provision in that example will take place in an unstructured informal manner: trade union branch educationals, periodic reports and invited outside speakers. The responsibility for the organisation, preparation and 'lay-tutoring' will be primarily with the employed members, although occasionally the unemployed, of that particular branch. It is these 'lay tutors' who will be participating in the residential school.

There are, then, significant contrasts between the AUEW model and the proposed white-collar model. Instead of working with unemployed trade unionists (the AUEW case), the main audience in the white-collar case, in the early stages at least, will be employed trade unionists. This does not entail a substantial change in the curriculum aims; there is still the social purpose concern of providing an understanding of the broader context surrounding unemployment issues, etc. However, there are differences for the educational providers in terms of their own roles, the extent of the educational provision, and the nature of that provision.

Establishing Relations with the Trade Unions

One overall lesson that has clearly emerged from all the case studies is the extensive preparation required before any 'classroom' developments materialise. In the AUEW case, for example, there were three months of detailed discussions between the tutors and the District Committee before tasks such as publicity and recruitment were begun. And comments were made earlier indicating the extensive time and number of meetings necessary before the first workshop for Centre workers took place. This, of course, is a problem which is common to all areas of Pioneer Work activity but is particularly problematic in working with, and through, trade unions. There are, however, obvious practical advantages in this approach. In three of the case studies, for example, the trade unions have been responsible for the recruitment of the courses.

Secondly, other courses and developments in the country have benefited from the Leeds experiences through National Officers' involvement. Thirdly, certain developments in this area of work would possibly not have taken place had there been no formal involvement with the trade unions, through, for example, national residential schools. And finally, although no fees are charged by the Department for courses involving the unemployed, there are additional costs to be found. The Regional TUC, for example, spends around £200-300 per three day workshop on travel and food for the parti-

cipants. The national residential weeks have so far
attracted some £5,000 to cover costs from a variety of trade
unions.

Pioneer Work has continually stressed the importance of
inter-agency collaboration: the four examples in this section
illustrate the advantages of such an approach. Collaboration
between an adult education provider and the trade unions in
no way compromises the autonomy and control of that
educational provision. In the Leeds experience, it has added
to the quality of provision through identification, by the TUC
National Officer (Services for the Unemployed), of approaches,
developments and problems encountered elsewhere in the
country.

Overall, then, it is clear that there are problems, but
also considerable advantages, in working with trade unions
over unemployment issues. In Pioneer Work, it has been
agreed that, given scarce resources, only selective
initiatives can be undertaken. There is an urgent need for
case studies to be provided from elsewhere so that problems
and questions which have been encountered in Leeds can be
examined in a more generalised format.

Monitoring the Effectiveness of the Provision

Central to all aspects of Pioneer Work has been the desire to
monitor and evaluate the nature, quality and consequence of
the educational provision (see Chapter 8). This is no less
the case in this area of work involving trade unions and
unemployed people.

The monitoring of the work can take, and has taken, a
variety of forms. Where possible, for example, there are
'recall' days or weeks: that is, inviting participants to
return, at some date in the future, to evaluate collectively
the usefulness of their previous courses in the light of
subsequent activity and experience. The idea of a 'recall'
course has proved most useful to all parties involved. In
the national residential 'recall' school (recruiting from
three previous residential courses) participants will complete
a detailed second questionnaire/survey that can be compared to
data collected from the first survey. Questionnaires, then,
are a second important means of monitoring developments and
additionally strengthening the course content. In addition to
the usual reports on courses and initiatives, it is important
to monitor a wide range of outcomes. In the AUEW case, for
example, a number of small but significant changes took place
as a result of the classes (eg. travelling expenses for
participants, a permanent 'unemployment' agenda item on the
District Committee and a system devised that allowed the union
to identify members recently unemployed). The UWC courses,
furthermore, have become the main educational vehicle for

Centre Workers and users in the region. 1986 has seen the beginnings of what it is hoped will become regular educational provision for users active in an around the Centres. In other words, new developments and needs arise from existing provision which increase the range and possibilities of educational opportunities for the unemployed in the area.

Overall, then, there is a need for monitoring devices which utilise systematically the views of participants, but which also record over a period of time the possibly unintended consequences of various initiatives.

Conclusion

It is appropriate that a university liberal adult education department, rooted in a tradition of 'social purpose', should be involved in work with unemployment and trade unions. Despite the economic and political pressures to the contrary, it is also appropriate that social and political issues are an important context within which this provision is developed.

As the comments above indicate, much of this work has been and will continue to be of an exploratory, 'pioneering' character. However exploratory this provision may be, it is necessary and important that liberal adult education contributes, albeit in a very minor way, through its educational provision, to a resolution of the complex collective and personal problems facing unemployed trade unionists in the West Yorkshire area.

REFERENCES

1. Education for Unemployed Adults, Advisory Council for Adult and Continuing Education, 1982, p6.

2. R Price and G S Bain, Union Growth in Britain : Retrospect and Prospect, British Journal of Industrial Relations, Vol XXXI, No 1, March 1983, pp.46-68.

3. See annual TUC Economic Reviews, TUC.

4. Report of 112th Annual Trades Union Congress, TUC, September 1980, p 382.

5. Ibid, p482.

6. Report of the General Council to Congress, p48 in Report of the 113th Annual Trades Union Congress, TUC, September 1981.

7. Ibid, p48.

8. For a summary of the development of the Centres, see
    K Forrester and K Ward, TUC Centres for the Unemployed,
    TUC, March 1985; also, by the same authors, Organising
    the Unemployed, Journal of Industrial Relations, 1986
    (forthcoming). For a critique of the Centres by Trades
    Councils, see Unemployed Conference Report, Tyne and
    Wear Association of Trades Councils, December 1984. For
    an analysis of trades unions' retention policies, see
    A Barker et al, Trade Unions and the Organisation of
    the Unemployed, British Journal of Industrial Relations,
    Vol XXII, No 3, Nov 1984.

9. Centres For the Unemployed, Bulletin No 1, TUC,
    March 1981.

10. Forrester and Ward, TUC Centres for the Unemployed; and
    Organising the Unemployed.

11. Ibid, 1985, p3.

12. Ibid; see also, TUC Centres in the South East : A
    Detailed Information Directory, TUC, 1985.

13. Southampton Unemployed Centre, Annual Report 1983-84.

14. Leeds Trades Council Unemployed Centre, Annual Report
    1983-84, p15.

15. Ibid, p8, where it is stated, '..over each of the last
    three quarters, the number of enquiries (and requests
    for advice) has doubled ...we expect the number in
    January 1985 to be well over 350-400. The figure for
    January 1984 was 100'.

16. For a report on this initiative, see C Hampshire,
    Unemployment and Unions - An AUEW Educational Initiative,
    AUEW Journal, August 1983, p26; see also K Ward,
    Beyond Tokenism - Unemployed Adults and Education,
    Department of Adult and Continuing Education, University of
    Leeds, 1983, Chapter 3.

17. For a report on this workshop, see K Forrester and
    K Ward, Making Unemployment Centres Work, September 1983,
    available from Department of Adult and Continuing
    Education, University of Leeds.

18. Working Party on Education for the Unemployed, UCACE,
    September 1984, p2.

19. Forrester and Ward, Making Unemployment Centres Work, p 3.

WORKING WITH WOMEN

The focus of this chapter is how gender shapes the relationship of working-class women to education and how consciousness of gender must inform educators' policy and practice if they are to respond to women's aspirations. It is based on some of the lessons learned through working with women as a community adult education tutor in Bradford in the period 1976-1985 and specifically as a member of the Pioneer Work team during the last three of those years.

One major theme of this book is that for education to meet the needs of working-class people its form and content have to develop and be negotiated in a diversity of ways with the different constituents of the working class. The book is concerned particularly with those groupings within the working class that have been marginalised traditionally in social and political analyses of class: unemployed people, women, black people, and retired people. Educational needs and demands spring as powerfully and persistently from gender and race as they do from class. Any approach to education which emphasises class without giving equal importance to gender and race will not be rooted in the real lives of the majority of working-class people.

Which Women are Working Class?

Definitions of working class have of course been particularly problematic for women. Until recently women were largely invisible within sociological studies of class which were based on the family as the unit for class analysis. Married women were categorised on the basis of their husband's occupation whilst single women were ignored for awkwardly failing to fit within the family unit. Recently, some sociologists have made attempts to recognise the autonomous aspect of women's position in the class structure either by adopting the individual as the unit for class analysis(1) or by introducing the concept of cross-class families.(2) Either way women (and men) who are outside paid employment continue to be marginalised. The debate continues and this is not the place to attempt to resolve it.(3)

The other major question which sociologists have as yet failed to resolve relates to the conventional practice of locating the manual/non-manual divide as the major 'break' in the class structure separating working class from middle class. This approach is based on a static occupational classification which fails to take account of processes of economic and technological change discussed by writers like Braverman.(4) Such changes have had a major impact on non-manual occupations, particularly in shops and offices, with a resulting proletarianisation of many primarily female jobs. The largest group of women in employment in Britain (about one third) are now concentrated in junior non-manual occupations (Registrar General's Class IIIN) which includes clerks, typists, shop assistants and office machine operators. The vast majority of women in junior non-manual work are concentrated in a narrow range of jobs bearing low status within this class category. When the schooling and family class background of these women is taken into account as well as the nature of their work, there would appear to be little justification for defining them as middle class. It is difficult to avoid the conclusion that the continued, albeit critical, acceptance of a schema of class categories that is less appropriate for women's jobs than for men's is evidence of continuing male bias in the social sciences.

Given all the problems associated with definitions of class for women, and because the focus of this chapter is on education, it is appropriate to define class in relation to educational background instead of occupation. This enables women's class position to be defined in individual terms whether they are married or single, in employment or outside it. Educational background has also been the major criterion used by the Pioneer Work team in deciding on priority groups for funding courses. The only statistics on class background of people attending courses which have been systematically collected are those relating to education. None of this is to imply, however, that women's own occupational background and, where married, that of husbands, is not significant in shaping women's lives and self-perceptions.

Although defining women's class on the basis of educational background is here appropriate and more straightforward than using occupational categories, a dual class model still requires a dividing line to be drawn between middle-class and working-class educational attainment. People who left school at minimum school-leaving age without any qualifications would be unquestionably defined as working - class. In addition there are grounds for including within the working class all those whose qualifications are less than the equivalent of the five O-levels which have traditionally given access to further and higher education. The vast majority of women who participated in the courses discussed in this chapter are women who left school at minimum school leaving age without qualifications.

Working-class women on this definition, or any other, should not be seen as a homogeneous mass. We need constantly to remind ourselves of the different experiences, demands and divisions created by such factors as race, ethnicity, age, generation, parenthood, marital status, joblessness and disability. All of us who are practitioners and policy makers committed to the development of working-class education have to come to terms with this diversity and reject the stereotypes that have so often been dominant.

This chapter focusses on specific case studies of particular women's courses which illustrate the issues and problems discussed. They have been selected from a wide range of courses some of which are set out below. A number of women's health courses have been run at different locations - council estate community centres, a community school, Asian community and women's centres, playgroups, an Afro-Caribbean community centre and a centrally based women's centre. A discussion group on 'Marriage and the Family' was organised with a council estate-based 'Mother-and-toddler' group. A course about 'Parents and Schools' ran on another council estate. An art course for lone parents was organised jointly with Ginger ALE (the educational project set up by Gingerbread in Bradford). And finally a group (mainly women) set up in conjunction with an inner-city community association initially to study the impact of a General Improvement Area Scheme continued to meet for over a year to discuss and inform the community association about other local issues such as roads, housing and pollution. All of the courses mentioned here were organised in partnership with other community work and community education agencies. The discussion in this chapter thus draws on a wide range of experience in organising community-based courses.

The Historical and Social Context

A social revolution affecting middle and working-class women's lives, consciousness and aspirations has been underway most noticeably in the last fifteen to twenty years (although with a much longer history). Most women are now in paid employment for all but a break of a few years in their working lives. (Nearly 60 per cent of all women of working age are now in employment.) Women have gained greater control over their fertility and have higher expectations of marriage. Motherhood remains a major aspect of most women's lives but increasing numbers of women across classes seek other fulfilling activities and a measure of economic independence.

120

The feminist movement of the 1970s and specific women's campaigns - for example for equal pay and abortion rights - have created a climate enabling women to question traditional assumptions about their role and to glimpse their own untapped potential.

However, these changes in attitudes and expectations have faced working-class women of working age with a major dilemma. The nature of the job market and male working lives are such that the only paid jobs available to working -class women with dependent children are poorly paid and part-time, thus often replicating the most routine aspects of domestic labour - for example cleaning and catering - without tapping most of the valuable skills and experience that motherhood has brought. Mass unemployment has clearly exacerbated the problems facing these working-class women, creating a wider gap between developing aspirations and shrinking opportunities. For black women racism, and racial discrimination, make matters very much worse.

A Case Study: Opportunities for Women

In different parts of the country the development of second chance educational provision aimed at working-class women has begun to demonstrate the latent demand for educational opportunities that now exists amongst these women. For the reasons discussed above, the women coming on to second chance courses are looking to education to help them resolve the personal dilemmas they face. However, an important aim of this type of provision is to enable women to recognise the social dimension of problems that they may initially perceive as individual, and to understand better how social factors often prevent individual needs from being satisfied. Courses are therefore needed that, in form and content, address individual needs and develop an understanding of the social context in which women's individual choices are made.

Such a course, called 'Opportunities for Women', has been running in Bradford since 1983 as part of the Pioneer Work programme. Altogether 120 women have attended the six separate courses that have run.

The Opportunities for Women course is provided free of charge, as are all Pioneer Work courses, and runs for one day a week over six weeks during school hours. It is held in Bradford Central Library and a creche is provided for pre-five children of women attending.

The course is intended primarily for women who left school at minimum school-leaving age without qualifications but literate in English, and who are now considering the possibility of further education. Its aims are: to provide women with information about and contact with the range of educational and training opportunities available; to give

121

women a taste of study and provide an introduction to study skills; to examine some of the issues affecting women at work, in education and in the home; and to assist women to make informed decisions about the next stage for them.

A crucial feature of the course is that it is based on a partnership with the Education Advice Service for Adults (EASA), an independent voluntary organisation providing educational guidance. The course was started in the general context of developments elsewhere in second chance education and specifically because EASA identified a gap in provision through its outreach and counselling work. Many women who had only had a basic education were looking for educational opportunities but were not generally able or ready to embark upon a costly or lengthy formal course. Something was needed that could bridge the gap between the individual counselling provided by EASA and existing routes into education for adults.

The women who come on the course are open and articulate about their reasons for coming.

'I want to find out what I am capable of'
'I need to do something for myself'
'I'm a lone parent and need to support myself and my children'
'I wish I'd tried harder at school'
'I feel frustrated at work. I know I am capable of more'
'I helped at my daughter's school. I would love to become a teacher.'

These women already have a wide understanding of the role of education. This emerges when they are asked how they see education and the benefits it can bring. Some of the comments that are made are as follows: 'learning about different points of view'; 'understanding how other people live'; 'becoming more self-aware'; 'learning greater confidence'; 'getting a better job'.

What these comments demonstrate is that women's motivation for attending courses of this kind is highly complex and cannot be regarded as either purely instrumental or simply the desire for education for its own sake. This would be regarded as a false dichotomy by these women who are aware of both the pleasure and personal satisfaction that education can bring and its practical applications. The nature of women's lives is such, especially when they have young children or other dependents, that personal satisfaction and development cannot be hived off from practical and financial problems. These women are managing, maintaining and servicing themselves and the people around them every day of the week and how these processes will be affected is always uppermost in their minds when educational choices are made.

Two important implications can be drawn. If barriers to education are broken down, increasing numbers of working-class

women are ready to take advantage of educational
opportunities which will enhance their understanding of
themselves and the world about them as well as helping them
tackle the practical problems they face in terms of poverty
and economic dependence. Education providers must recognise
that these two needs coexist and are interrelated, and must be
tackled in an integrated way rather than hived · off into
separate areas of instrumental and liberal education.

The second implication is that educational providers do
not just have responsibility for teaching. It is their task
to ensure that the support that people require to complete a
course successfully is available, whether this involves
childcare provision, help with financial problems or
individual counselling. Educational providers have a
particular responsibility when they seek to attract on to
courses women who lack any previous experience of educational
achievement. These women must not be left to grapple alone
with their problems and possibly 'drop out', with all their
doubts about themselves and their abilities thereby
reinforced. Unfortunately, the systems of accountability
under which educational providers operate, often militate
against a 'holistic' approach to education. This is
especially so where achievement is measured only in terms of
teaching hours and student numbers.

The Women on the Courses

On the second week of the course the women are asked to fill
in a questionnaire.(5) The information provided throws
interesting light on how these women perceive their economic
status.

Table 1: Employment Status

	Number	Percentage
Unemployed (registered)	17	20.5
Unemployed (unregistered)	20	24.1
Employed part-time	21	25.3
Employed full-time	3	3.6
Full-time mother/housewife	22	26.5
Total providing information	83	100.0

Fewer than half the women (45%) perceive themselves as
unemployed, with a slightly higher proportion of these being
unregistered. Another quarter of the women are employed part-
time, generally in cleaning and catering jobs. These women
typically come on the course because they would like more
fulfilling work which taps experience they have acquired,
particularly as mothers. Slightly more than a quarter (27%)

of the women see themselves as full-time mothers. These women come because they want to do something to develop themselves and generally are looking to future work when their children are older. Some of the women find it difficult to place themselves in a single category. A number of the women who are unregistered unemployed also see themselves as full-time housewives as do some of the women who have part-time jobs.

The perceptions these women have of their own economic status are consistent with conclusions drawn in recent studies of women and unemployment.(6) Women who are actively seeking paid employment are less likely to define themselves unambiguously as unemployed. Unemployment for women often does not have the same inactive connotation it has for most men, particularly where they have children or other dependents. In fact the poverty associated with unemployment intensifies and expands the unpaid work necessary to care for a home and family. Moreover the current official definition of the unemployed excludes many married women:'people claiming benefit at an Unemployment Benefit Office... who are able and willing to do any suitable work'.(7)

In the mid-1980s, although about 64% of women in the labour force are married, only 40% of the women officially counted as unemployed are married. A significant part of this difference will be explained by the fact that married women are less likely to be claimants. Women who are excluded from the official unemployment statistics because they are not claiming benefit often do not perceive themselves as unemployed: 'I am a housewife looking for a job, but I don't class myself as unemployed. I think you class yourself as unemployed when you're being paid for being unemployed'.(8)

Ineligibility for benefit also puts pressure on married women who need or want their own income, to accept whatever paid, usually part-time, employment is available. This provides a partial explanation for the high proportion of women on the Opportunities for Women course who have part-time jobs but are generally dissatisfied with the work they are doing.

Table 2: Educational Background

	Number	Percentage
Basic education only	61	68.5
Some qualifications (to O-level standard only)	10	11.2
Vocational training	18	20.2
Total providing information	89	100.0

Table 2 gives a summary of the educational backgrounds of

women attending the course. Of the women who completed the questionnaire 69% had had only a basic education: that is, they had left school at the minimum school-leaving age without qualifications and had not had further education or formal training since.

A further 11% of women had some qualifications up to O-level standard. Most of these had taken O-level courses as mature students. The remaining 20% had received some vocational training, mostly in office skills. Because of effective pre-course counselling none of the women on the course had educational qualifications above O-level standard.

Information was also collected on the jobs the women had had on leaving school. Just over a third had gone into office work and just under a third into factory work. A fifth had worked in shops. The remainder (13%) were split fairly evenly between hairdressing, nursing and laboratory work.

Black women are under-represented on this course. On each of the last four courses there has been a small number of Asian women, either single unemployed working-class women or married middle-class women whose qualifications from Pakistan, India or Iran do not provide access to professional posts or training in Britain. It is significant that the course has failed to attract married working-class Asian women. One explanation for this is that it is a monolingual course which assumes literacy in English. The course has also failed to reach Afro-Caribbean women, although a few younger unemployed women did attend one of the earlier courses. A priority for future courses should be to involve a black woman tutor on the staffing of the course. This is essential if the course is to be seen by black women as a course for them. Black women want opportunities to define and provide the kind of education that they see as appropriate. These are important issues that will be discussed further below.

Teaching Content and Method

Within the women's courses discussed above, the major emphasis is placed on activity-based learning methods which concentrate on developing interaction between the students rather than focussing on the relationship between tutor and group. The teacher becomes facilitator and participant, learning with the group.

These methods are now well established and accepted as highly effective in many areas of education but they bring special benefits on a course for working-class women. Each individual woman is given an active role in the group and is able to draw on her experience and move on from existing areas of confidence and skill. The women begin quickly to develop greater self-awareness and a more positive self-image. One useful exercise which assists this process involves a

125

comparison of job descriptions for a housewife/mother and for a managing director of a small firm.(9) Moreover, by sharing experience with each other the women discover that they are not alone in the problems they face and the dilemmas that confront them.

These methods provide the context in which the women are able to write about their lives after the first week of the course. This exercise is very useful in terms of self-reflection and the development of writing skills which are analysed and discussed in later sessions culminating in a visit to Bradford and Ilkley Community College (BICC) Communication Workshop. Students can follow a programme of work here if they wish to improve their writing skills. Various other visits are made which give a practical insight into further courses the women can take subsequently. Visits to the BICC Maths. Workshop where the women all try out a diagnostic test, and the BICC Computer Unit where everyone has a chance to use a computer, ensure that the course does not concentrate on the traditional areas of education for women. There is also a visit to the National Museum of Photography, Film and Television Education Unit, the aim of which is to develop a critical awareness of visual images. Again, this may lead to a follow-on course for those women in the group who are interested.

In addition to activity-based learning and visits there is a need for sessions which concentrate on giving the women reliable and up-to-date information on such topics as employment, training and educational opportunities, social security benefits, grants and other financial aspects of education. A major aim of the information sessions is to familiarise the women with the network of information and advice-giving agencies so that they learn where to go for further information.

An important and difficult question to resolve is the extent to which feminist ideas should be explicitly studied on courses of this kind. Here I would suggest a rather different approach from that of Jane Thompson. She makes the case for a clear feminist perspective to be presented by tutors in second chance education based on her experience of the much longer courses in which she is involved in Southampton.(10) She also recognises that some women have withdrawn from the courses because they have found the ideas being put forward either threatening or objectionable.

Tutors working in any area of radical education must constantly face the question of how much it is appropriate to present a challenging ideological framework to the group, and how much it is preferable for the diversity of views and feelings in the group to be given expression and legitimacy. It is important to reassess continually whether the balance between these objectives is correct.

In a short, women only course where the emphasis is on getting the group to explore and build upon their strengths and the untapped potential within themselves, and on activity-based learning, tolerance of different viewpoints and an understanding of the diverse circumstances within which women find themselves, are crucial aspects of the course. Discussion about feminist ideas arises out of statements made by women in the group rather than being initiated by the tutor. The role of the tutor should be to explain that the course aims to support women in their attempts to gain both equality with men in society and greater recognition by society of their specific experience and skills. In this respect it is helpful to explain the different traditions within feminism rather than presenting feminism as a single ideology. In particular, there has been a spectrum of views historically which can be divided into those that have emphasised equal rights for women and entry for women into areas of work and education dominated by men, and on the other hand those giving greater weight to the way society treats women's reproductive role.(11)

All education should provide a combination of challenge and support for the individuals participating within it. The balance between these two objectives will be different on different kinds of courses. It would seem legitimate to argue that the way in which this balance is achieved will differ between a feminist course for women and a feminist course for men; just as the approach to anti-racist teaching would clearly be different as between a white and a black group. Education should be seen in the way that Paulo Freire interpreted it, in a different context, as the means by which people who are oppressed can perceive, interpret, criticise and transform the world about them.(12)

The Value of Women only Courses

At the end of the Opportunities for Women course the women are asked to complete an evaluation which includes the following question: 'Are there any advantages in the course being for women only, or would you have preferred a mixed course? If so please say why.'

These are some of the responses:

It was definitely better for women only, to get our views put forward in depth.

I prefer a course for women only. I feel that we have similar experiences giving common ground for discussions and yet there are enough differences of point of view to make it interesting.

Women are more at ease with one another and feel free to talk without being interrupted.

I felt more confident to come on a women only course.

Women only is fine with me.   Told my father it was   for women only, so he agreed.

I enjoyed women only but I would love to hear   a   man's point of view on certain subjects.

Mixed course preferred.   Unemployment is now affecting both equally and maybe then men would understand women's difficulties about returning to work as well.

Of the 46 women who answered the   question   about   the respective advantages of women only and mixed courses, a large majority(39) stated a preference for a women only course.   The remaining women felt there was a definite role for   a   mixed course either because unemployed men had similar needs or because they would be interested in discussing issues with men.

The vast majority of women attending these courses welcome the fact that they are for women only.   The view that there are many advantages in a women only course is not however in conflict with a recognition that there is also a role for mixed courses and that there are similarities as well as differences in men's and women's experience of unemployment.   In fact, a mixed course modelled partially on the Opportunities for Women course, entitled 'New Directions', was organised for the first time in 1985 within the Pioneer Work programme.   It, too, was based on a partnership with EASA.   It was successful in attracting a mix of mostly older unemployed men and women, and demonstrated the value of running mixed as well as women only courses of this kind.

From the experience of running the course and the comments of the women, it is possible to draw out a number of different arguments for women only courses.   The first point is that a wider cross-section of women is likely to identify with the publicity for the course than would be the case if it was presented as a course for unemployed people.   As has been stated, fewer than half of the women who have come on the course have perceived themselves as unemployed.   Many of the women who apply to come on the course do so in response to an article in the local free newspaper under a title such as 'Mums - pick up the threads'.   A lot of women comment on how immediately they identified with the aims of the course when they read about it. This gave them the confidence to apply.

For some of the Muslim women on the course the fact that it is for women only has been crucial in getting support from their families to attend.

The collective experience of the women only course itself also has great benefits.   There is great value in the sharing of common experience and common problems, especially for women who have felt a sense of social isolation in the communities in which they live and work as mothers and housewives.   The freedom to talk and the confidence that others will listen is an ongoing theme expressed by the women and identified as an aspect of a women only course.

It is also much easier for women to identify and evaluate positively their own skills and experience, particularly as mothers, in a women only context. Women by themselves more quickly perceive the areas of strength and confidence they already have. The awareness that women's skills and experience are downgraded by society in general and employers in particular, is already present to be built upon. Feeling positive about oneself is important for all people who are looking for a new direction in their lives. But because gender divisions in society create in women a specific sense of inferiority and subordination, learning to feel positive about oneself often only happens as part of a collective experience with other women. Personal development is thus part of a social process and self-awareness is linked to a social perspective.

Moreover, women often come on the course saying that they have reached a point in their lives when they need to do something for themselves, possibly for the first time in many years. The course enables the women to see themselves in the context of the rise in women's aspirations that has taken place generally in recent years. It enables them to recognise the legitimacy of their desire to have fulfilment for themselves and a measure of independence. It enables them to begin to examine and overcome the areas of guilt and conflict which may constrain their own personal development or vocational aspirations.

Working with Black Women

It has been noted that the courses discussed so far have attracted white women primarily, although not exclusively. These courses have all been defined, planned, organised and taught by white women. Many questions are thus raised for the women involved. What support can be given to black women in their attempts to define and provide the education which they see as appropriate? In what ways should courses where black women are under-represented or absent, be changed in terms of staffing, organisation and content?

The most successful black women's courses within the Pioneer Work programme have been those planned, organised and based at Afro-Caribbean and Asian community projects. Two particularly successful Black Women's Health Issues courses taught by a black woman health visitor were organised at the Bradford West Indian Parents' Association.

Most of the women who came on the courses were married or single mothers in their forties, born and educated in the West Indies with children at or beyond school age. Some of the women had very low levels of literacy. They were mainly part-time hospital auxiliaries and nursing assistants or unemployed. A small number of women were younger (about twenty) and single, born and educated in Britain and currently unemployed or studying. A small number of white women also attended the course, friends of, and brought by, black women in the group.

Altogether, fourteen women attended the two courses with nine women attending both. For several of the women these courses provided their first opportunity ever to talk in a semi-formal group. The women who were particularly lacking in confidence and reluctant at first to attend the course gained enormously from the opportunity it gave them to express themselves. For them it was particularly important that the course was set up by an organisation with which they could identify and was held in a venue where they felt at ease.

The tutor was able to put the women at their ease by talking about her own experiences and things she had in common with the group. A very relaxed and trusting atmosphere was quickly established. The fact that the tutor was a black woman assisted a great deal in this process. The tutor had been concerned about whether she would be able to establish a good relationship with the women because she was born in Africa rather than the West Indies. But this difference did not emerge as a problem because she was able to share with the group the experiences of being a black woman in Britain: for example, racism and problems of diet.

It was also important that a majority of women in the group were themselves black and that the course, although being about women's health, could focus on how black women specifically experience health problems. This enabled the group to look at certain health issues which are specific to the black population (eg. sickle cell anaemia). However, more significantly it made possible an open discussion of the particular ways black women experience problems that are more widely shared, problems of dealing with GPs, for example. If a majority of the women in the group had been white, the black women would have had less confidence to express themselves and the focus of the course would have been quite different. As it was, the women were able to use the greater confidence gained through the group to cope more effectively with their own GPs and to go for health tests which previously they had been too intimidated to undertake.

Other community-based health courses have been organised with Asian women's groups. In some cases these have involved bilingual Asian tutors and in others they have been taught jointly by an English health worker and an Asian interpreter.

Efforts to build upon these small scale initiatives could be greatly extended if black women were employed as members of the Pioneer Work team. As long as we fail to tackle the institutional barriers which have so far prevented this occurring, the seriousness of our commitment to education for all working-class women will be questioned. These issues are returned to in the final chapter in the context of university attitudes to positive action.

Conclusion

Gender has a significant effect on how education is perceived by working-class people. A common feeling among working-class women is that they never had a first chance because education was assumed not to matter for girls. As a result many women who received only a basic education do not have a sense of personal failure so much as a feeling that they never found out their potential. The changing consciousness and aspirations of women generally is encouraging these women now to take what chances offer themselves. For working-class men who received only a basic education a sense of personal failure may be more significant unless awareness of class gives them a strong sense of the social context in which people 'succeed' and 'fail'. Second chance education programmes have generally found it harder to attract unemployed men than women. The 'New Directions' course referred to above successfully recruited a mix of older unemployed men and women by deliberately gearing the course away from formal educational opportunities towards more informal, practical and leisure- oriented opportunities. A great deal more thought needs to be given to the different perceptions and feelings adults have about education. Unfortunately, working-class attitudes to education have rarely been examined in sufficient depth to take account of gender and other differences within the working class.

Much community education work has been based on the assumption that working-class women in general feel alienated by education because of experiences at school. It is undoubtedly the case that the majority of working-class women who have had no previous involvement in education as adults are often lacking in confidence and easily put off by formal educational initiatives. However, the experience on which this chapter is based demonstrates that many women, once involved in a community education atmosphere, quickly develop the confidence to explore educational opportunities further.

What is clear is that working-class women want a whole range of diverse provision. On the one hand there is a need for courses at particular community centres for the women who use those centres and who can be involved in defining and planning the kind of education that they see as appropriate. On the other hand, it is important for women to have accessible routes out of the community so that a whole range of educational opportunities can be made available.

REFERENCES

1.   E O Wright, <u>Class, Crisis and the State</u>, New Left
      Books, 1978.

2.   N Britten and A Heath, Women, Men and Social Class, in
      (eds) E Gamarnikow, D H J Morgan, J Purvis,
      D E Taylorson, <u>Gender, Class and Work</u>, Heinemann,
      1983.

3.   For further recent contributions to the debate see
      J H Goldthorpe, Women and Class Analysis: In Defence of
      the Conventional View, <u>Sociology</u>, vol 17, No 4, November
      1983; M Stanworth, Women and Class Analysis: A reply to
      John Goldthorpe, <u>Sociology</u>, Vol 18, No 2, May 1984;
      A Heath and N Britten, Women's Jobs Do Make a Difference:
      A Reply to Goldthorpe, <u>Sociology</u>, vol 18, No 4, November
      1984. For a summary of the arguments see S Dex, <u>The
      Sexual Division of Work</u>, Wheatsheaf Books, 1985,
      Chapter 6.

4.   H Braverman, <u>Labor and Monopoly Capital</u>, Monthly
      Review Review Press, 1974.

5.   The information analysed here is based on questionnaires
      from five out of the six courses.

6.   A Cragg and T Dawson, <u>Unemployed Women: a study of
      attitudes and experiences</u>, Department of Employment
      Research Paper No. 47, 1984, Chapter 3.

7.   Social Trends 1985, Central Statistical Office.

8.   Cragg and Dawson, Unemployed women: A Study of
      Attitudes and Experiences, p 17.

9.   J Morris, <u>No More Peanuts</u>, National Council for Civil
      Liberties, 1983, p22.

10.   J Thompson <u>Learning Liberation</u>, Croom Helm, 1983,
      pp 182-186.

11.   For a useful summary of the debate between 'new
      feminism' and 'old feminism' see R Delmar's Afterword
      in V Brittain, <u>Testament of Friendship</u>, Virago, 1980.

12.   P Freire, <u>Pedagogy of the Oppressed</u>, Sheed & Ward, 1972.

13.   J Thompson, Learning Liberation, p 150.

Chapter 7

ONE ADULT IN FOUR: WHO CARES? EDUCATION AND OLDER ADULTS

One adult in four is a pensioner; for there are currently well over nine million people entitled to a retirement pension. The majority left full-time school aged 14 years or younger; yet the educational needs of such a large segment of the population have only recently begun to receive serious attention.

Now, in the 1980s, there is at last a growing body of opinion, both professional and voluntary, concerned about the inadequacies of adult educational provision for retired and elderly people. The Forum on the Rights of Elderly People to Education (FREE) was set up in 1981 to disseminate information and campaign on the issue. A self-help educational organisation, the University of the Third Age (U3A), came to Britain in 1981-82, inspired by the success of U3A groups in the French-speaking world. And more recently, a professional grouping, the Association of Educational Gerontology, was formed in 1985. Along with these new alliances, there have been many accounts published of different local initiatives around the country, a number of conferences, and a flurry of postal questionnaires.

Yet despite this welcome growth of activity and of reports, I have experienced difficulty in finding detailed accounts of any but fairly small-scale, one-off developments.(1) So I hope that this chapter goes some way towards remedying this apparent gap. It describes the development of 39 daytime classes, held over a three year period, 1983-85, and based in one of Yorkshire's major industrial cities, Bradford. Like the other areas of Pioneer Work described in this book, the courses have been funded mainly through the grant aid to the Department of Adult and Continuing Education of Leeds University from the Department of Education and Science(DES). Partly because the number of pensioners is so huge, and partly because other accessible daytime provision remains so slender, the classes for this age group have tended to recruit rather higher student numbers

than other areas of Pioneer Work.   The average class size is
about nineteen students*, with nearly two-thirds having a
school-leaving age of 14 years or under.   And with these
large numbers, and the enthusiastic and often stable groups
that have resulted, has emerged a different range of problems
from those facing other areas of Pioneer Work.   Particularly
taxing in the current political climate has been the
experience of trying to locate other educational agencies
equally committed to free daytime education for older working-
class people to whom these well-established classes could be
handed over.   Another dilemma has been the questionable .
logic of adult educationalists - like myself - with years to
go before reaching retirement, acting as advocates for a group
to which we do not yet belong - and which our higher education
experience prevents us anyway from ever realistically
joining.   These and other such problems inevitably surface
throughout this account of work with older students.   The
primary stress in this chapter, though, is upon the value and
success of this kind of educational outreach work, and I hope
that the case made here leads towards the adoption of similar
initiatives nationally.

     Bradford Metropolitan District has a population of nearly
half-a-million, of whom 76,000 are retired.**   These
pensioners represent almost one in four of Bradford's adult
population.   Among these 76,000 retired people, women
outnumber men by well over two to one.   And of these 52,000
older women, three out of every five are either unmarried,
widowed or (less likely) divorced.   Indeed, over 40% of
retired people are single women.(2)   The great majority of
the 76,000 pensioners were, of course, born and brought up in
Britain.   Only about 700 pensioners (about 1%) live in
Pakistani or New Commonwealth households.(3) By contrast, the
number of Bradford pensioners born and brought up in Eastern
and Central Europe is far higher.   Most came to Britain in
the 1940s, and they total about 12,000 people, of whom the
Polish and Ukrainian groups are by far the largest.   The
majority of the 12,000 are now retired and perhaps comprise
about 10% of Bradford's pensioners, which is a rather higher
proportion than for Britain as a whole.(4) Information about
older adults' educational experiences is less easy to come by;
but it seems that at least three-quarters of pensioners
finished their full-time education at 14 years old.(5)   For a
minority, now aged 76 or older, who grew up in a woollen and

---

*   See statistical analysis of classes at the end of this
chapter.
** 'Retired' is used here to refer to all men over 65 and all
women over 60.   'Elderly' is used only to refer to the
minority of retired people (under one-third in 1981) who are
aged 75 or over.

worsted area like Bradford, the age for leaving full-time school was thirteen or even twelve, for in the traditional textile regions of Lancashire and West Yorkshire, early school-leaving was formalised into the 'half-time system' whereby children of working-class families, once they reached the minimum age, could spend half a day at school and the other half at the mill. For retired people among Bradford's ethnic minority communities - whether Pakistani or Eastern European - school-leaving age may fall below 12 years old. Information here is, understandably, much less readily accessible: school-leaving ages of nine or ten seem not unusual, while a few may have no experience of formal schooling at all.

After leaving school fifty, sixty or even seventy years ago, most pensioners will have received no real opportunity to gain educational qualifications, and the proportion of retired people with experience of any form of higher education is tiny indeed. The exact numbers of pensioners who are currently involved in adult educational activities in the country remains unclear. The most frequently quoted figure is taken from the government's General Household Survey 1976-77 which indicates that only 2% of people of pensionable age attended a leisure class during the previous year. Other more recent surveys suggest that using different phrasing of questions gives a slightly higher (and possibly more realistic) proportion of pensioners involved in adult education. Even if the figure is rather higher than 2%, there still seems a marked falling off of older students once they reach retirement age.(6)

The largest single group of pensioners, then, are women who are retired but not yet elderly (ie. are under 75 years old), who are single (either unmarried or widowed), who left school aged fourteen and who have had few chances to gain educational qualifications since then. It is difficult to flesh out these abstract statistics and imagine what the educational needs of such a person would be. Case studies of particular people are much more vivid, and for this reason I have interviewed two of the retired students who attended Pioneer Work courses over the last two-and-a-half years, and supplemented this with information about a particular Polish pensioner. The three women, born in 1909, 1919 and 1922, are currently aged between seventy-six and sixty-three, and may speak for the largest single group of pensioners: single women who left school at the minimum school-leaving age.

The eldest of the three, Ginny, has lived all her life in Queensbury, a hill-top textile village on the borders of Bradford Metropolitan District. Born at Easter 1909, she missed becoming a half-timer by just a few months. Ginny remembers her mother's annoyance at this; a widow with many mouths to feed, she would have welcomed her daughter's half-timer wage.   Instead, Ginny had to wait two years till she was fourteen before she could leave school and start work in the spinning-room of Queensbury's Black Dyke Mill.

That was in 1923.   Since then Ginny has spent much of her adult life working in Black Dyke.   She married in 1930 and, looking back to those years, she felt that she and her husband 'were very lucky in that we both worked at the mill, because there was very little unemployment there - just a week here and there'.   By 1937 they had two children, one at school and one at home, but Ginny still went back to work, 'putting my little boy out to nurse...'. Even at the very end of her working life, Ginny was back at Black Dyke, this time in the mill office, doing the calculations.

Ginny was widowed in 1970:   her husband was sixty-four when he died.   She now lives alone, in a small terraced house in the centre of Queensbury.   An owner-occupier, she pays no rent, and her rates - just over £3 a week - are paid for her. She is entitled to a basic pension of £38.70 per week, and has just over £300 saved in the bank.   She receives no occupational pension from the mill, either for herself or for her husband, and she has only very recently realised that she might be eligible for a heating entitlement as well.   Yet Ginny, despite difficult family problems, is very contented. She remains a very active chapel-goer, and a very keen member of the Pioneer Work class for retired people in Queensbury.(7)

Because of the generation to which she belongs, Ginny had no chance to receive any but the most basic school education, and did not take part in any adult educational activity till she was in her mid-seventies.   Mrs S, who came to Britain from Poland just after the war, not only experienced such generational disadvantages; she is also further disadvantaged by the process of ageing itself.   Mrs S is ten years younger than Ginny.   Born in 1919, the daughter of a small peasant farmer in eastern Poland, she grew up in an isolated village, the youngest of seven children.   Like all the children in that particular village, Mrs S received only the basic education of four classes in the country school;   her father was scarcely in a position to send her on to higher education in the town.   She remained in her village up to the outbreak of war in 1939 when she was twenty.   The village came under occupation, by Russia and then by Germany, and Mrs S was forcibly taken away and put to work in a munitions factory in Germany.   After the war, when few members of her family remained alive and when her part of Poland was annexed to Russia, Mrs S took the opportunity of coming to Britain as a volunteer worker in Bradford.   Here she found a job in a textile mill, became part of Bradford's sizeable Polish community, married a Polish man, and together they managed to save for a deposit on a house of their own.

But growing older made Mrs S's life more difficult.   The

area of Bradford where they bought their house had deteriorated. And particularly since she was widowed a few years ago, Mrs S has retreated more and more within herself and within the Polish community. She goes to the local Catholic Polish church two or three times a week with two other ladies, but otherwise seldom goes out. Mrs S never learnt to write English though she used to speak the language quite well; more recently, however, she prefers to speak Polish rather than English with her daughter. In other words, Mrs S not only experienced the educational disadvantage of other working-class children of her generation; widowhood and the experience of ageing has increased her sense of isolation and powerlessness. Educational provision for Eastern European pensioners would have to be sensitive to the needs of a woman like Mrs S, as well as those of her peers who have become fully fluent in their second language, English.

Three years younger still, Helen was born in Hull in 1922, the daughter of a navvy. With her father often unemployed during the 1930s, Helen's schooling had to end abruptly - in 1936, at the end of the term in which she became fourteen. Jobs for girls in a depressed city like Hull were scarce and ill-paid. It was a choice between shop work, factory work - or domestic service. So Helen became a 'morning girl',

> helping with all the household chores, from nine o'clock in the morning until about half-past two in the afternoon. I wore a green dress with a white apron cap. Occasionally I was asked to stay on later in the afternoons, when I donned a tea-apron and served afternoon tea to visitors. I earned five shillings a week, plus sixpence when I worked a couple of hours extra.

After war broke out, Helen's mother heard from a neighbour that there were good jobs for girls at Salt's mill in Saltaire, and in November 1939 Helen became a cap spinner in the mill. Three years later, when she was 20½ years old, Helen was called up and joined the ATS. Demobbed in 1946, she was at last given an opportunity to train for the job she really wanted - for the ATS ran short child-care courses. Shortly afterwards she got a job as a nursery assistant at a Day Nursery not far from Saltaire; and right up to her retirement in spring 1982, Helen spent virtually all her working life as a nursery assistant or nursery nurse.

Indeed, in many ways life has got better for Helen as she has grown older. She shares a small terraced house with her sister (who is blind), and they both feel themselves to be comfortably situated. Helen receives a retirement pension of £37.13, supplemented by her superannuation from West Yorkshire

County Council.   With a weekly income of about £65, coupled
with her sister's pension, they 'both consider we're quite
favourably off;   and with there being two of us, it's a lot
easier to pay all the bills.   Yes, we've no grumbles'.(9)
Yet, nevertheless, Helen remained one of the many, many older
adults who had to leave school at the minimum age and who
have had virtually no contact with adult education since.

The case studies of Ginny, Mrs S and of Helen, though
widely diverse in some ways, all share the characteristic of
minimal educational opportunities.   And it was the life-
histories of such pensioners that were to shape the direction
of this section of Pioneer Work.   However, it was some months
after I began my job in Bradford before my path and theirs
crossed.   In October 1982 I was appointed on a half-time one-
year contract and so joined the Pioneer Work team.   When
I first began my job in Bradford and was encouraged to develop
accessible daytime courses for older adults, little of the
analysis summarised earlier in this chapter was clear to me.
I received considerable support from my Pioneer Work
colleagues, but still spent the first term rather in the dark,
stumbling around and wondering which groups I should contact
and which communities I should work in first.   I wondered
whether I should focus Pioneer Work provision on retired or
elderly people;   and whether age-segregated classes were
really what pensioners want.

I began to work out in my own mind why older adults should
be more involved in adult education.   Was it because their
educational needs were so much greater than those of younger
people?   Or because they had established rights to education,
by dint of paying their rates and taxes all their working
lives?   Or because if they weren't offered access to education
they would be less able to live independent lives;   and so be
increasingly dependent on the state and the community?

As I began to try out these and other ideas, one of my
strongest feelings during these early months was of isolation.
Although nobody was openly hostile, of course, there seemed to
be no-one else in Bradford doing similar work.   Gradually the
picture began to fall into place.   I read some of the
literature on the subject, and realised that what I was trying
to do was not wholly new.   There were imaginative precedents
elsewhere, both in Britain and abroad.   And I began to meet
people active in similar fields.   One of the first contacts I
made was with the major local college, Bradford and Ilkley
Community College (BICC), which organised a retired people's
forum with a programme of speakers, and ran fee-paying pre-
retirement courses.   But rather than duplicating BICC's
provision, I turned instead to the needs of a slightly older
post-retirement group. Here I found it easier to make initial
contact, not with the statutory Social Services, but with the
voluntary sector.   The major voluntary body, the then

138

Bradford Metropolitan District Federation of Old People's Welfare Committees, as its rather cumbersome and traditional name implies, acted as an umbrella for the local groups of volunteers providing practical and much-needed help: meals-on-wheels in particular, but also outings and Christmas parties. The individual welfare committees' great strength was their deep-rootedness in their particular communities. But inevitably, development work and District-wide strategic planning remained weak; and a critic might suggest that the Federation and its local committees had somehow got stuck in the 1950s; for instance there seemed little recognition of Bradford's sizeable ethnic population.

Although the feeling of operating out on a limb persisted, by the spring term 1983 I had organised two Pioneer Work courses for retired people.(10) The first was based in Saltaire - in the neighbourhood, it turned out, where Helen lived, the area of compact working-class housing, still overshadowed by Salt's celebrated mill. During the crucial development stage of the course before Christmas, I made contact through the Federation with two local 'havens' for retired people, each meeting weekly in Saltaire's two church halls. Although I was very much sandwiched in between the bingo and the cups of tea, I was warmly received; and I followed up these two talks by home visits with a tape recorder. In order not to exclude more isolated pensioners, I also made contact with Saltaire Post Office and leafleted pensioners on the favourite pension day - Thursday. (Additionally, I did a more routine leafleting of Saltaire's almshouses, shops and libraries - though this seems to have been considerably less effective than more personal contact.) The class started in January in the Methodist Church hall straddling Saltaire Road and Titus Street; and as a result of the development work, nineteen retired people from the Saltaire area came along on the first morning. The following week four more students joined: among these were Helen and her sister, who had somehow missed the first week but heard the class announced at their church on Sunday and had thought it sounded interesting. Indeed, the word generally went around Saltaire: by the fourth week student numbers had mushroomed to 26.(11) Of these, at least four of the more elderly had left school aged 12 or 13, the majority at 14 or younger, with about half the class having worked some of their lives in a textile mill - usually, of course, Salt's. Helen's experiences were therefore fairly typical of the group.

The second class, a 'Writing and Listening' course, was organised in conjunction with Bolton Royd, one of BICC's local adult education centres, in Manningham about a mile out of the city centre. The tutor was a retired English teacher, herself an enthusiastic believer in education _for_ retired people _by_ retired people, as well as an early convert to the

139

University of the Third Age (U3A). (For instance, she was actively involved in the Wakefield branch of U3A, the first in West Yorkshire, formed in mid-1982.)

Publicity methods were less intense than for Saltaire: leaflets were distributed largely through Bolton Royd's own networks, and additionally information about the course was published in the local evening newspaper. There were eleven students at the first meeting, with 17 eventually registering. However, largely because the course was based in an adult education centre rather than in, say, a local community centre, it was less able to reach such a broad range of working-class pensioners. Only about a third of those who came had left school at 14, and none at 12 or 13 (despite the fact that the giant Manningham Mills still towers near the area); and more were already attending one of the centre's existing classes or groups. Nevertheless, both the 'Writing and Listening' course and its tutor proved extremely popular: by the following autumn term it had expanded to two classes, with a total of over 50 students.

By the next year, 1983-84, I also began to develop other more adventurous initiatives: a 'Come and Write' course on Holmewood, Bradford's largest council estate; and a 'New Opportunities for Retired People' course based in the Central Library. And the following year, 1984-85, the provision was expanded to include mother-tongue courses for retired members of the Ukrainian community; and a people's twentieth-century history course, 'The Changes We've Seen', for the keen group of students attending the class at Saltaire church hall. And in 1985-86, courses included an estate-based 'Growing Older: Feeling Healthy' course, a bi-lingual Polish course on pension rights, and a class based in a local authority residential home. Plans for the future include a health class for Polish pensioners and course provision for the elders of Bradford's Asian community.

But rather than painstakingly describing how the development of all these classes proceeded, I shall try and isolate the different processes involved: identifying the particular group and community centre; finding a tutor with the appropriate skills and jointly working out a relevant course outline; publicising the course with the help of local groups; teaching the course; detailed monitoring and evaluation; and, finally, finding out whether the class wants to continue and, if it does (but Pioneer Work can no longer act as its organisational umbrella), trying to arrange for a 'handover' to a more appropriate provider.

The first process, that of identifying the educational needs of specific groupings, is perhaps the most complex and lengthy of the six stages. It becomes complex because a project _may_ begin just as an informal hunch or information mentioned in casual conversation; but then has to be tested

out more rigorously with people with local knowledge and
experience; and then perhaps backed up - or rejected - by a
glance at statistical sources. This becomes clearer by
citing specific examples. For instance, I knew from studying
Bradford's census for 1911, that a very high proportion of
children - especially working-class girls - left school aged
12 to start work in the mills as half-timers. Although I was
not able to find current figures to confirm this, it seemed
reasonable to deduce that those elderly working-class
pensioners now 76 years old or more were among the most
educationally disadvantaged of pensioners. I therefore felt
it would be appropriate for Pioneer Work provision in a
textile district like Bradford to be heavily focussed on the
communities centred on the big worsted mills - like Fosters'
Black Dyke Mill at Queensbury and Salt's at Saltaire.(12)

A second example concerns work with ethnic minority
elders. I made contact early on with a social worker
responsible for work with elderly Asians. But his job, he
explained, was only just getting underway, and at the time I
felt it was premature to go much further. Instead, I began
to look at Bradford's Eastern European communities, the first
generation of which comprises a markedly ageing population, as
most of them - like Mrs S - arrived in Britain from Prisoner
of War or Displaced Persons camps during or shortly after the
last War. I was soon able to establish links with the major
communities, Polish and Ukrainian, because I was a member of
an advisory group to an oral history project, the Bradford
Heritage Recording Unit, which included a major interviewing
programme with local Eastern European immigrants. At the
same time, Bradford Social Services had begun to take the
problems of growing isolation and dependency of the older
Eastern Europeans (like Mrs S) increasingly seriously; and in
January 1983 a special Social Worker for East and Middle
European Ethnic Minority Groups (herself an Estonian) was
appointed, funded through the Community Programme. By this
route, then, I came to appreciate how urgent - though usually
invisible - were the growing needs of this particular group of
ethnic minority elders.

Other groups were identified in less circuitous ways.
The majority of retired people left school at 14, of course;
and so it is appropriate that much of Pioneer Work provision
should be geared towards their educational needs. But within
this majority there are, as already noted, key sub-groupings
experiencing different levels of social and educational
disadvantage - in particular, single women, elderly widows,
those living on their own, those lacking occupational
pensions, and those too proud to claim the supplementary
benefit that may rightfully be theirs. Poverty, of course,
affects pensioners whether they live in older housing or in
the sprawling post-war council estates beyond Bradford's ring-

road system; but older people living on the isolated housing estates are much more likely to be cut off from children and grandchildren, from their childhood roots and from their traditional communities. So the 'Come and Write' course was developed in the library at Holmewood, an estate housing over a thousand pensioners. And more recently the 'Growing Older: Feeling Healthy' course was tried out on Buttershaw, a bleak hilltop estate with a pensioner population of nearly 700, few of whom seemed to be involved in regular community activites.(13)

Although there were one or two near failures, this first process of identifying groups and their needs worked well on the whole. The second stage is the equally important one of recruiting a tutor, usually a part-time tutor, who combines the appropriate subject skills with adult teaching experience, and then working out the most appropriate course outline with them. In almost all cases I preferred to fit the tutor to the group - rather than vice versa.

The only exception here was Angela Black, the tutor who taught the 'Writing and Listening' classes, and whose energetic commitment to education for older adults pre-dated Pioneer Work. (Angela Black's enthusiasm was contagious and fired the imagination of many around her. So, in December 1983, a Bradford branch of U3A was launched, with support from myself: I acted as branch secretary for the initial nine months, till the first AGM. In order to involve as wide a range of pensioners as possible, membership was fixed at just 50p, and an interesting programme of small study groups in members' own homes, plus trips and social events, was publicised.)

In the remaining instances, however, tutors were recruited to suit the needs of particular groups. This was sometimes a fairly straightforward process. When some students said they wanted a chance to polish their spelling and punctuation, I contacted BICC and was recommended an experienced adult literacy tutor: the class in Holmewood library quickly followed. Similarly, I was able to model the 'New Opportunities for Retired People' class on the successful 'Opportunities for Women' courses which had run previously; the model had to be adapted so that, for instance, sessions about job opportunities and training for employment were omitted, and a session on voluntary work was added. But I was able to recruit the same, or similar, tutors to help teach the course: a 'study skills' tutor from BICC's Mature Students' Certificate course; and the outreach worker at EASA, Bradford's Educational Advice Service for Adults which is based in the Central Library. Likewise, my contacts with the Bradford Heritage Recording Unit enabled me to meet one of the Ukrainian-speaking interviewers. His rare skills, coupled with his oral history experience, made him an ideal tutor -

even though he lacked higher education qualifications. As a result, I spent slightly longer discussing the course beforehand than I would have done with a more experienced tutor. We broke down into their component parts each of the 'Ukrainians: Then and Now' sessions - on school, work, customs and religion - discussing where excerpts from interviews might help stimulate discussion: and this helped give the tutor the confidence to face two dozen of his elders.

From this class grew a Ukrainian 'Welfare Rights for Pensioners' course nine months later. The hiatus between the two classes was caused precisely by the problems of identifying specialist tutors referred to earlier in the book. However hard I scoured the Bradford area, I could not find a tutor combining conversational Ukrainian with adult education pension rights and skills. Indeed, it is unlikely such a person existed. Therefore the course needed two tutors: a Ukrainian interpreter and a pension rights expert. It then became difficult to find two tutors who were both free at the same time of day, especially (as so often happens) after one of the tutors was offered a secure teaching job and so had to withdraw. Eventually, by June 1985, these problems were ironed out, and the tutor and interpreter (himself a teacher at the Ukrainian Saturday school) were able to meet to discuss bi-lingual teaching methods and materials. The course eventually got off the ground quite smoothly, and a Polish 'Benefits for the Retired' class followed it.

To summarise, such unusual - but extremely important - classes could only be developed through a growing network of local organisations: the Heritage Recording Unit, Social Services, the Bradford Resource Centre (which trains welfare rights tutors) and EASA. For instance, Social Services made a major contribution towards the cost of employing the bi-lingual Polish interpreter. Without such inter-agency support, Pioneer Work would be hard going and time-consuming. For instance, I was always keen to organise a pensioners' health course, but for a long time found it difficult to make contact with skilled and committed tutors. Only later did I discover that the local Health Education Unit, based in nearby Shipley, had in fact appointed in September 1983 a Health Education Officer with specific responsibility for older people. Because of the structural isolation of this area of work, our paths crossed only after she had been in post for over a year; and so it was not till autumn 1985 that the first 'Growing Older: Feeling Healthy' course was developed. (And, once again, the original officer left her job for another elsewhere: luckily her successor agreed to take on the course and, after lengthy discussions, produced a very thoughtful and sensitive course outline.)

Once the group has been identified, the appropriate tutor secured and a syllabus agreed, the third process is, of course, publicising the class. When everything proceeds smoothly, this usually emerges naturally from earlier discussions - with the group, with the people running the community centre, and with the specialist tutor. Put another way, publicity works best when it is done, not by yourself, but by other people who are already personally well-known to potential students.

An example of good educational practice was the development and publicising of the 'Queensbury: Our Memories, Our History' course during 1984. The original contact, made early on at the Bradford Metropolitan District Federation of Old People's Welfare Committees, was with the hard-working secretary of the local Queensbury committee. Queensbury had had its own urban district council till local government reorganisation in 1974, and as an old hilltop community it still deeply resented having been forced to 'go into Bradford'. The secretary, impressed by the success of the Saltaire class, was keen for something similar to be organised locally. I contacted him towards the end of spring 1984, and attended one or two of his committee meetings. Here I had a chance to meet local activists - a Queensbury councillor, and representatives from the Civic Society, local schools, the Friendship Club, the handicapped club, and the many chapels. By the autumn, when the publicity leaflets were ready, I had a tailor-made distribution list and merely had to drop off packages of leaflets with the representative of each of the groups. (And later I took up an invitation to speak briefly at Queensbury Civic Society, as well as more routine leafleting of the old people's bungalows and local shops.) Having local people, who already knew me, help persuade local pensioners to come along to the class made all the difference. Thirty-nine people came to the first meeting: the headmaster of the school where we met was luckily on hand to help move dozens of extra chairs into the classroom. The following week forty-nine people turned up; and I had to enlist the assistance of a part-time tutor to help cope with the crowds and noise. At this stage it is perhaps important to mention a set of changes that made developing and publicising Pioneer Work classes easier than it had originally been in 1982-83. In September 1983 the traditional voluntary sector began to be given a new lease of life. To bring it more into line with the rest of the country, the Federation of Old People's Welfare Committees' ponderous name was changed to the more succinct Bradford Metro Age Concern. More importantly, the following summer, in June 1984, an Age Concern Development Officer was appointed. Her brief was to promote work on a broader basis than previously - a far from easy job since local voluntary committees still jealously guarded their own parochial ways of doing things. Then, in August 1984, three development officers (for north, central and south Bradford) were seconded by Social Services to work with the elderly. Soon the Age Concern Development Officer and the Social Services officers proposed to Bradford Metro Age Concern that an 'activity week' should be held the following year, in autumn 1985. This met with an enthusiastic response, and a meeting was arranged to bring together interested people: the voluntary sector, Leisure Services, Social Services, the Health Education Unit and, of course, Adult Education - Bradford and Ilkley Community College, Pioneer Work, the WEA, and the newly-formed Bradford U3A branch.

The timing of 'Age Alive' week at the beginning of October suited Pioneer Work perfectly. And I used the event to launch 'taster days' and 'drop-in afternoons' to help publicise the Pioneer Work classes planned to start the following week in different venues. These included a community centre on Buttershaw estate, the Polish Parish Club in the city centre, and Mayfield, a local authority residential home in an inner-city neighbourhood by a busy six lane carriageway. Particularly valuable, 'Age Alive' week gave potential students an opportunity to meet the course tutors in an informal relaxed way before the classes started.(14)

After publicising the class, teaching began. Like Adult Education generally, all Pioneer Work classes share the same broad principles here: that teaching should be as informal as possible, with little or no straight lecturing, and plenty of time for discussion and participation. Tutors are urged to start from where the students are, rather than from where the tutor might feel they ought to be. Chairs are usually arranged in an informal circle beforehand, and much of the work is done in small groups, sometimes with report-back sessions afterwards. Students are always encouraged to relate what is being discussed to their own lived experience as far as possible. In this respect, the teaching and learning processes in the Eastern European pension rights courses, say, are probably not markedly different from those of the welfare rights courses described earlier in this book, while the 'Growing Older: Feeling Healthy' and 'New Opportunities' classes will share similar teaching methods with similar courses for women.

But beyond this there are important differences between teaching methods in Pioneer Work generally and in classes for retired and elderly students in particular. Each older student brings to a class a lifetime of experience, stretching back, perhaps, to a peasant childhood in the Ukraine, or to a Victorian or Edwardian childhood in pre-1914 England, and certainly to a young adulthood in the last war. This is a rare and important strength which no mixed class or a group of younger students can match. It provides an extra resource for a tutor trying to democratise the learning process and to break down the teacher-taught dichotomy. It proved an important basis for, say, the 'Writing and Listening' classes, which subsequently went on on to produce their own anthology of poems and short stories. And, of course, it was vital to the success of the community history courses taught at Keighley, Shipley, Saltaire, Queensbury and Mayfield. At least three of these five groups have gone on to undertake their own local research project, to participate in the lengthy but enjoyable process of editing their writings, and to produce a typescript of publishable length. The Shipley class, for instance, was rewarded for its time-consuming work on lengthy oral history tapes and transcripts with a grant from West Yorkshire County Council towards the cost of publishing its class booklet. And the Saltaire and Queensbury classes have both created considerable local interest by celebrating the publication of their booklets with an exhibition of photographs, attracting many friends and neighbours.

Another difference is that older Pioneer Work students tend to want to remain loyal and active members of the class for rather longer than younger students, yet are usually reluctant to travel into the city centre to attend classes. For this reason, 'bridging courses' have been devised for the community history classes at both Saltaire and Queensbury.(15) These courses, titled 'The Changes We've Seen', try to provide a link between the reminiscence-based community history classes of the first year and the rather more structured history teaching of conventional adult education. Topics include the dole-queue image of the 1930s, changes brought about by the 1939-45 War, the coming of the Welfare State, and the 'never-had-it-so-good' 1950s; and teaching combines the same oral history input of the previous year with a reading of other (and often very challenging) accounts of those decades. One or two of the elderly students have found this transition to a more comparative approach and to a more rigorous periodisation too much to cope with; but most of the students have thoroughly enjoyed this kind of 'people's history' course.

The next process after teaching is monitoring - although the collection of information on the register by each tutor naturally takes place during the course itself. Compiling the detailed data from each register, alongside the tutor's class report, throws considerable light on the excellent response to this area of Pioneer Work.

As the statistical appendix at the end of this chapter makes clear, a total of 39 classes has been taught over the three years, 1983-85. Of these, 38 ran successfully and one failed to recruit. The total number of students enrolled (ie. whose names were entered on the register by the tutor) totalled over 700, an average of about 19 students per class. Of these, 73% attended two-thirds or more of the sessions each

term.(16)   In   sheer   size,   the largest class was that at
Queensbury, with 64 names on the register;   after the second
week the class had to be divided in two. The 'Saltaire: Our
Memories, Our History' classes, 'Writing and Listening', the
first 'New Opportunities' course, the two Ukrainian classes,
and the Polish Welfare Rights class have also been large, with
over 20 students registered for each. But more important than
numbers has been the loyalty and commitment of the students
themselves. Registers are a crude measure of enthusiasm, but
they do perhaps point to how high a proportion of those
pensioners registering subsequently attended all - or nearly
all - the sessions. This is markedly the case for the classes
taught in Saltaire, and in Keighley and Shipley, where,
perhaps because the groups were each working intently on their
own project, attendence was remarkably high.
       The   information given on the Pioneer Work registers is
quite detailed.   (See statistical analysis at the end of this
chapter.)   It indicates that women students outnumber men by
over two to one - as would be expected from the population
profile - but that courses for East European elders recruit a
noticeably higher proportion of men.   It also shows that
nearly two-thirds (64%) left school aged 14 or under - perhaps
slightly fewer than in this age range as a whole, though still
an impressive proportion. What is particularly interesting is
the information given about first job after leaving school and
last job before retirement.   Of the thirteen students listed
on one of the registers for the Keighley community history
class, for instance, eight had worked either in textiles or in
clothing: one was a weaver who became a newsagent, another a
spinner who became a sheet metal worker, a third, a tailoress
who became a grocer. This makes an interesting contrast with,
say, the 'Welfare Rights for Retired Ukrainians' students.
There, five of the men (though none of the women) had begun
their working lives in farming, one having left school aged
nine; and six (four men and two women) had <u>ended</u> their working
days in a textile mill, three having turned to textiles in
later life, probably on arrival in Bradford.
       The final process, after teaching and monitoring, is
finding out whether the class would like to continue;   and if
it would, but Pioneer Work can no longer act as its
organisational umbrella, finding another hospitable home for
the class - ie. one that has a commitment to this kind of
liberal adult education, and will not charge fees. It is here
that this section of Pioneer Work has encountered almost
insuperable problems: its very success in recruiting large,
stable, enthusiastic groups conflicts with the aims of Pioneer
Work, which was conceived as <u>short</u>-term provision, with some
groups eventually being handed over to other more appropriate
agencies. After a while, Pioneer Work in Leeds, for instance,
has been able to achieve a smooth handing-over with many of

the courses for unemployed people.

But there seems no parallel wide-scale policy commitment, yet, to underwriting free classes for older students, no longer of working age. So arrangements have had to be made on a woefully ad hoc basis, occasionally satisfactory in the short-term, but seldom perfect or fair in the long-term. Pioneer Work's commitment to the education of disadvantaged retired and elderly people is not yet equally shared by other adult education agencies. Yet, of course, there has been a considerable shift in attitudes, if not actual funding, since I was first appointed in 1982.

Nationally, the initiatives begun in the early 1980s, by The Forum on the Rights of Elderly to Education (FREE) and the University of the Third Age (U3A) continue, and now are joined by the newer Association of Educational Gerontology. U3A continues to offer a direct challenge to the institutions of adult and higher education, accusing them of becoming over-centralised and over-professionalised. One response to these accusations of institutional ageism in education has been the flowering of local U3A groups up and down the country. The current national membership has now reached about 6,500, organised into 90 local groups. One of the largest is Huddersfield, immediately south-west of Bradford. Formed in spring 1984, it had 655 members by the summer of 1985; and by the following autumn this had risen to over 900. Such visible popularity offers a direct challenge - some might say threat - to the traditional adult education providers in the area who still have to ask pensioners to pay the usual fees for classes, albeit reduced for retired people.(17)

Elsewhere, the Unit for the Development of Adult Continuing Education (UDACE) has recently set up a development group on Education and Older Adults; the project worker is attempting to map all the forms of older people's involvement in education - from formal courses to 'informal and individual learning, in mutal learning groups and as contributors to other people's learning'. Similarly, UDACE is working alongside FREE to send out thousands of postal questionnaires, from the returns of which will be compiled a 'Directory of Educational Initiatives'. The value of this directory will be to offer a national picture of an area where a million small and energetic flowers bloom - but there is as yet no one field map.

On a more local scale, there have, of course, been comparable developments over the last three years. The series of appointments from early 1983 onwards, in Social Services, health education and the voluntary sector, indicate this. Critics might say this reveals merely a further professionalisation of ageing as a 'problem' to be 'solved' by younger people; and for this reason, the founding of the Bradford U3A branch is perhaps a particularly important development. Although it has not mushroomed at the spectacular rate of the Huddersfield group, it has about 140 members, with a programme of social events and a number of study groups (in Alternative Medicine, Making Music, Bridge, History of Local Villages, Travel, Spanish etc) each meeting in a member's home. It currently receives a modest amount of support from BICC (use of rooms for meetings and help with printing), but otherwise is genuinely a self-help educational organisation by retired people, for retired people. Since I ceased to act as secretary after the first nine months, the branch has been run by a committee elected by members from various study groups plus co-opted members from Age Concern, BICC, and Pioneer Work, who play a supportive role from 'the back seat'. U3A participated in Age Alive week in October 1985, for instance, which helped bring together some of the people newly involved in this field in Bradford.

But these developments, both nationally and locally, though welcome, are not without problems. First, the most powerful advocates of the educational rights and needs of retired and elderly people are not so much pensioners themselves, as professionals (sometimes near retiring age, sometimes not) speaking on behalf of an older generation. Such are the extremely modest expectations of pensioners like Ginny and Helen, that local U3A groups, for instance, are more likely to make small one-off demands (eg. the use of local authority rooms for events), than to ask, say, the local education committee to waive all pensioners' class fees. Yet should retired people be demanding their own educational 'rights'? If the education expansions of 1918, 1944 and the 1960s have been financed from the rates and taxes of today's pensioners, should they not be asking - on the grounds of natural justice alone - that they be entitled to, say, one-sixth of all educational expenditure?

The question of rights to education raises the issue of educational standards. If pensioners have a right to demand educational standards similar to those offered to children and young adults, should the teaching be undertaken exclusively by paid professionals - ie. under retiring age? Yet this goes against much of the radical thinking in education. Certainly, those of us demanding Women's Studies courses in the 1970s insisted they should be taught by women; and there are of course similar arguments made elsewhere in this book about ethnic minority provision. Yet trade unions may insist on sticking to the letter of their 65-year-old ruling; and with teacher and graduate unemployment being as prevalent as it is, there are additionally moves to encourage early retirement at 55 or even 50. Would this mean retired people had the right to learn - but never to teach? Or does it indicate, as I would suggest, a dual approach - with classes such as those developed by Pioneer Work being taught by paid professionals (ie. normally a generation younger than their students), parallel with more informal U3A groups being taught (if at all) by retired volunteers with teaching skills or knowledge to share?

Among the other problematic areas are how and what might be taught. Pioneer Work's pedagogic roots are fairly libertarian ones; yet in the classes I have taught I have not always felt persuaded to adopt a completely democratic approach. This is partly because of the large numbers involved. (And at Queensbury, one of the students expert at wood-carving made me a gavel to bang on the desk so I could be heard, and for hard-of-hearing students not to feel left out.) But it is not just a question of size and noise: students of Ginny's and Helen's age recognise that, through no fault of their own but just because of their class, their generation, and their gender, they received only a very basic elementary education, and so are keen to come along to a course and follow the guidance of an experienced tutor. Premature proposals for 'syllabus negotiation' may well lead to grumbles that the tutor 'hasn't got a clue'.

Yet, within the course structure introduced by the tutor, students like Ginny and Helen are relieved that the atmosphere is friendly and informal, that there is no pressure to take examinations, and that students are free to write about their own personal recollections. Pioneer Work classes, especially the community history classes with their strong personal emphasis, have proved extremely popular and productive. Yet do community history classes, which focus exclusively on these streets, these shops, these schools, often to the virtual exclusion of the world beyond the parish boundary, really fall within the pale of liberal adult education, with its commitment to open discussion and critical analysis? May they not encourage parochialism and status-quoism? In a multi-cultural city like Bradford, this may well mean confirming many elderly people's conservative attitudes towards newcomers - rather than gently challenging racist ideas.

These are all real dilemmas which have to be faced in developing and teaching courses for older adults: the professionalising of ageing as a 'problem', the proud modesty of the majority of pensioners' own educational demands, the question of teaching by the retired as well as for the retired, of the most appropriate teaching methods, and of whether students' preferences for the status quo ante should be further validated - or gently challenged.

My own preference is for a pluralistic approach to education for older adults, an approach which recognises that the history of adult education includes an important voluntary tradition - particularly through the WEA branch structure. There should be room for the voluntary sector, operating independently of institutions like the DES and HMIs, and based within, say, local U3A groups with informal teaching (where it is done at all) undertaken by retired and elderly people themselves. Parallel with (but separate from) this would be the statutory providers, whether university adult education departments, local education authorities or others. These institutions have an obligation to organise classes, taught by experienced tutors, that offer comparable educational standards to those obtaining elsewhere in the education system. Why <u>should</u> working-class retired and elderly students have to accept second-rate education any more than any other class or generation?

What might this 'good educational practice' entail, then? The experience of developing Pioneer Work courses in a city like Bradford suggest that five points are important.

First, that the classes are accessible. This means that time is spent, long before the groups meet, ensuring that the courses are all held during the daytime, in a nearby community centre (preferably one already used by pensioners), in a ground floor room. Fees should either be waived completely, or charged at not more than about 20p, paid weekly; the ILEA practice of offering unlimited classes at £1 per head to resident pensioners provides an admirable example of good local authority practice.

Second, that the classes should be organised through the appropriate educational institution - rather than through, say, the local authority's non-educational sections. It would, of course, be cheaper for local authorities to organise classes through leisure or social services, because tutors would no longer have to be paid an educational hourly rate and because there would be little or no commitment to providing books and other essential teaching aids. But the price paid for this cheapness would be that the wages and conditions of already vulnerable part-time tutors would probably deteriorate further, and the commitment to <u>liberal</u> adult education would be weakened. Only provision funded through the appropriate <u>educational</u> structures can guarantee both that tutors' employment is not further casualised by 'lay tutors' and that working-class retired and elderly people are not offered second-rate education.(18)

Third, and linked to this, students should be offered a real choice between attending a 'segregated' class designed especially to meet pensioners' needs (eg. a 'Growing Older: Feeling Healthy' course) and more general classes open to every age. Older students often feel they have been out of education for so long that they could not match the pace and confidence of younger people; they welcome a gentle start in a supportive atmosphere with members of their own generation. After this, if they choose to, one or two may enter the hurly-burly of a local college. However, the ready access of individual students from, say, a 'New Opportunities for

Retired People' course, to, for instance, a college-based 'Mature Students' Certificate' course, is only really practicable if the introductory 'Opportunities' course is part of (or very closely linked to) established local adult educational provision - rather than existing in its own organisational ghetto, separate and (in all probability) second-rate.

Fourth, there should be a commitment to detailed monitoring of both the courses and the students, particularly at the outset, to ensure the provision is meeting the educational needs of the groups it was designed to help: disadvantaged retired and elderly people in general, and specific groupings within that population in particular.

Fifth, and as a corollary of monitoring, there should be a commitment to recognising that the nine million people in the country entitled to a retirement pension do not, in any educational sense, form a homogenous group, but rather a number of groupings. The largest grouping is the one Helen falls within: those pensioners who had to leave school at 14 and who have since felt cut off from educational opportunities; some of them can afford the fees of mainstream adult educational classes because (like Helen) they have more than one pension coming into the household; but others cannot, because their weekly income is around the supplementary benefit level.

Helen belongs to the largest grouping, Ginny to a smaller one: those elderly (over 75 year old) pensioners, many of whom in areas like Bradford had to leave full-time school at 12 or 13 to work in the mill. In this elderly grouping, women greatly outnumber men (by four to one amongst those aged 85 or more); and loneliness (through widowhood or perhaps the death of a sister) and poverty are felt most keenly here. Two other small but vitally important groupings are those pensioners isolated from their families and other supportive services by living on large, new housing estates, an intimidating walk or bus ride away from the nearest adult education centre. And finally the grouping Mrs S falls within: the first generation ethnic minority elders, whether from Eastern Europe, the New Commonwealth or Pakistan, whose own schooling may have been extremely rudimentary, and whose feelings of isolation and dependency are likely to be exacerbated by old age.

Courses for pensioners, or courses including a high proportion of pensioners, are easily organised: computer classes in a local adult education centre or local 'village history' courses, for instance. What the Pioneer Work experience in Bradford, very small scale though it has been, has tried to argue for is provision that goes beyond this, and offers relevant, accessible, community-based courses for those key groupings among the retired population most likely to be left out of adult education activities unless special consideration is given to their needs.

REFERENCES

1. I looked for accounts of how classes had been
    organised and taught, in a variety of venues, for
    different kinds of groupings amongst the elderly and
    retired. Although I found nothing quite comparable to
    the scale, variety and detailed monitoring of Pioneer
    Work, I was very interested to note the following
    accounts:

    (ed) F Glendenning, Outreach Education and the Elders:
    Theory and Practice, Beth Johnson Foundation, 1980;
    E Midwinter, Age is Opportunity: Education and Older
    People, Centre for Policy on Ageing, 1982, pp 32 ff;
    Inner London Education Authority and Age Concern Greater
    London, Joint Project Report 1981-83; (eds) S Johnston
    and C Phillipson, Older Learners: The Challenge to Adult
    Education, Bedford Square Press 1983: this includes
    J Bornat's account of 'Learning in Later Life: A Special
    Programme for Older People at the Polytechnic of North
    London, April-July 1981', for which 54 people enrolled
    at a cost of £3 for each pensioner; Diane Norton notes
    that the forthcoming directory also highlights the
    range of projects currently based in Scotland.

2. Bradford Metropolitan District, with a population of
    nearly half-a-million (454,198), has a slightly lower
    percentage of pensioners than the country as a whole:
    16.9% compared to 17.7%. The percentage of pensioners
    within the adult population (aged 16 and over) is:
    Great Britain 22.75% and Bradford 22.4%. In
    neighbouring Calderdale (ie. Halifax) it is as high as
    24.7%.

    For those involved in adult education a more useful
    figure, though, is pensioners as a percentage of the
    adult population aged 19 and over: the figure for
    Bradford is 23.9%. In Bradford, the number of men
    over 65 is 24,180, and women over 60 is 52,461. Of
    the 52,461 women, 31,105 are unmarried, widowed or
    divorced (ie. 59.2%). The national picture is
    similar. There are 6.4 million women and 3.2 million
    men who are of pensionable age; 30% of pensioners live
    on their own, of whom 4 out of 5 are women. Britain's
    Elderly Population, Office of Population Censuses and
    Surveys (OPCS), 1984, pp 2 and 7-8.

3. Bradford in Figures, City of Bradford Metropolitan
    Council, 1984, p 145. However, the figure aged between
    45 and pensionable age is 6,065; some of these 'middle-

153

aged' people may already be counted as 'elderly' within their own community, and this suggests the need for adult educators to be aware of the ethnocentricity of their own definitions of old age. Britain's Elderly Population, p 7, gives a figure of 0.4 million as the number of pensioners born outside the UK in 1981; of these, the biggest grouping is those born in the Irish Republic, followed by the New Commonwealth and Pakistan, and, in third place, Europe.

4. Eastern and Central Europeans are invisible in the official statistics: instead I have relied on the figures supplied by Bradford Social Services.

5. Figure cited by Mark Abrams, 'Education and the Elderly', Alice Foley Memorial Lecture, 1980, p4.

6. The most frequently quoted figure (2%) is taken from 'Education and the Elderly', p 2. Midwinter in Age is Opportunity also suggests 2% based on research done in 1982, though again it might be argued the question was too narrow. Thus the ILEA/Age Concern Joint Project Report p 14 implies a much higher percentage; more accurate research is badly needed here.

7. Information received from student.

8. Information based on case study notes.

9. Interview with student recorded 30.9.85; quotation from An Ordinary Lot, Pioneer Work publications No 5, 1985, p 4.

10. I was also involved in teaching in other areas of Pioneer Work , and in non-Pioneer Work classes.

11. Many thanks to Carol Greenwood for her assistance at this large class.

12. The other people contributing to Pioneer Work here as members of the Department were David Goodway, whose interest and experience of using oral history techniques in teaching led him to develop two community history courses, one in Shipley and one in Keighley; and Gina Bridgeland, also a historian, who taught 'The Changes We've Seen' course at Saltaire. This overlapping of interests helps to explain why so many of the classes described here (nearly two-thirds) are history courses of some kind.

13. Bradford in Figures, pp 20-24 gives the percentage of

pensioners on Bradford's council estates: Holmewood
13% and Buttershaw 11%. District Trends 1984: The
Changing Face of Bradford, City of Bradford
Metropolitan Council 1984, looks at the 'Dependency
Ratio', that is, the number of people depending on each
working person, a calculation which includes 'the
elderly' (ie. of pensionable age) and is used to
illustrate 'the growing gap between the haves and the
have nots'. Unfortunately, in all other respects this
booklet ignores the experiences of pensioners.

14.   In addition, Colin Neville from EASA brought his
      displays and leaflets out to these new venues. And
      tutors had an opportunity to re-think their course
      outlines in the light of potential students' comments;
      this was particularly helpful (and necessary) for the
      health course at Butttershaw.

      Apart from this, Age Alive Week proved a little
      disappointing: despite city-wide publicity the response
      was lower than had been hoped.

15.   See references 9 and 12. Pioneer Work students, with
      help and advice from tutors, have produced the following
      research booklets, published by the Department of Adult
      and Continuing Education, University of Leeds: Saltaire:
      Our Memories, Our History (1984); Listening and Writing
      (1984); Lazy Tees (1985); An Ordinary Lot (1985).

16.   It is only fair to say that the Pioneer Work method of
      counting students (each new term as a new course, and
      therefore each student as a new student) rather
      distorts the statistics here. A higher proportion of
      students is therefore being counted twice and thrice
      than in other areas of Pioneer Work.

17.   U3A seems to thrive extremely well in the self-help
      traditions of West Yorkshire. West Yorkshire
      comprises about 20% of national U3A membership, and no
      fewer than three (representatives from Wakefield,
      Huddersfield and Keighley) out of the seven members of
      the U3A national committee.

18.   However, it is very important that links with social
      services and library provision are maintained, even
      though their role is supportive rather than
      organisational. For instance, Pioneer Work and
      Bradford Social Services have co-operated on a joint
      report on adult education and ethnic minority elders.

PIONEER WORK CLASSES FOR THE RETIRED 1983–85

Note 1. All courses are of 10 weeks, unless otherwise stated

2. Courses which continue on after the 1st term are counted as separate courses for each term, and are open to new students.

COURSE TITLE (& length)	Total student number	Male	Female	No of effective students (2/3rd+)	Age of leaving school −13	14	15+
1. Saltaire: Our Memories, Our History (i)	26	5	21	19	4	7	9
2. Writing and Listening (i)	17			12	0		9
Autumn 1983 – summer 1984							
3. Saltaire: Our Memories, Our History (ii)	18	3	15	14	3	6	9
4. Writing and Listening (ii)	27	4	23	15	0	4	5
5. Writing and Listening (iii)	26	4	22	22			
6. Writing and Listening (iv)	15	2	13	11			
7. Writing and Listening (v) (11 wks)	23	4	19	21	0	8	10
8. Saltaire: Our Memories, Our History (iii)	21	5	16	17	3	9	6
9. Saltaire: Our memories, Our History (iv)(3 wks)	21	5	16	19	3	9	4
10. Understanding Psychology (6 wks)	8	5	3	4	0	2	3
11. Shipley Community History (i) (6 wks)	11	5	6	6			
12. Shipley Community History (ii) (6 wks)	15	6	9	9			
13. What Do You Remember (Keighley i) (11 wks)	18	6	12	11	1	8	6
14. What Do You Remember (Keighley ii)	15	6	9	9			
15. Come and Write (Holmewood)	10	3	7	7	0	6	3
16. New Opportunities for Retired People (i)	21	6	15	19	0	12	8

Autumn 1984 - summer 1985

17 & 18. Queensbury: Our Memories, Our History (i and ii)

Course							
17 & 18. Queensbury: Our Memories, Our History (i and ii)	64	17	47	44	5	31	16
19 & 20. " Our Memories, Our History (iii & iv)	56	13	43	44	5	29	16
21 & 22. " Our memories, Our History (v & vi)	43	9	34	36	4	23	13
23. Ukrainians: Then and Now (4 wks)	22	11	11	14			
24. Welfare Rights for Retired Ukrainians (6 wks)	20	12	8	8	5	6	6
25. New Opportunities for Retired People (ii)(6 wks)	12	4	8	9	0	9	3
26. The Changes We've Seen (Saltaire v)	19	8	11	17	1	12	5
27. The Changes We've Seen (Saltaire vi)	18	7	11	13			
28. The Changes We've Seen (Saltaire vii)	19	8	11	13			
29. Shipley Community History (iii)	10	5	5	8	0	6	4
30. Shipley Community History (iv)	11	5	6	9	0	6	4
31. Shipley Community History (v)	10	5	5	8	0	6	4
32. What Do You Remember? (Keighley iii) (12 wks)	14	6	8	13	1	9	3
33. What Do You Remember? (Keighley iv) (12 wks)	13	6	7	8	1	9	3

Autumn 1986 -

Course							
34. The Changes We've Seen (Queensbury vii)	32	8	24	18	3	26	3
35 & 36. Welfare Rights for pensioners (Polish)(i)	41	16	25	32	2	3	17
37. Growing Older: Feeling Healthy (Buttershaw)	16	1	15	14			
38. Do You Remember Marshfield? (Residential)	15	4	11	9	1	2	3

Total number of courses for which information available: 38
Total student number: 727
Average number of students per class: 19
Total number of men: 208 (30%)
Total number of women: 487 (70%)
Total number of effective students: 532 (73%)
Total leaving full-time school aged 13 or younger: 42 (9%)
Total leaving school aged 14: 248 (55%)
Total leaving school aged 15 or older: 163 (36%)

Chapter 8

REFLECTIONS ON RESEARCH

Introduction

The need for adult education to develop detailed monitoring and evaluation procedures was discussed in Chapter 3. Reference was made there both to the overall continuous action-research procedures adopted within Pioneer Work, and also to the specific Research Project funded by the DES from 1984-86, primarily to develop user and tutor surveys from work with unemployed people.

A final report on this Research Project with unemployed people is being presented to the DES in September 1986, and, at the time of writing, the results of the surveys have not been analysed. The aim of this chapter is to examine briefly the methodology which has been adopted, and discuss a number of general issues which have arisen during the designing and implementation of the research.

Continuous Evaluation Methods

It is important to stress that the Research Project has developed from the continuous monitoring and evaluation which has been used generally in Pioneer Work.

Since its inception, Pioneer Work has adopted a number of methods of evaluation. Registers contain information of a statistical nature relating to age, sex, unemployment status (ie. registered or not) and educational background. And various types of reports - including organisers' reports, tutors' curriculum plans and their post-course reports - are also used in the evaluation process. Discussions between organisers, tutors and students are another crucial element in continuous course monitoring.

These methods, then, both quantitative and qualitative are used throughout the work. Once extrapolated, this information gives the Pioneer Work teams concrete data upon which to base decisions. Strategies and future plans depend heavily on the interpretations of past evaluation.

The ongoing evaluation, using these methods, looks at how

contacts are best established in the community, the processes involved in organising courses, and the types of students who attend those courses. During the process of evaluation, an approaches and categories model has been developed in order to simplify the task of analysing courses. This model reflects the different subject areas and locations used in Pioneer Work.(1)

The Research Project

Building on this overall evaluation, a research assistant has been employed to examine aspects of Pioneer Work with unemployed people in more detail. The aim of the research is to gain a clearer insight into the perceptions of students and tutors involved in the Pioneer Work programme, and the learning outcomes which emanate from the courses. Thus, user-surveys and tutor-surveys have been carried out. It is hoped that information arising out of the research will be valuable not only to Pioneer Work, but also to the development of adult education provision for unemployed people in general.

In order to enable generalisations to be made, it was felt that as many course participants as possible should take part in the research. Moreover, a substantial sample would show whether team members' preconceived notions of students' and tutors' opinions and attitudes were correct. These notions have usually been obtained from discussions with a selected number of course participants. Fordham et al encountered this phenomenon when studying residents' attitudes in their research into non-formal education on a housing estate:

> Residents' attitudes towards living on the estate were shown from the survey to be very positive, whereas the general impression we gained from some groups reflected negative attitudes to life on the estate! This general impression had been gained from discussions with small groups of people.(2)

The size of sample will affect the choice of research method. Some qualitative methods, such as discussion and in-depth interviews, can be used successfully only with large numbers if the resources, in terms of researchers/ interviewers, are available. The Project piloted the method of individual discussion-based interviews. The findings revealed that this technique could produce extremely useful information. Also, because of its flexible structure, important matters would sometimes arise only when respondents were able to deviate from the subject. Unfortunately, this method is very time-consuming, both in terms of interviewing and analysing the data.

This interview technique, then, was used with the tutors as this sample was relatively small. With the students, on the other hand, it was decided that the resources were not available to implement this method effectively. Another reason for this decision, was that Pioneer Work staff felt that a certain amount of quantification of students' attitudes would benefit the research. Comparisons could then be made betwen students in different approaches and categories, and between students of different ages, educational background, sex, etc.

A sample survey seemed the most efficient and reliable way to interview a substantial number of people. Thus, a questionnaire for the user or student survey was designed which included questions relating to the following:

students' changing educational and vocational expectations, previous educational background, their unemployment background, barriers to access (including transport, childcare(3)), students' assessment of courses in terms of content and approach, social aspects of courses, discussion of teaching methods, the significance, if any, of courses to students' lives, and the influence of liberal education.

It also consisted of both open and closed questions.(4)

Given the much smaller numbers involved in the tutor-survey, it was possible to include mostly open questions. The topics covered included course content, teaching methodology, curriculum planning, teaching philosophy, analysis of progress and outcomes for students and courses, level of support for tutors, tutors' attitudes to working for a university department, counselling, the demands of informal teaching, and tutors' educational and vocational backgrounds.

The interviewing took place during the spring and summer of 1985 both in Leeds and in Bradford. A total of 76 students and 14 tutors was interviewed from 16 courses.

Discussion of Research Methods

The research methods used must be seen in the context of action-research which is 'conceived with the ongoing developmental work rather than a one-off evaluation of routinised activities'.(5) The research can only be justified by the action and therefore it must 'adapt itself to the programme environment and disrupt operations as little as possible'.(6)

If sample survey methods are being used, then, they must in some respects be adapted for use in a changing and dynamic environment. There are other reasons for altering the techniques of the sample survey. They include the principle that people should not be treated as objects but should be encouraged actively to participate in the development of the research, whether by discussing methodology or by having the opportunity fully to air their views relating to Pioneer Work courses.

The selection of the sample also differs from that in traditional sample surveys because of the nature of Pioneer Work, where courses are short, and are staggered throughout the year; moreover, they begin when a need for a certain subject area has been identified. Therefore, it was impossible to draw a sample from the total population beforehand as that population could change quickly. In order to overcome this problem, it was decided that a sample of students who had attended two-thirds or more of courses (which had been selected from the various approaches and categories) would be interviewed. A sample could only be drawn when individual courses were near completion. A proportionate sample of two-thirds of each course was drawn from class registers. The sample gives a true representation of the population at the time of interviewing, in terms of age and sex. Between 75% and 80% of the total population was interviewed.

The sample survey was, however, in certain respects similar to those used in traditional research, in that a uniform questionnaire was used, a coding frame was designed and standardised techniques implemented for quantitative analysis: ie. cross tabulations, graphs and statistics. Moreover, only two interviewers(7) were used in order to lessen bias, although a certain amount of flexibility was incorporated so that the interviews could take place in a relaxed and friendly fashion. Nevertheless, questions were asked in a standard order, and extensive piloting had tried to overcome the problem of 'loaded' questions.

The use of sample survey as a method in this research, therefore, deviates somewhat from traditional survey techniques. Ongoing practical work is not disrupted and also participant involvement is encouraged. However, some standardisation is seen as necessary, in order that valid generalisations can be made.

Although sample survey methods have been criticised by some adult educators,(8) they can, if used flexibly, be an efficient way of obtaining information as well as maintaining a degree of involvement by participants. It is recognised in this research that a sample survey cannot provide the depth of information that may be possible with some qualitative methods; nevertheless, valuable data can come to light. With this research, the survey data is being used as a basis for in-depth studies into various course categories.

Other issues arising out of the development and the direction of the research will be discussed briefly.

Personal Background

The personality and background of a researcher are bound to affect the techniques which are used, and the findings. Ruddock sees findings as being as much a function of the personality of the researcher as they are of the data. Other researchers, he feels, could produce an altogether different set of findings.(9) However, in the case of Pioneer Work, the researcher was given very clear directions and guidelines as to how the research should be conducted. Moreover, the collective way of working has limited, to a certain extent, the researcher's influence.

Nevertheless, her previous experience, both academic and practical, had an effect on the methods used and the way they were implemented. As Halsey states: 'The researcher does not begin as an impartial evaluator of the action, for his discipline has contributed to the conceptualisation of the problems in question and has adopted a stance towards them'.(10)

In this case, there was initial conflict between the research worker's social science research background, her experience of being unemployed and, more recently, her work undertaken as a tutor/organiser with unwaged people. Whilst wishing on the one hand to adopt a critical, 'objective' approach to the research, she also wanted it to contribute to the action in some tangible way. This inner conflict resolved itself in the flexible approach, as described above, being adopted within the framework of a traditional social science methodology.

Researcher Involvement in Pioneer Work

The researcher continued to have a small organising role in developing work with unemployed people, in order to keep in contact with grass-root organisations and other relevant agencies. The research, it was hoped, would benefit from the researcher having a clear understanding of key issues such as outreach, identifying tutors, etc. 'If educators are aware of the hidden agendas of individuals and groups at different levels in the community, and only if such groups are convinced that educators can be trusted, will information be offered that is authentic and revealing'.(11)

One problem that arises with the researcher's involvement in the action is the possibility that she may seek only those results which support the programme's effectiveness. Attempts have been made to overcome this, by discussing the research with relevant contacts outside the immediate environment: a colleague from the University's Social Policy department acts as a consultant, giving advice on methodology, especially relating to the quantitative data (ie. he gives expert advice on the SPSS computer package). He also acts as a further check on basic factors and assumptions that Pioneer Work may take for granted. An external researcher, on the other hand, might have difficulty being accepted by team members and conflicts of interest might arise between them. Also, an outsider might not have a proper awareness of the aims of the research. A researcher involved in Pioneer Work provision is likely to generate less friction; because of this, the research will cause little upheaval and will be seen to fit into the ongoing evaluation process.(12)

Pioneer Work works collectively as a team. Colleagues are kept up to date with the progress of the research and are actively encouraged to criticise all stages of the research process. Often in university departments, research assistants are not considered as integrated members of staff and do not take part in the decision-making process. This does not happen in Pioneer Work, where, as far as possible, the research assistant is on an equal footing with her lecturer colleagues.

Accountability

The Research Project is accountable to a steering committee, which is not always in agreement about the aims, methods and scope of the research.

The DES's main objective in funding the research is to aid policy-making in the field of Adult Education with the unemployed. The University sees rigorous academic research as an a priori justifiable university function. The Department of Adult and Continuing Education, whilst sharing such objectives, wishes also to examine the connections, at all levels, between Pioneer Work provision and liberal adult education objectives. Where such connections appear tenuous, the Department tends to argue for changes in Pioneer Work practice and provision. On the other hand, one of the main aims of Pioneer Work staff is to ensure that information from the research is used to improve the quality of the services provided for unemployed people, and that a sound research basis is provided to encourage the funding and development of 'good practice' elsewhere.

Conflicts can arise betwen these aims. One example of this was that in the first drafts of the student questionnaire, several questions were devoted to the sociology of unemployment, on the basis that such material is fundamental to education and the unemployed. However, others felt that such questions lengthened the questionnaire considerably and that areas such as health, home environment and personal problems related to unemployment have been dealt with elsewhere. The latter argument prevailed.

A second example concerns the tutor survey, where it was

necessary to reconcile the interests of those whose prime concern was with technical aspects of pedagogy, such as teaching methods and curriculum planning, and those who wanted to assess the degree to which people's overall political/ social awareness has been affected. The final questionnaire is a compromise between these two positions and includes questions on both topics.

In general, researchers are accountable to people in authority - steering groups, management committees, and funding bodies. But they should also be accountable to the people taking part in the research. Participants should be allowed to comprehend the reasons underlying the study and be involved in determining its aims and objectives. They should also be in a position to veto anything that is written about themselves or the particular groups in which they are involved.

Ideally, the way to do this would be to hold regular meetings that could discuss the research. Unfortunately, previous experience in Pioneer Work has shown the difficulties of getting tutors and students from different groups to come together. Lack of finance, transport, childcare, and an understandable reluctance to become entangled in organisational structures, combined with the sense of alienation often encountered in unemployed/unwaged people, have resulted usually in the failure of this kind of attempt. These factors do not mean that accountability can be jettisoned; it is the responsibility of the researcher and interviewer to keep people informed of progress and to encourage feedback.

Language

The issue of language arises both during the research and afterwards. During piloting of the questionnaires, questions thought to be intimidating, unproductive and redundant, were removed. However, in spite of numerous reworkings of certain questions, paraphrasing still proved necessary. A researcher often wishes to probe topics that to most people are 'non-issues' (teaching styles or teaching methods, for example). After all, there is no reason why people should know the necessary language to describe such specialised areas of work. Therefore, asking technical questions is problematic if detailed information is being sought.

After findings are collated, there is the question of what type of language should be used when discussing data - that of pedagogy for the DES and HMI, academic terminology for the university, adult education jargon for practitioners, or everyday language for students, tutors, and the general public. Glotelenschen makes the point that it is important to understand the criteria, standards and indicators that various audiences have in mind as they consider a programme and to prepare findings for dissemination that address those concerns in a language that the audience have in mind as they consider a programme and to prepare findings for dissemination that address those concerns in a language that the audience will understand.(13)

But can one type of language accommodate such a variety of audiences? In this respect, there is a huge comprehension gap between academic institutions and large sections of the population, with language acting as a barrier, both excluding the population and imprisoning the institution.

Interviewing

Interviews can be an artificial way of making contact with people.(14) Moreover, it is unrealistic to pretend that absolute equality has been achieved between researcher and participants. There cannot be an equal relationship where one person is initiating and directing the interview. Furthermore, unlike the respondents, the researcher is being paid. Nevertheless, in this research, interviewers tried to create a relaxed atmosphere where respondents felt free to voice their own opinions. It was emphasised that their views were very important to future course planning. It is hoped that the participant population 'gains not only from the results of the research, but from the process itself'.(15)

The process of setting up the student interviews was time-consuming, but crucially important both in establishing an initial relationship between the research and the students (the researcher already knew the tutors involved from her previous and current practical work), and also helping to demystify the research. The students discussed, not just the methods used for the research but also the reasons for it, its funding, and their involvement in it, not just as passive providers of information, but as equal partners.

Ways of breaking down the barriers between the researcher and the respondents included not just these initial discussions, but also continued individual discussions on visits to courses and also by the researcher's becoming a temporary participant on courses. On one occasion the researcher was incorporated into a role play relating to DHSS tribunal appeals.

The involvement by the interviewer in courses and the fact that most interviews took place before, during and after classes, not only helped the research to become an extension of the educational process but also hopefully assuaged people's fears of being interviewed. 'It will not be an unfamiliar occurrence for researchers into informal learning to realise that individuals may have experienced a number of interviews in which they have been cast in the role of offender against institutional norms and conventions'.(16) Unemployed people, in particular, are often subject to this in interviews with the DHSS. Despite this, everyone in the sample, who was asked, agreed to be interviewed.

Whenever possible, the interviewer used the opportunity to give general and educational advice on relevant information/advice agencies. One woman who was not registered as unemployed subsequently signed on to take advantage of concessions for adult education courses. Some others started going to new courses as a direct result of the interview. This was one practical way in which the 'research' was related to the 'action'.

The tutors' interviews did not take the same amount of 'setting up' as the students' had. Most tutors already knew the researcher because of her practical work in this field of adult education. She was not viewed as an outside professional, monitoring their livelihood. The interviews merged into frank discussions regarding teaching methods and related problems.

In addition, the interview provided an important means of support, giving tutors the opportunity to 'sound off' about the lack of resouces, support, money and the plight of 'part-timers' in general.

Conclusion

The purpose of this chapter has been to raise certain issues which have emerged in the course of the research to date. I have not tried to resolve them, partly because several, at least, do not allow for final resolution. The researcher must nevertheless confront such issues, rather than ignore them because they interfere with the neat packaging of the research. The other reason for being unable to resolve certain matters is that the research is not yet complete. In fact, the surveys, even when analysed, should be viewed as merely the first step of an in-depth study of Pioneer Work. Participant observation, group discussion, experiments in curriculum development and a longitudinal survey will all be utilised to build on the work undertaken so far.

The measure of the effectiveness of the research, whatever the methods used, is not only the impact of findings on academics or administrators, but rather the capacity of the collated data to offer a basis for improving the quality, relevance and efficacy of provision offered to the unemployed, in Pioneer Work or elsewhere. The importance of the method lies in its ability to operate effectively on different levels as 'an approach to social investigation, an educational process and a means of taking action'.(17)

The research has proved valuable, in so far as course planning is already taking initial findings into account. Some subject areas, like community issues, are being increased; further means of extending support and training to tutors are being discussed; and new ways of attracting people to courses have been given fresh impetus by the fact that so many participants in the research feel that this type of provision for the unemployed is both worthwhile and life-enhancing. The research, therefore, has already made a contribution to the action, and it is assumed that this contribution will be increased substantially when the results of both the tutor and student surveys are analysed.

REFERENCES

1. The approaches are (i) Community (ii) Institutional (iii) Organisational (iv) Trade Union. There are six categories of courses. They include (a) welfare rights (b) general and educational counselling, discussion groups (c) subject courses (d) interest courses (e) courses related to local issues, expressed need (f) women's courses. For discussion of these see Chapters 3 and 4; and K Ward, Beyond Tokenism - Unemployed Adults and Education, Department of Adult and Continuing Education, University of Leeds, 1983, Chapters 2 and 3.

2. P Fordham, G Poulton and L Randle, Learning Networks in Adult Education, Routledge and Kegan Paul, 1979, p 147.

3. Barriers of access are defined in Continuing Education: from policies to practice, ACACE, 1982.

4. Examples of these are:-
   (a) What, if anything, have you learnt from the course? (An open question)
   (b) Would you say that the tutor's teaching style was
      1. very satisfactory
      2. satisfactory
      3. neither satisfactory nor unsatisfactory
      4. unsatisfactory
      5. very unsatisfactory.
   (A closed question)

5. R Lees, Research Strategies for Social Welfare, Routledge and Kegan Paul, 1975, p 15.

6. C H Weiss, Evaluation Research: Methods for assessing

programme effectiveness, Prentice-Hall, 1972, p 103.

7. Lindsey Fraser in Leeds, Roger Higginbottom in
    Bradford. In the tutor survey, the interviewing was
    undertaken by Lindsey Fraser.

8. See B L Hall, Breaking the Monopoly of Knowledge,
    Research Methods, Participation and Development, in
    (eds) B L Hall and J R Kidd, Adult Learning: A Design
    for Action, Pergamon Press, 1978, pp 155-168; and
    M Pilsworth and R Ruddock, Some Criticism of Survey
    Methods in Adult Education, Convergence, Vol VIII,
    No 2, 1975, pp 33-43.

9. R Ruddock, Evaluation: A consideration of principles
    and methods, Manchester Monographs 18, 1981, p 67.

10. (ed) A H Halsey, Educational Priority, Vol 1, EPA
    Problems and Policies, Report of a research project
    sponsored by the DES and SSRC, HMSO, 1972, p 170.

11. H L Polshey, Community Needs Assessment - another
    viewpoint, in (ed) C Klevens Materials and Methods in
    Continuing Education, Klevens Publications Inc, 1976.

12. For discussion of who should evaluate projects, see
    M Key, P Hudson and L Armstrong, Evaluation Theory and
    Community Work, YVFF Papers on Community Work and
    Youth Work, 1976, pp 25-27.

13. A D Grotelenschen, Program Evaluation, in (ed)
    A B Knox, Developing, Administering and Evaluating
    Adult Education, Jossey Bas, 1980, p 103.

14. For discussion of interviews see M Berney and
    E Hughes, Of Sociology and the Interview, in American
    Journal of Sociology, 62, July 1956, pp 137-147.

15. B L Hall, Breaking the Monopoly of Knowledge, Research
    Methods, Participation and Development, p 161.

16. S Brookfield, Adult Learners, Adult Education and
    Community, Open University Press, 1983, p 138.

17. P Fordham, Participatory Research and the Non-formal
    Idea: some lessons from a Community Project in (ed)
    M Hays, Papers on Adult Basic Education, Adult
    Education Training and Research Unit, Department of
    Adult Education, University of Southampton, 1980, p 35.

Chapter 9

ADULT EDUCATION AND THE WORKING CLASS: POLICIES, PRACTICE AND FUTURE PRIORITIES FOR COMMUNITY ADULT EDUCATION

Introduction

The core of the argument on which this book is based is that, in education as elsewhere in contemporary British society, there is gross inequality; that, in the post-school sector, there is an unacceptably low level of working-class involvement which must be ameliorated on grounds of both principle and pragmatism; and that, further, traditional definitions of 'working class', based on the manual occupation classification of the male head of household, are no longer relevant to large sections of the adult population. The central concern of the book has been with the analysis, within this overall context of societal inequality, of one particular example of adult education provision for particular groups of working-class people.

In this concluding chapter a brief assessment of Pioneer Work, and its achievements and problems thus far, will be followed by a discussion of the implications the experience has, not only for the West Yorkshire region, but for adult education provision nationally. Finally, some proposals are made for the reform of the post-school education system, and suggestions made for the development of more flexible and innovative structures.

Such aims may be criticised, perhaps rightly, for building major (albeit hypothetical) structures on limited, even flimsy, evidence. It should be emphasised, therefore, that the proposals in the latter part of this chapter are tentative, and intended more as areas for discussion than fully worked out structural initiatives for reform. Nevertheless, the overall crisis in education generally, which is manifested not only in economic but also in ideological uncertainty at a number of levels, is so acute that the need for serious discussion of 'alternative futures' is critical. This chapter - and, indeed, the whole book - is intended as a contribution to that debate, focussing on adult education and its potential in this context.

Pioneer Work Objectives and Performance

The developments described in earlier chapters have taken place within an established and deep-rooted tradition of adult education. Thus Pioneer Work, and other similar developments, are neither wholly autonomous nor wholly new. The concern of adult educationists with the working class has been a consistent theme since the formation of University Extension in the 1870s - and indeed before that.(1) Similarly, the orientation towards informal and student-centred teaching approaches, which has been noted earlier in relation to Pioneer Work, has also been an integral part of the adult education method. The objective within this tradition has been one primarily of social purpose, construed in the past largely as assisting the working class to develop the knowledge, ability and commitment to play a leading role in the creation of a better - more democratic and egalitarian - society. Pioneer Work has been motivated by that same educational dynamic, though, as is discussed below, both its methods and its objectives have differed in some important respects from the earlier adult education movements (eg. the Joint Tutorial Classes movement).

In many other respects, too, Pioneer Work represents the continuation of a well-established approach. The search for innovation and experimentation has always characterised the best of adult education: unlike most educational institutions, adult education has had to innovate continually in order to survive and develop. In its inter-agency approach, too, Pioneer Work has followed the increasing patterns of varied collaboration which UAE departments and, more significantly, other adult education agencies have developed since the 1950s. And, finally, in its concern with educational access, Pioneer Work has been a small part of a major, and welcome, trend towards the institutional networking of provision, and the creation of counselling mechanisms, leading to linked progression through AE, FE and HE, within the whole of the post-school sector in the 1970s and 1980s.(2)

Given all this, it might be argued that Pioneer Work, and other comparable developments (the Liverpool Second Chance scheme, for example(3)), are wholly orthodox adult education enterprises - worthy, perhaps, but with little of originality to interest others in the field. This would be a misinterpretation, however. There are significant departures from traditional established practice which should be noted. Perhaps most important of all is Pioneer Work's interpretation of working-class adult education. This broad interpretation, which is discussed below, has been adopted in practice by many community-based adult education providers in recent years. These include LEA and a wide range of other adult education workers. Unfortunately, important issues and lessons emanating from such provision have often been lost, since little has been documented.

As was noted in Chapter 1 - and exemplified in some detail in subsequent chapters - Pioneer Work's educational concern has been with certain specific, sometimes overlapping, disadvantaged groups of people and not exclusively with the traditionally defined manual, male working class. Thus, educational approaches have been developed to make · provision for working-class people who are suffering double or multiple disadvantage: because they are unemployed, because they are black, because they are retired, or because they are women. This is a significant departure from much traditional AE practice. The overwhelming preponderance of liberal AE activity with the working class in the post-war period and before, has been within the formal parameters of trade union provision: and this has been almost exclusively (until very recently) with white, manual, male workers. Just as the wider labour movement has had, and continues to have, problems in broadening its framework - conceptually as well as practically - to move beyond the traditionally defined working class, so AE has had similar difficulties in coming to terms with other areas of disadvantage and inequality, where different methods and approaches are called for. Moreover, provision via the trade unions is well-established and, despite serious logistic and political problems, easier to establish. The 'target groups' Pioneer Work is aiming for are, necessarily, more amorphous, less easy to contact and, generally, less receptive to 'education' per se.

It is crucially important that such work is attempted, however. As socio-economic structures change, so educational needs, amongst other things, change also. New modes have to be developed for all the groups with which Pioneer Work is concerned: paid employment until 65 is no longer the norm; perceptions of women's roles, and hence needs, have altered radically since the 1960s; the identity and consciousness of Britain's black communities are now being recognised, belatedly, and their educational requirements coming to the fore at all levels; and the significance of the increasing proportion of the population now retired is also beginning to be appreciated.

The 'social purpose' dynamic has also to be redefined. In the past, within the RB sector, the social purpose orientation was based upon a dual conception of a belief in 'education for citizenship', stemming from liberal democratic ideology, and an attachment organisationally and politically to the democratic socialist mainstream of the labour movement. No longer is such a definition of social purpose sufficient.(4) There is now a different, and more complex, array of interests that,in terms of educational provision, creates both opportunities and problems. Pioneer Work has been careful to

171

develop specific ad hoc provision appropriate to the needs of the particular group concerned. Moreover, the notion of social purpose has been construed in more directly educational terms. Whereas in the 1920s and 1930s AE was seen, by many on the Left at least, as essentially a means for attaining political ends, in recent decades, social purpose AE has concentrated much more upon education as an 'enabling' process.

Pioneer Work has thus aimed to devise approaches and curriculum content which is relevant, and perceived as being so, by working-class communities. The initial emphasis has therefore been upon innovative educational processes, which will enable working-class people subsequently to develop both individually and collectively.

Thus provision within Pioneer Work has had two central guiding principles: that there must be considerable groundwork undertaken before courses are offered, in order to ascertain the real, felt needs of the particular target group; and, second, that the provision should be community, rather than institution, based and normally concerned with 'issues' rather than 'subjects', in order to overcome the alienation from 'education' which most working-class people have.

This attempt to merge community orientations with the social purpose concerns of working-class AE is not of course unique to Pioneer Work: many other AE examples from recent years can be given but, as was stated earlier, much of the work has not been documented.(5) In terms, however, of the overall monitoring and evaluation, the nature of the curriculum content, and the continuity of the programme over a number of years in two contrasting northern cities, Pioneer Work should be in a position to highlight significant general issues and lessons.

One such issue is that of 'access'. There is an increasing emphasis within the post-school sector on 'access' generally. But this is normally constrained by two factors: the assumption that all the provision will be institution-based; and, second, the notion of the 'educational escalator', with its assumption of educational progression. With Pioneer Work, and similar developments, however, the concept of access is considerably more open-ended. For a minority of students, access will lead on to qualification-oriented courses, and, on occasion, to degree level work. But for the majority that is not, and cannot be, the primary aim. Access, in this context, has two major dimensions: access to knowledge and education in order to achieve either personal or community goals (or both); and access to build self-confidence, minimise social isolation, and, above all, counter-act the alienation which so many people feel in the social groups with which Pioneer Work operates. (Although it should be noted, as was discussed in Chapter 6, that not all working-class people, and especially not all working-class women, are alienated from education per se.)

To an extent, all this replicates the traditional WEA motivations, of course. But there are two points to be noted in this context. First, the WEA is no longer primarily committed to this area of work: its main bulk of provision for many years has been in general liberal education of a more conventional type. And, second, the emphasis in Pioneer Work is very much upon devising community education processes and approaches, radically different from traditional subject-based courses, in order to make provision relevant to working-class communities. Again, some such work has been undertaken by the WEA in recent years, but only as a minority strand in its provision.

Finally, in terms of inter-agency links Pioneer Work has again moved beyond the purely formal institutional network, important though this is. Thus, as was indicated in the case studies cited in Chapters 4, 5, 6, and 7, not only has Pioneer Work worked jointly with statutory educational providers, it has also developed a wide range of community- based contacts both statutory and voluntary, and both educational and general, in nature. Such linking has been central to the operation of Pioneer Work, as was discussed in Chapter 3. Only through building appropriate links within the community can Pioneer Work provision attract local working-class people, and provide them with what is useful, relevant and needed.

A key aspect of this process, however, is the handing over of Pioneer Work courses and students to other agencies. On occasion, of course, this will be to the mainstream UAE programme or to the WEA - as in the case of some local history and 'New Opportunities' courses, for example. But more often the provision required is more appropriately undertaken by other educational bodies - the LEA, the local FE college - or by non-statutory bodies - such as the Citizens' Advice Bureau, and community associations. Pioneer Work's function is thus not primarily to recruit students who will progress onto mainstream UAE courses; but rather to enrol people in educational provision relevant to their needs, who would probably not otherwise have become involved in any educational context; and subsequently to hand over that provision, once established, to whichever agency is best equipped to meet the group's needs. Of course it is never quite as straightforward and simple as this. As was argued in Chapter 7, there are often practical problems in handing over, especially when all agencies are experiencing both financial and human resource problems because of educational 'cuts'. And the whole problem of maintaining free provision of courses has proved difficult in many instances. Moreover, quite often there are simply no other agencies to which work can be handed over.

This leads on to two problems of principle in this area, which also affect fundamentally the whole Pioneer Work process. First, to what extent is Pioneer Work exclusively concerned with <u>liberal</u> AE? And, second, to what extent should Pioneer Work be <u>wholly</u> concerned with innovatory, experimental courses?

Plainly, Pioneer Work, located as it is within a Department and a tradition whose central reference point has been the liberal tradition,(6) is concerned to promote the values of the liberal social purpose approach. But Pioneer Work's philosophy has been considerably more flexible and libertarian on this point than orthodox defenders of the liberal tradition would consider justifiable. Which of the 'founding fathers' would have regarded as viable - 10 week courses on 'Rock 'n Roll' or 'Photography', for example? Pioneer Work's argument, however, has been that such courses are legitimate, <u>provided</u> they are taught within a liberal context. A great deal of time and effort - in terms of syllabus construction and tutor counselling and discussion - is spent within Pioneer Work ensuring that all courses are taught within the liberal,critical, open-ended framework. Such courses often provide a point of contact with local working-class communities, and have resulted in a broadening out from the original subject matter into critical analysis of the societal context within which this takes place. In short, therefore, Pioneer Work has argued that virtually any subject matter (aside from the purely practical or vocational)(7) is legitimate, provided it is taught with the dual objective of ensuring a critical awareness of the context, and of 'opening out' the students' perceptions in order to develop a wider awareness and interest. In this sense, again, the experience of Pioneer Work in curriculum design and development, and the achievement of liberal objectives within a seemingly 'non-liberal' context (as exemplified in the case studies cited in earlier chapters), provide useful examples of how similar developments might be undertaken elsewhere.

On the second question - concerning innovation - Pioneer Work has always seen one of its primary purposes as innovation and experimentation in terms of both curriculum and target group. The whole programme could not consist of such experimental courses, due for handover to other agencies at an early stage, however. To devise, maintain and develop a continually evolving Pioneer Work programme would require both greatly increased resources, and a high level of long term originality and creativity. Moreover, a continually changing programme could have no stability and would make medium-term course planning virtually impossible. Thirdly, given the general financial climate, there is considerable pressure on all RBs to concentrate upon 'productivity' in terms of student numbers (and hence Effective Student Hours). Finally, there are very often no agencies, at least in the short term, which have the resources, the expertise and the commitment to take on extra course provision. Thus, not only does Pioneer Work have to initiate the provision (on an inter-agency basis) in the first place, it has also to negotiate with other agencies in order to avoid duplication and explore the possibilities of 'handover' where appropriate.

In the circumstances, therefore, there has to be a balance in Pioneer Work programming between continuity and innovation: and it is significant that in its three years of existence Pioneer Work has handed over approximately one quarter of its successful provision to other bodies. (In some cases, of course, it is appropriate for Pioneer Work to continue beyond the initial stage: where, for example, groups develop more advanced interests in subjects which are within the liberal area and in which Pioneer Work full-time staff have a particular expertise.) Partly because of resource problems, however, it has been necessary on occasion to take some very hard decisions, in terms of programme priorities, between continuing with successful and much needed provision, and devoting resources to developing new and experimental areas of work. Sometimes this has meant withdrawal from certain areas leaving no other agency to take over - although on other occasions the group has developed strongly enough to create its own support and informal educational systems. In general terms, therefore, problematic though the balance has been, it has been possible to maintain a coherent and viable programme, allowing for extensive innovation but also keeping a core of legitimate Pioneer Work provision in the programme from year to year.

In these senses, therefore, Pioneer Work has operated as innovator, catalyst, and both short and medium-term provider of courses for the disadvantaged groups in question. Of course, much more could have been accomplished with greater resources, and it must be stressed once more that Pioneer Work has involved only a tiny proportion of total numbers in the target groups. But before moving on to discuss funding problems, brief note must be taken of two further crucially important Pioneer Work functions.

Emphasis was placed in both Chapter 3 and Chapter 8 on the centrality for Pioneer Work of research and monitoring. Indeed, in many ways, Pioneer Work is seen, especially by Leeds University, as an action-research project, with the only real justification for the University's involvement in the programme of courses being seen as the provision of the raw material for subsequent analysis and research codification. As will have been abundantly clear from the preceding chapters, the authors of this book (and all others involved in Pioneer Work) do not share this attitude. For Pioneer Work staff, the programme provision itself is of at least equal value to the research.

Nevertheless, the research is of crucial importance - not autonomously, but within an action-research framework. This involves critical evaluation of practice by Pioneer Work staff, together with participants, rather than an abstract, 'academic' exercise, which regards participants as merely raw material for research. The development of this type of experimental programme of work needs rigorous research and monitoring of provision in order to be able to disseminate ideas of 'good practice'. Thus, one of the key functions of this book itself is to explore and analyse critically, for a wider public, the experience of Pioneer Work over the 1982-85 period.(8) The point need not be laboured, but it is significant to note the dearth of rigorous research evidence in the field of community adult education: and the insistent demands from a whole range of agencies (including the DES) for such research, especially in the rapidly developing field of work with the unemployed.

The other major area of Pioneer Work achievement, with considerable potential for further development, is the consultancy work referred to in Chapters 3 and 4. Again, the research and monitoring experience within a UAE context gives those involved in Pioneer Work both the opportunity and the responsibility to engage in regional and national consultancy work. Such work is a valuable way of disseminating 'good practice' and ensuring that scarce resources are used effectively.

In all these ways, then, Pioneer Work can claim to have made a useful, though small-scale, contribution to the field. Its value, it may be suggested, lies in three broad areas: the provision itself, which has proved to be of benefit for at least a limited number of the disadvantaged people in the target groups concerned (as the preceding chapters have illustrated); the experimentation and innovation in both structures and curriculum content which have been devised and subsequently disseminated to others in the field; and the extension of the existing tradition of social purpose liberal adult education into new and significant areas of work, indicating again (albeit in a small way) that there are legitimate ways in which AE can help to counter the inequalities that persist in contemporary educational structures. In all these senses, therefore, Pioneer Work, and other similar developments, can act as <u>catalysts</u> for more dramatic subsequent changes in structures of provision in post-school education.

Pioneer Work Problems and Failures

Despite these not inconsiderable achievements, there are immense problems for Pioneer Work. And, by extension, though the detail may vary according to local situations, the fundamental problems are common, at least in the short to medium term, to all similar AE developments. These may be grouped under two heads: the resources crisis; and the inherent tension between innovatory and unorthodox developments of the Pioneer Work type, and the deeply ingrained conservatism of the parent institutions concerned.

It is tempting, given the prolonged and ever worsening financial crisis within post-school education that has existed through the 1970s and 1980s, to become paranoid, and see always politically reactionary motivations behind the successive rounds of 'cuts' and restrictions. Nevertheless, such self-indulgence must be resisted. Within a general climate of unprecedented attacks upon HE in general, and universities in particular, work with disadvantaged groups in AE has received some (minimal) governmental encouragement and support. The REPLAN initiative, which was discussed in Chapter 3, is an example of this: and at the more parochial level, the positive attitude of the DES towards Pioneer Work is another indication that such developments are looked on with some favour.

However, the resources crisis is extremely grave. For the combination of reasons outlined in Chapter 3, the DES 'new formula' for grant aid discriminates very heavily against such initiatives. Moreover, the UGC cuts in the universities sector and the LEA cuts in the local context, render parent institutions even less willing, or able, to support such initiatives to any substantial degree.

Such funding as there is, tends increasingly to be short-term: and this creates further serious problems. In Pioneer Work, the experience has been that continuity of planning, and the integration of staff into the team structures, have been essential ingredients of coherent development. And yet the majority of posts have been of two years' duration or less. (And this omits mention of the high turnover and job insecurity factors affecting the organising tutor - 'Group 2' - positions which were referred to in Chapter 3.) This short-term funding has led to uneven planning, and, on occasion, to the abrupt withdrawal, at a crucial stage of development, of key staff members from whole areas of work, because of failure to renew funds. Moreover, the large proportion of time spent by full-time Pioneer Work staff in negotiating for successive short-term contract renewals, all with different agencies with different criteria for appointment and diverse bureaucratic procedures, has been highly frustrating, and, arguably, a misuse of scarce resources.

Under the new funding arrangements for RBs no allowance is made for the time-consuming developmental, outreach and research work which is central to Pioneer Work's operation.

These activites, though vitally important (and agreed to be so by both the DES and the University) are not directly productive of 'output' in terms of Effective Student Hours, and are thus not credited for grant aid under the 'new formula'. New procedures and criteria for grant aid in this area are desperately needed. Thus, despite all the support and prominence given to Pioneer Work and similar initiatives, they are, in fact, under real and short-term threat unless urgent action to resolve the resources crisis is undertaken. This must involve not only more favourable criteria for funding, but also <u>longer term</u> commitments to finance developmental work of this type.

Such funding and resource problems are not confined to one sector, of course. All providing agencies are undergoing similar cutbacks and, if Pioneer Work's 'networking' approach is to be maintained, then it is important that the broader resource problems are solved also. All these resource questions lead, therefore, towards a national initiative and structure, a possible outline of which is discussed in the final section of this chapter. In the specific case of Pioneer Work, however, there needs to be recognition by the educational bodies concerned (principally the DES and the parent university) that such areas are inevitably more labour-intensive and time-consuming than 'orthodox' provision. Moreover, if the work is to be planned and subsequently analysed effectively, a considerable amount of staff time must be set aside for this purpose. Courses eventuating from such schemes usually cater only for small numbers, if they are to be taught effectively, thereby reducing still further their 'grant earning power' under the 'Effective Student Hours' system of the 'new formula' for grant aid. What is needed, therefore, is a separate agreement on 'output' measured in terms which take account of the very special circumstances obtaining in this crucially important area of work; and, subsequently, an agreed funding grant on a year-by-year rolling basis.

Obviously, the details of finance cannot be entered into here. But the central, simple fact is that there must be recognition, translated into funding terms, of both the value and the special nature of this area of work.

The DES, to be fair, has shown a very positive attitude over such questions. Universities' attitudes are more ambivalent.(9) UAE, after all, is both a marginal and an atypical university activity: and the community-based AE of the Pioneer Work type is still further removed from the norm. Universities are concerned primarily with high level research, and with elite education at both undergraduate and postgraduate level. The reasons why universities should, in our view, be closely involved with community-based AE action-research of the Pioneer Work type, were discussed in Chapter

3.   But such arguments tend to carry relatively little weight
inside university structures.   By their nature,   universities
tend to be somewhat removed from their communities in general:
and to have virtually no contact with the disadvantaged groups
on   which   this   book   is   focussed.   It is   not   generally   a
question   of   explicit   university   hostility   or   coherent
ideological   opposition to such developments: rather,   there is
a   cultural   and   ideological   incomprehension   which   makes
problematic   the relationship between this aspect   of UAE   and
the   university authorities.   (And it is in this context   that
the research emphasis within Pioneer Work becomes so important
as   a   validating reason for UAE engaging in the provision   of
what,   by every other 'normal' university criterion,   is 'low-
level' work.)   There is thus always an underlying   structural
tension in UAE work of this type.

There now exists, generally, a modus vivendi: but if this
work   were   to develop into a major aspect of UAE in terms   of
quantity   and   staffing levels,   it is unlikely   that   such   a
fundamentally   uneasy   relationship could continue to   operate
satisfactorily.   To an extent,   Pioneer Work   and   similar
developments   are tolerated by universities because   they   are
very small-scale,   insignificant and almost incidental.   This
raises   larger questions about the proper relationship between
universities,   UAE   and   working-class   education,   which   are
touched upon in the concluding section of this chapter.

However,   even at the present minimal level of   activity,
there   are   occasions when this 'culture clash' causes   severe
problems.   One important example of this,   already referred to
in Chapter 3,   occurred in Pioneer Work over the   University's
attitude   towards   appointments   to develop   work   with   black
groups.   Two quite separate appointments,   at different times,
were involved.   In the first,   the UAE Department had received
from NIACE,   as part of the REPLAN programme,   a grant,   over two
years   and in conjunction with Harehills Housing Aid (HHA)   (a
voluntary association in a predominantly Asian area of Leeds),
to appoint two half-time workers to develop community-based AE
primarily   with   Asian women.   The   management   committee,
comprising representatives of Pioneer Work staff,   HHA workers
and local LEA workers,   agreed that,   whilst it was   important
that   one   appointee   should   have   higher   educational
qualifications,   AE   or   related   experience,   and   research
ability,   it   was equally important that the   other   appointee
should   have appropriate language skills,   local community and
cultural knowledge,   and   be able to identify directly with the
local women.   Ideally,   of course,   both appointees should have
had   all attributes,   but this was always unlikely to   be   the
case.   Whilst HHA was somewhat dubious about the importance of
the 'academic' criteria they were,   rightly,   insistent on the
need for the 'community' attributes.   The University,   on the
other hand - as the formal employing body - was insistent that

in neither case should anyone without adequate qualifications be appointed. They were prepared to accept appropriate alternative qualifications, but not to countenance experiential background as satisfactory. The Pioneer Work staff were thus left in the unenviable position of being 'go-betweens', vilified by both bodies (which had, of course, no direct contact with each other).

After complicated and protracted negotiations, workers were appointed who were acceptable to all parties and the project (as was discussed in Chapter 4) has developed well. Nevertheless, the example is indicative both of the clash of criteria involved, and of the delicate position in which Pioneer Work found itself.

The second example put the same problem into sharper relief. In 1984 the DES agreed to extend the funding of a temporary post for two further years to develop work with unemployed people. It was agreed in the UAE Department that the post would be divided, and that one half-time appointee would work in Leeds to develop the existing work with the unemployed, and the other in Bradford, to develop work with black unemployed groups. The posts were advertised, short-listed and interviewed for jointly. It was quite clear to the Pioneer Work staff involved that, as far as the Bradford post was concerned, it was unlikely that a white person, however talented, hard-working and 'empathetic' could develop such work satisfactorily, especially within such a short time span. Moreover, there was a strong feeling that, in the Pioneer Work section, that there should be, on grounds of principle, at least one black full-time staff member. In other words, on grounds of both educational practice and moral and political principle, there was an overriding argument for 'positive discrimination' in this particular case. Whilst the short-listing was undertaken with this in mind, the University appointing committee (on which Pioneer Work had one representative out of five) felt unable to accept the argument for positive discrimination, and appointed a white person to the post.

It is important to emphasise that this was in no way an example of overt racial prejudice. It was the result of the application of the normal university criteria: who had the best academic record, who had the most experience of higher education teaching, who 'came across' in the interview as the person most generally suited to a university environment, where the ability to conceptualise, to engage in research and so on, are of key importance. The result was the appointment of an extremely able, well-qualified, and committed person, who was inappropriate to undertake this particular post.

Either universities must change their attitudes in such cases, allow 'positive discrimination', and accept criteria other than, or in addition to, the orthodox academic ones -

which was explicitly ruled out of order by the Registry on this occasion - or they must accept that universities cannot operate in this crucially important field.

These are not isolated examples. Nor are they restricted to the development of AE with the black communities. Similar problems are almost certain to arise in a large number of adult and continuing education contexts where purely academic criteria are insufficient grounds for selection.

There are, then, problems for Pioneer Work development, which should be borne in mind by other agencies in analogous contexts if similar developments are contemplated. But they are not insuperable problems. Given commitment and institutional support they can be accommodated, if not solved.

There is, however, another range of more general problems relating to the place of such work within the wider national context, which must also be discussed briefly.

Community-based Adult Education:
Some General Contextual Considerations

The first, and very obvious, point to re-emphasise is that community adult education for disadvantaged groups is minuscule in scale, compared with both educational expenditure in toto, and expenditure on vocational training programmes (largely via the MSC). In Chapter 3, the reasons for there being little cooperation between Pioneer Work and the MSC were discussed. But it remains true that, however galling it may be to those involved in AE, a huge proportion of public expenditure is allocated to these functions, and a tiny fraction of this amount to AE development of work with the disadvantaged. Should there be made in future a greater effort by AE, to make viable and legitimate links? An amount of joint work already takes place, of course, through the FE college system. But little such work is undertaken in the RB sector. It must be borne in mind, of course, that, as was indicated in Chapter 3, MSC's overall orientation is towards work with young people rather than adults.

Nevertheless, and bearing in mind all the caveats that must be made, there is a strong case for including a review of future possible collaboration within the structural proposals discussed in the final section below. The old distinctions between vocational and non-vocational are, if not redundant, at least in need of a more careful and sophisticated definition. And there are areas of overlapping concern and interests that possibly could be developed. Similarly, within the consultancy field, there may also be opportunities for fruitful collaboration.

An equally acute problem for those in the social purpose, liberal adult education tradition has been how best to use scarce, indeed minimal, educational resources. Should the concentration be upon the elite, opinion-forming stratum of the working class, in the hope of reaching through them to far larger numbers? Or should the aim be to try to make appropriate provision for 'ordinary', non-elite members of the disadvantaged groups, in the hope that such provision would act as a catalyst, both in terms of stimulating further educational provision, and in terms of 'educational liberation' for larger numbers of working-class people in the community concerned? The first line of development has been broadly that adopted in the Liverpool developments,(10) and the second has been Pioneer Work's approach, as detailed in this book. Both models have their advantages and disadvantages, and, in practice, a sensitive combination of both approaches is needed. However, it is, in our view, always desirable wherever possible (and it is not always possible, of course) to democratise the educational process and break down the barriers of inequality. Thus, to concentrate exclusively on the already activist and involved sections of the working class, may lead to the educational equivalent of 'vanguardism' with all the dangers that the political experience of the twentieth century has shown inhere in that model of development. On the other hand, care must be taken to avoid spreading scarce resources so thinly that they have no effect at all. Here, again, it is argued by Pioneer Work staff that the development of the consultancy role as an ancillary part of provision may counteract this latter and inherent danger within a small scale organisational structure, and enable 'good practice' to be disseminated rather more widely through professional networking.

A related danger of the Pioneer Work approach, at least as seen by critics from the Left, is that it may fall into wholly liberal assumptions and ignore the wider socio-economic, structural problems which, it is held, give rise to the local and specific situations of disadvantage. This is a criticism made of much single issue, and community work, practice, unrelated to specifically educational concerns.(11)

However, the liberal social purpose tradition of education is based essentially upon the need to link the specific to the general, and the practical to the theoretical. Certainly, it is argued, 'start from where the students are' in terms of their life experience and cultural parameters; but the intention of the liberal educational process is precisely to make those links, to broaden and open out students' perceptions. In this respect, therefore, the Pioneer Work type of provision within the RB sector is far less likely to have this problem than are other sectors of provision. Of course, the ideal is often not attained: but the framework, both conceptually and practically, exists to enable the provision to be made in such a way that this particular set of dangers inherent in one view of the liberal tradition, is avoided.

Some critics on the Left, however, argue that there is a more fundamental danger still with the Pioneer Work type of development. It can be used, so it is argued, for either social control purposes, or for 'bread and circuses' provision, or indeed for a combination of both. In other words, the positive attitude of the authorities stems from their need to 'keep the unemployed off the streets' and maintain some sort of ideological control over their activities (and those of the black minorities) so that they are susceptible neither to criminal or 'hooligan' elements, nor to political 'subversives'. And, of course, one well-tried method of maintaining such control is to provide determinedly apolitical, undemanding leisure and educational activities.

Again, these are - or may in the future be - real dangers. But the dynamic of the liberal social purpose tradition is quite opposite in intention. Pioneer Work has aimed to stimulate people's critical faculties, and to 'raise their consciousness' in the educational, not the directly political, sense. To the extent that the authorities may try to impose a cultural hegemony (and this may be more often unconscious than conscious), this pressure must be resisted. But it is equally important that this resistance is seen to be, and genuinely is, on educational rather than political grounds.

Many people argue that such dangers can best be avoided by voluntary involvement. Only through voluntary involvement and eventual control, so the argument goes, can educational provision be made genuinely democratic and responsive to felt needs. Moreover, such arguments enable the avoidance of awkward funding problems - a critical point in the severe financial climate of the 1980s. There is much that is of appeal in such 'libertarian' educational arguments (and of course many community adult education activists have argued in such a way). However, given the alienation from the educational system, which many working-class people feel, and, not least, the very acute economic problems that abound, it is unrealistic to advocate the abandonment, even in the long term, of professional involvement. Of course, for both ideological and financial reasons, the Conservative Governments of the 1980s have been keen to extend the principle of 'voluntarism' throughout the public sector. But the reality is, surely, that professional services have never been needed so much as in the contemporary context. In practical terms, the experience of Pioneer Work is that to withdraw professional involvement from an area of previous programming, results either in a severe diminution of activity or lowering of educational standards, or, in extremis, in the cessation of educational activity altogether.

There is, then, a strong case for retaining professional AE input, although of course this must be within the context of the liberal adult education tradition which lays great emphasis upon the democratic structure of the educational process.

However, over and above these important practical considerations, there is a point of principle relating to the whole question of voluntarism in AE (or any other sector in the educational system). There does reside, or there certainly should do so, within the institutions of higher and further education, a body of theoretical and empirical knowledge which cannot, by definition, be shared to anything like the same degree by the population at large. Part of the justification for educational institutions is precisely that they should develop such knowledge (through study, research, scholarly activity and so on), and then disseminate it through the community.

This is the traditional model which radical educationists (Freire, Illich et al) have criticised so strongly.(12) And we, too, would agree that this traditional view is an inadequate, 'top down', model for AE provision. However, it is also true that AE is a symbiotic process: as Edward Thompson put it some years ago, a combination of 'Education and Experience'.(13) Thus, whilst we would agree that life experience is a key factor in any AE approach, so too is the articulation by a professional of the body of educational knowledge relevant to the topic under discussion.

The relationship between the paid professional and the participants must be one of joint responsibility and equality. This should not be misinterpreted to mean a rejection of 'expert' or specialised skills and knowledge which the professional may possess or have access to. The crucial point is the basis on which this knowledge is provided. In a wholly voluntary situation, ad hoc, haphazard arrangements would develop whereby working-class groups would inevitably not have access to such resources and would have to make do with second or third-rate provision. Professional input, then, will always be essential, although one of the priorities for adult education should be the identification and support of people from working-class groups who can themselves act as enablers and educators.

Future Provision

Three contextual points of considerable importance should be made at the outset of this concluding discussion. First, inequality, which is so prevalent at all levels of British society, is nowhere so gross as in the post-school educational system. The universities, in particular, are overwhelmingly bourgeois, both in outlook and in terms of the social composition of their student bodies. What is needed, therefore, in general terms, is a reformed structure which provides greater equality of opportunity and more sensitivity to community needs. Similarly, and crucially important, the long-established hierarchy of both institutions and subject areas must be reformed: this is as much a matter of attitude as of structure.

Any reforms of post-school education must thus bear these overriding egalitarian aims in mind. And this applies, of course, to the proposals below for AE reform and restructuring.

The second contextual point, again already touched on in an earlier chapter (Chapter 2), is both more controversial and in some respects more fundamental. It is, quite simply, that the days of full employment, and eventually of the dominance of the work ethic itself, are in all probability over. Already, in all modern industrial societies, the importance of paid work has diminished, and that of leisure, in all its forms, increased. The pattern is the same in all sectors: the youth culture explosion since the 1950s (music, fashion et al), the growth of recreational, 'hobby', and sporting activities, the large increase in foreign holiday expenditure, the increasing pattern of early retirement (and premature redundancy), and the greater number of the very elderly in the population. Within this changed context AE has, or should have, a very major role indeed to play. At the 'soft end' of the market this has already been exploited, of course. Those who already have educational experience, who are intellectually and culturally integrated into an educational framework, have capitalised - quite rightly of course - on the educational opportunities available. But in relation to the majority of the population, alienated to a greater or lesser degree as they are from education per se, there remains an enormous job for all sectors of AE.

There are problems, in social as well as economic terms, for those large and growing sections of the population with increasing amounts of leisure. This is often enforced leisure, of course, as with the chronically high levels of unemployment: but it is often the result, too, of changing age structures and hence of a greater proportion of retired people in the population (as was discussed in Chapter 7). In this context AE may again be 'used' by the authorities as a means of social control or 'bread and circuses' provision. However, as was noted earlier, it is the responsibility of adult educationists to ensure that such pressures are avoided, and resisted where necessary.

Thirdly, and perhaps most important of all in the context of specific, practical proposals, it must be emphasised that AE as a whole is only a part of the post-school educational and training environment; and that Responsible Body AE in general, and Pioneer Work and similar developments in particular, are a relatively minor part of AE. There is no sense, then, in which generalised proposals for working-class post-school education can be seen as co-terminous with the perspectives and objectives described in this book: the field is very considerably wider than this, and includes not only other sectors of AE but HE, FE, MSC, and others.

Nevertheless, it is equally important to note that one of the major problems in the field of working-class post-school education has been the disparate and incoherent nature of provision. In all sectors attempts have been made, with varying degrees of priority, to develop provision appropriate for working-class people. But such provision has been predicated primarily upon the priorities, assumptions and structures of the institutions in question, and not upon any over-arching concept of working-class education per se. In other words, there has been no coherent, rational, inter-institutional policy for working-class post-school educational development.

This book has been concerned with the analysis of one small - but we believe significant - development in one sector of this work. But if such developments are to have real and long-term impact, they must be linked in to an overall national structure which focusses upon the very diverse educational provision for working-class adults that is needed in the various sectors of the educational system.

It is for this reason that we would propose that a major national review of working-class post-school education be undertaken (using our broader definition of working class), with the objective of making recommendations on how best to establish a coherent structure for the inter-linking of existing provision and the development of a more focussed national policy. The Pioneer Work type of development would be only a small part of such a structure, obviously. But, in this as in other sectors, no viable developments can be made in the long term without such linkage and coherence. If working-class post-school education is to be seen as a whole, and as a high priority,'then some such initiative is necessary to give focus, dynamism and coherence.

In relation to specific development in the field discussed in this book, we would propose the establishment of a limited number of five year projects to develop community-based AE on a similar model to Pioneer Work. This would involve close monitoring and analysis from the DES and, dependent on the results, could lead to more permanent provision being undertaken, under the separate funding arrangements proposed earlier, within the RB sector.

Developments such as this, in various sectors, should be linked, both conceptually and practically, within the structure proposed earlier. Without such linkage they run the danger of becoming merely short-term, tokenistic experiments with no real long-term benefits for the community.

These arguments lead, finally, to a broader proposal for the establishment of a national body with responsibility for the overall development of AE with the working class. It is not within the scope of this book to discuss in detail the composition and functions of such a body: obviously, RB participation, although important, would be a relatively minor part of the much larger institutional complex of involvement (FE colleges, MSC, LEAs et al). But it is our experience that there is an urgent need for such a national co-ordination in order to make the best use, through constructive inter-linking, of the considerable resources, both human and financial, that exist potentially for development in this area.

Again, it is beyond the scope of this book to discuss the structures and developments in other sectors. But the complexity of the context in the RB sector, which has been the location of Pioneer Work and thus the focus of attention here, merits brief discussion in order to illustrate the need for the Development Body proposed.

Both the WEA and UAE departments have a longstanding concern with working-class adult education, as was discussed in Chapters 1 and 3. In the contemporary context this manifests itself primarily in three ways: Trade Union courses; the participation of working-class people in the mainstream provision of the WEA and UAE departments; and specific community-based provision for particular groups of disadvantaged adults, which has been the concern in this book.

All these activities are important, and a part of the overall programme of provision for working-class adults. But they are not co-ordinated and focussed nationally: nor are they normally linked together coherently and given priority, even in individual WEA districts or UAE departments! Here, then, is a prime example of the need for a coherent and focussed linkage.

In the specific area of community-based adult education for disadvantaged groups, there is a plethora of initiatives, organised on an ad hoc, piecemeal basis, and funded on short-term contracts by central government.

These are focussed on specific target groups and/or broad educational issues (such as counselling and guidance). For example, linked to NIACE, there is: (i) the Adult Literacy and Basic Skills Unit (ALBSU) with field consultants, local short-term development projects and a training programme nationally through the regional advisory councils; (ii) the Unit for the Development of Adult Continuing Education (UDACE) with development groups on educational guidance for adults (with short-term pilot projects and development officers), and Education and Older Adults; (iii) REPLAN (DES

Programme for the Adult Unemployed) with field officers, short-term development projects and a national staff development programme through the regional advisory councils.

There are, of course, strong arguments for establishing programmes which focus on specific needs and contribute to the debate about such issues as unemployment, the needs of retired people, etc. The focus on particular target groups and issues, however, is only of maximum value if it is located within a broader overall framework, rather than in the present compartmentalised structures, and extends beyond the short term. Many adult educators, struggling with major cutbacks anyway, are confused by the current proliferation of specific schemes, which leads to a danger of overlap and duplication. A national development body could prevent overlap, and co-ordinate the development of all specific programmes within an overall framework of education for the 'missing millions'.

This is but one example of the useful role that a national Development Body could fulfil. Analogous networking could be undertaken in other sectors. In this context, the central point is not the detail of the proposal but the emphasis upon the need for a national focus, and a coherent policy, for post-school education for the working class. Of course, this would need detailed discussion throughout the various sectors, and it would be essential to create appropriate local structures (possibly in the form of local forums) to give real meaning to the initiative. But without such an initiative it is difficult to see how the valuable, but disparate, provision now taking place in this area can be built into a substantial and effective educational programme which will enable working-class people to benefit from the educational system.

We should return, finally, to the role of Pioneer Work in this overall process. Pioneer Work's motivation throughout has been to contribute to the process of making available educational resources to groups which have previously not had access to them, and thus to help break down the barriers of inequality and create a more democratic society.

Although Pioneer Work's contribution has been small in terms of the quantity of provision, we hope that, together with similar initiatives, it may act as a catalyst for other larger and more important subsequent developments.

REFERENCES

1. See R Peers, Adult Education: a Comparative Study, Routledge and Kegan Paul, 1958; and, on University Extension, N A Jepson, The Beginnings of English University Adult Education, Michael Joseph, 1973.

2. See, for example, the North West Open College Federation

(involving a number of FE colleges, Preston Polytechnic, and the University of Lancaster); and the similar structure emerging in the 1980s in West Yorkshire, the West Yorkshire Open Learning Federation.

3. See B Ashcroft and K Jackson, Adult Education and Social Action, in (eds) D Jones and M Mayo, Community Work One, Routledge and Kegan Paul, 1974.

4. It is this relationship which has been the cornerstone of the 'social purpose' strand within the liberal tradition which has characterised both UAE departments and the WEA.

5. See, for example, C Kenner, No time for Women, Pandora Press, 1985; T Lovett, Adult Education, Community Development and the Working class, Ward Lock Educational, 1975; R Bryant and T Addy, Crisis in Community: A Resource Programme for Local Organisations and Leaders, William Temple Foundation, 1985.

6. On the liberal tradition, see R Taylor, K Rockhill and R Fieldhouse, University Adult Education in England and the USA: a reappriasal of the liberal tradition, Croom Helm, 1985.

7. It should be noted, however, that in principle vocational courses can be, and have been, taught from within a liberal perspective. For example, Pioneer Work colleagues have recalled shorthand and typing courses, provided at another institution, in which tutors adopted a critical view of both commercial practice, and of conventional 'boss/secretary' relationships, in order to develop students' social awareness. Similarly, there were liberal, critical elements in the early days of the MSC's Youth Opportunities schemes.

8. Since its inception in 1982 the following research articles have been produced by Pioneer Work:

K Ward, A University Adult Education Project with the Unemployed, Studies in Adult Education, Vol 15, September 1983.

R Imeson, Unemployed Adults and Education, Bulletin of Social Policy, No 14, Autumn 983.

R Taylor and K Ward, University Adult Education and the Community Perspective: the Leeds Pioneer Work Project, International Journal of Lifelong Education, Vol 3, No

1, March 1984.

K Ward, What Response Can Adult Education Offer to the
Unemployment Crisis?, Convergence, Vol 17, No 14,
International Council for Adult Education, Toronto,
Canada, 1984.

K Ward, Free and Relevant Education: a University
Response to Adult Unemployment, International Journal
of University Adult Education, Vol 23, Nos 1-3, 1984.

K Ward and K Forrester, Servicing the TUC Centres for
the Unemployed, TUC, March 1985.

K Ward, The Unemployment Bandwaggon, in (ed) B Spencer,
Adult Education with the Unemployed, Leeds University,
1986.

R Taylor, A rationale for universities' involvement in
education for unemployed adults, in (ed) B Spencer,
Adult Education with the Unemployed, Leeds University,
1986.

J Gardiner, Women and unemployment: a case study, in
(ed) B Spencer, Adult Education with the Unemployed,
Leeds University, 1986.

K Ward and K Forrester, Organising the Unemployed? the
TUC and the Unemployed Workers' Centres, Industrial
Relations Journal, 1986 (forthcoming).

In addition, Pioneer Work students, with help and advice
from tutors, have produced the following publications,
published by the Department of Adult and Continuing
Education, University of Leeds, and all representing
areas of original, local research and students' work:
Saltaire: Our Memories, Our History, (1984);
Listening and Writing (1984); Lazy Tees (1985);
Queensbury: Our Memories, Our History (1985);
An Ordinary Lot (1985).

9.   The focus here and throughout the chapter is on
      universities and UAE as that is the context within which
      Pioneer Work operates. In many cases, however, similar
      considerations apply to LEA and other sectors. In this
      particular instance the general attitudes of LEAs will
      vary to some extent of course, according to the
      political perspective of the authority concerned.

10.   See Ashcroft and Jackson, Adult Education and Social

Action

11. See R Taylor and K Ward, Community Politics and Direct
    Action: the non-aligned Left, in (eds) D Coates and
    G Johnston, Socialist Strategies, Martin Robertson,
    1983.

12. See, for example, P Freire, The Pedagogy of the
    Oppressed, Sheed and Ward, 1972.

13. E P Thompson, Education and Experience, Fifth Mansbridge
    Memorial Lecture, Leeds University Press, 1968.

Educational Priority Areas
43
Education Support Grants
43
Edwards E G 11
effective student hours
(ESHs) 19, 63, 174
English as a Second
Language (ESL) 12, 42
ethnic minority provision
(see also black groups,
provision for) 71-72
(Extension: see University
Extension)

feminists, feminism 35,
126-127
Fordham P 159
Forum on the Rights of
Elderly People to
Education (FREE) 133,
148
Freire P 127, 184
Further Education Unit
(FEU) 42

Gorz A 35

Halsey A H 162
Hannington W 29
Harehills Housing Aid (HHA)
93-95, 100, 179
Harrison J F C 52
HMI 53, 150, 164
Honeyford R 90

Illich I 184
industrial studies
provision 20-21, 52-53,
and Chapter 5 passim
inequality Chapter 1 passim
- of age 6, 7, and
Chapter 7 passim
of education 8-21
- of gender 5-6, 31-32,
and Chapter 6 passim
- of geography 4-5
- of race 7
- of social class 1-8, 11
institutional approach (in

Pioneer Work) 68-70,
85-88,96

Jarrow March 29
Jenkins C 105

labour movement 13-14, 171
- and unemployment in the
1930s 28-30, 34-35
Labour party, government
17, 31, 33-34, 36
Leeds
- unemployed people in
44-46
Leeds Centre Against
Unemployment 70-71, 91,
106-107, 109
liberal approach (to
education) 9, 16-21,
52-53, and Chapter 9
passim
literacy programme 12-13
Liverpool 'second chance'
scheme 170
Local Education Authorities
(LEAs) 12-13, 15, 41, 64,
66, 68, 70-71, 81, 84,
86-88, 91, 95, 97, 170,
179, 187
Local State 38-39

McDonald J 42
McLeod I 3
Manpower Services
Commission (MSC) 30,
36-38, 40, 42-44, 107,
181, 186-187
Mansbridge A 14
Marcuse H 35
Marsden 3
Marx, Marxism, Marxist 14,
34-35
Miliband R 8

National Council of Labour
Colleges (NCLC) 14
National Council of Social
Service 28
National Council for
Voluntary Organisations 39

193